In Search of Asylum

UNIVERSITY PRESS OF FLORIDA

Florida A&M University, Tallahassee
Florida Atlantic University, Boca Raton
Florida Gulf Coast University, Ft. Myers
Florida International University, Miami
Florida State University, Tallahassee
New College of Florida, Sarasota
University of Central Florida, Orlando
University of Florida, Gainesville
University of North Florida, Jacksonville
University of South Florida, Tampa
University of West Florida, Pensacola

IN SEARCH OF ASYLUM

THE LATER WRITINGS
OF ERIC WALROND

Edited by

Louis J. Parascandola
and Carl A. Wade

Foreword by Joan Stewart

UNIVERSITY PRESS OF FLORIDA
Gainesville ❖ Tallahassee ❖ Tampa ❖ Boca Raton ❖ Pensacola
Orlando ❖ Miami ❖ Jacksonville ❖ Ft. Myers ❖ Sarasota

22 21 20 19 18 17   6 5 4 3 2 1

First cloth printing, 2011
First paperback printing, 2017

Library of Congress Control Number: 2017937027
ISBN 978-0-8130-3560-4 (cloth)
ISBN 978-0-8130-5491-9 (pbk)

The University Press of Florida is the scholarly publishing agency for the State University System of Florida, comprising Florida A&M University, Florida Atlantic University, Florida Gulf Coast University, Florida International University, Florida State University, New College of Florida, University of Central Florida, University of Florida, University of North Florida, University of South Florida, and University of West Florida.

University Press of Florida
15 Northwest 15th Street
Gainesville, FL 32611-2079
http://upress.ufl.edu

To my siblings: John Parascandola, the late Maryann Barbieri, and Judy Bilello—LOUIS J. PARASCANDOLA

To my late mother Gwendoline Estelle Wade, and to my daughters Lisa Karima Wade and Alisha Nicole Wade—CARL A. WADE

CONTENTS

FOREWORD

I yearned for the writings of Eric Walrond long before I knew they existed, long before I knew that my grandfather, Eric Walrond, was a writer of some renown during those days of feverish creativity and imagination known as the Harlem Renaissance. I never met my grandfather nor did I hear much about him within my family until my teenage years. "My father was a writer," my mother, Dorothy, said to me abruptly one day. "He left us when I was three." Her sadness was palpable, the sound of anguish unmistakable, the longing of a child for a father who could never be. I ran to my brother, David, several years older. "Did you know grandpa was a writer?" I asked excitedly. He brushed me off as older brothers are wont to do to annoying younger sisters. "I knew that," he said in an exasperated tone. "But we don't know much about him." Family secrets such as they are. And so our journey began to discover Eric Walrond, the writer whose blood coursed through our veins but who we had never set eyes upon.

On our bookshelf was an old weathered out of print copy of *Tropic Death*. I gently removed it from the shelf and made a mental note to myself that my mother had never shown it to us nor mentioned it in passing. This was surprising to me, since we were all voracious readers who were eager to explore and expand our repertoire of good works—especially writing that was infused with discussions of race and cultural identity.

Looking back, it is interesting to note that indeed all my siblings and I had a deep thirst for literary writing that attempted to explain and analyze the dichotomy of blackness in North America. This was a subject that Eric knew well as a Guyana-born immigrant to the United States, who also spent his formative years in Barbados and Panama.

Like us, African American children of West Indian descent living in the most improbable of places, a small town in central Connecticut, Eric was always the outsider looking through a lens at the cultural nuances and idiosyncrasies of those whom we often make our own and others whom we distance ourselves from. Like Eric, my siblings and I belonged nowhere but managed to fit in everywhere like the chameleons that we and my grandfather learned to be.

Few writers have had the ability to express so vividly and so viscerally to me the intersection of cross-cultural connections, of being from one place and embracing the traditions, beliefs, and values of another—or not. In terms of the African diaspora, the breadth of cultures merging and colliding forcefully together in unity or dissonance, few writers have so seamlessly re-created the diversity of peoples, their differences, their commonalities evoked against a background of a lush Caribbean world that is at once romanticized and clearly real, as Eric does in *Tropic Death*. His descriptions of Caribbean life are alive with the patois and colorful language of places that are unique and yet comfortably familiar to those of us of West Indian descent. His ear for dialect and his uncompromising view of life in the Caribbean and beyond are forceful renderings of a particular time and place. As we all struggle, as African Americans in particular, with the cultural, racial, and class divisions within the Americas, Eric was able to look sociologically and philosophically at how and why we become who we are and how and why we chose to be who we are.

Like many writers, Eric's life was a peripatetic one, moving from place to place, drinking in his current surroundings and then moving on to the next. He left my grandmother, Edith, to raise three young daughters, all under the age of three, alone. Perhaps, Eric's destiny was not to be the faithful husband and the dutiful father. Instead, his legacy to our family and the world is the decidedly pointed, clearly articulated perspective on the world that we as people of color inhabit. Edith went on to remarry and remarry well, Dr. Egbert Evans, a dentist, who came from a prominent Jamaican family. She raised two daughters, Jean and Lucille, in comfortable surroundings in

Kingston. My mother, Dorothy, was raised by Edith's sister Maude and Dr. Frank Gray, a physician in a staunchly middle-class but segregated section of Washington, D.C. They were loving and kind people, but my mother's sense of abandonment never faltered. She held tight to her own children, not wanting them to feel the loss of family in the way in which she had.

Eric's journey would be a less traditional one. His journey would be fraught with unanswered questions for those he left behind. However, it was one that dared to provoke and explore the standard values and norms held by people of color in the Americas and beyond in the years before integration.

This collection of the Roundway Papers and other writings is evidence that Eric continued to be a prolific and highly opinionated wordsmith, although most of his time spent in Roundway Hospital is shrouded in mystery as was much of his life.

So yes I yearned for Eric Walrond long before I knew he existed, because I yearned to understand the complexity of race and class and culture as it impacted my family and others. Eric took the less traveled road, and, although I never met him and my mother barely knew him, he has left us with a rich and lasting repertoire of artfully drawn, clearly imagined, and definitively stated perspectives on timeless issues that are as current today as when he wrote them more than fifty years ago. Yes, I still yearn for the father my mother never knew and the grandfather who would never hold me on his knee. Yet, in its place he has left a different kind of legacy—his writing—and that we can share with the world.

Thank you, Louis and Carl, for your unfaltering determination and dedication to bringing Eric's unsung works to light. And for your deeply considerate understanding of how personal and highly emotional our feelings toward Eric could be as well as your tacit acknowledgment of how both difficult and freeing this experience has been, I thank you as well. It is finally time to let go of old wounds and move forward. Through your generous efforts, it is time to let the world see the whole breadth of Eric Walrond's writings. It is a time to heal. We find great comfort in knowing that his journey was not in vain. Thank you again for revitalizing interest in an oft forgotten but talented writer by the name of Eric Walrond.

Joan Stewart

ACKNOWLEDGMENTS

Much has happened in Walrond research since the hardbound publication of this book in 2011, particularly three recently published works: the reissuing of *Tropic Death,* with an introduction by Arnold Rampersad (2013); Parascandola and Wade's edited volume *Eric Walrond: The Critical Heritage* (2012); and James Davis' biography, *Eric Walrond: A Life in the Harlem Renaissance and the Transatlantic Caribbean* (2015). We also wish to thank Assistant Acquisitions Editor Stephanye Hunter at the University Press of Florida for her help with this paperback edition.

In addition to those listed in our notes to the introduction, we wish to thank the following in particular: the institutions that made material available including the Schomburg Center for Research in Black Culture, the James Weldon Johnson Collection at Yale University, the Woodruff Library at Atlanta University, the Moorland-Spingarn Research Center at Howard University, Fisk University, the Guggenheim Memorial Foundation, the Barbados Archives and the National Library Service, and the Wiltshire Heritage Museum and Library. We would also like to thank the late Robert Bone, as well as Amritjit Singh, James Davis, Cary Wintz, Kathy Wildfong, and George Hutchinson, for encouragement and support; Debora Bone for allowing us to use her translation of "Harlem"; Mary Walker, who spotted more typos than we can count; the staff at the University Press of Florida, including the director Meredith Morris-Babb and our editor Amy Gorelick, project editors Jacqueline Kinghorn Brown and Marthe Walters, and copy editor Elizabeth Detwiler as well as Heather Hathaway and Gary Holcomb for their helpful comments on the manuscript; Dorothy and Joan Stewart for allowing us to use Walrond's manuscript material; Joyce Harris, Angela Trotman, Kerry Lucas, Alison Johnson, and Neisha Applewhaite of the University of the West Indies, Cave Hill Campus, Barbados, who helped with the preparation of the manuscript; Chris Cox, formerly of Green Lane Hospital, Wiltshire, who supplied copies of Walrond's stories and information about his life; the *Journal of Caribbean Studies* for allowing us to reprint parts of our introduction; Andrea Butler Ramsey, who was a rich source of information on Walrond's family history; Ms. M. Cummings of the General Registrar's Office, Georgetown, Guyana, who facilitated access to Walrond's birth records; Ronald Hughes, for his early genealogical research on Walrond.

Louis also wishes to thank his students and colleagues at Long Island University, including those in the Honors program, Latin and Caribbean Studies, Africana studies, and the English Department, especially Maria McGarrity, Vidhya Swaminathan, Leah Dilworth, and Sealy Gilles; Dean David Cohen and Provost Gale Stevens-Haynes; the memory of his parents, Ann and Louis Parascandola, who will always remain a part of his life; his wife, Shondel Nero, whose love and support have enriched his life in ways too innumerable to count.

Carl also acknowledges for their encouragement and support his daughters Lisa and Alisha, many friends, especially Sandra Osborne, C. Walter Harper, his colleague Curwen E. Best of the Cave Hill Campus, Paul Gibbs of Cave Hill, and the University of the West Indies, for facilitating the research that went into this book.

A NOTE ON THE TEXT

In choosing the pieces, we have tried to select works reflecting the diversity of Eric Walrond's literary and political interests from the 1930s until his death in 1966. Collectively, we believe these works add greatly to his reputation as a diasporic writer as well as one of the leading figures of the Harlem Renaissance. To our mind, they put to rest the common misconception that his writing career had finished after he left the United States in 1928. We are happy to restore material that would otherwise be lost forever, and we are particularly pleased, thanks to the generous cooperation of Walrond's family, to publish, for the first time, several pieces of his manuscript material.

Walrond's work appeared in numerous publications, each with its own editorial policies. We have silently corrected a number of obvious typographical errors. Our goal, however, has been to adhere to the texts as they were originally published. Therefore, spellings, italics, and capitalizations have not been regularized. We have tended to include complete texts except in a few works (such as "The Second Battle" and "The Panama Scandal"), which contain material that seems extraneous for modern readers. Omissions are marked by ellipses in brackets. We have also selectively provided annotations (marked by an asterisk) that may be unfamiliar to a contemporary audience, at the end of the text.

SELECTIVE CHRONOLOGY

1898 (Dec. 18) Eric Derwent Walrond born in British Guiana (Guyana) to William and Ruth Walrond

1906 Ruth Walrond and children migrate to Barbados

1906–10 (ca.) Eric attends Saint Stephen's Boys' School in Black Rock, Saint Michael

1909 William Walrond migrates to Colón, Panama Canal Zone

1910 (ca.) Ruth Walrond and children migrate to Colón

1910–16 Eric furthers education in Panama

1916–18 Eric employed as reporter with the Panama *Star and Herald* newspaper

1918 Migrates to New York City via Ellis Island; employed as secretary to recruiting office in British Mission

1920 Works as secretary to architect, New York City; employed with *Weekly Review*, run by Marcus Garvey; becomes secretary to superintendent, Broad Street Hospital; marries Edith Melita Cadogan in New York City

1921	Wins first prize for "A Senator's Memoirs," published in *Negro World*
1922	Meets Edna Worthley Underwood, linguist and editor, who offers assistance with his fiction; becomes part owner, assistant editor, *Brooklyn and Long Island Informer*; sails to Latin America
1922–23	Fills positions as assistant editor, associate editor, business and contributing editor, *Negro World*
1923	Divorced from Edith Walrond
1922–24	Attends the College of the City of New York
1924	Writes Alain Locke about anxiety and depression and the lack of progress with a novel
1924–26	Attends Columbia University
1925	Publishes "The Palm Porch" in *The New Negro*, edited by Alain Locke
1925–27	Employed as business editor, *Opportunity*
1926	*Tropic Death* is published by Boni and Liveright
1927	Receives Harmon Award in recognition of achievement in literature; second edition of *Tropic Death* is published; travels to Panama gathering material; named a Zona Gale Scholar; awarded Guggenheim Memorial Foundation Fellowship
1928	Guggenheim Grant extended for six months
1928–29	Visits Dominica, Barbados, U.S. Virgin Islands, and other countries in the region; travels to Paris and joins community of American artists in exile
1931	Travels to New York City and visits parents in Brooklyn
1933	Interviewed in Paris by Jacques Lebar for *Lectures du Soir*.
1935	Travels to Ireland as publicity manager of a "negro revue"
1938	Arrested in London and charged with "causing grievous bodily harm"; charges later dropped

1939	Moves to Wiltshire in South of England; publishes in *New York Amsterdam News*
1940	Writes letter to Henry Moe of Guggenheim, accompanying articles published since 1932, and regretting failure to honor terms of award; applies unsuccessfully for Rosenwald Fellowship
1944–46	Publishes articles in the *People's Voice*
1952	Admitted to Roundway Hospital, Devizes, Wiltshire, as voluntary patient
1953	Writes letter to Henry Moe listing publications in *Roundway Review*
1954	Eldest daughter Jean visits from Jamaica; Walrond expresses intention to donate material to Countee Cullen Collection at Atlanta University in letter to Harold Jackman
1957	Discharged from Roundway Hospital
1958	Presents "Black and Unknown Bards"—an evening of music and poetry at the Royal Court Theatre, London; publishes book with same title
1960	Informs Moe about meetings in London with Richard Wright and W.E.B. Du Bois; expresses regret about not fulfilling commitment to Guggenheim
1965	Hospitalized following heart attack
1966	Signs contract with Arthur Pell of Liveright for reprint of *Tropic Death*
1966	Dies August 8, in London; buried in September in Abney Park Cemetery, London
1972	*Tropic Death* reissued by Collier Books, New York
1998	*"Winds Can Wake Up the Dead": An Eric Walrond Reader* published
2009	Gravestone erected in Abney Park Cemetery

INTRODUCTION

Noted historian David Levering Lewis cites a chance meeting between Harlem Renaissance enfant terrible Richard Bruce Nugent and writer Eric Walrond "in a London railway station in late 1929." According to Lewis, that brief encounter "was about the last heard of [Walrond]" (234). Indeed, it is a common misconception among scholars of African American literature that when Walrond left North America in 1928 he simply stopped writing (or at least publishing), and the life that he led in Europe until his death in 1966 has been largely unknown. The purpose of this anthology is to dispel the belief that he did not publish after leaving America and to clear up some of the mystery of his European years. We have managed, in part, because of the generous cooperation of members of Walrond's family, to put together the most important work in the almost forty years following his departure from America. The result is a diverse collection of fictional and nonfictional writings, which not only belie the myth of Walrond's being nonproductive, but also greatly enrich the scope of black diasporic literature. The writings herein, often first published in the *Roundway Review*—the organ of the Roundway Hospital, a psychiatric facility in Wiltshire, England—where Walrond was "a voluntary patient" from May 11, 1952, to September 5, 1957, reinforce several of the themes from the writer's earlier years, including alienation, the search for identity, "otherness," racism, hybridity, and imperialism, issues that still resonate today.[1] As Walrond's grandson Frank Stewart observes, "Walrond kept a unity and consistency to his repertoire after *Tropic Death*" (34). The publication of these works should help establish his place as one of the earliest and most significant anti-imperialist black writers who, among other things, espouses the vision of a global community made up of those with a "shared history of colonialism and European exploitation" (Stephens, *Black Empire* 2).

Walrond's European writings consist of fictional narratives, articles on race and other social issues, and an unfinished fifteen-part history of the Panama Canal ("The Second Battle"), likely a sequel to the long awaited but never published "The Big Ditch." Among the narratives is the lengthy "Success Story" (1954), set mainly in New York City, but encompassing the landscapes of Barbados, Panama, and British Guiana (now Guyana) as well. To be sure, not all the last fictions equal the achievements of the critically acclaimed *Tropic Death* (1926).[2] The best fiction, however, such as "Inciting to Riot" (1934), "Morning in Colon" (1940), "Two Sisters" (1953), "The Iceman" (1953), "The Coolie's Wedding" (1953), "Bliss" (1953), "Success Story" (1954), and the previously unpublished "Shadow in the Sun" demonstrates that much of his creative power remained intact. Some of the nonfiction prose, including "Harlem" (1933), "White Man, What Now?" (1938), "On England" (1938), "The Men of the Cibao" (1945–46), and the previously unpublished "The Panama Scandal" also enhance his reputation. Walrond continued writing and, with fitful success, particularly in the pieces set in the Caribbean and New York, remained committed to his craft, ever mindful of his contractual obligations to the publishers Boni and Liveright, and the Guggenheim Foundation, as his correspondence to Henry Moe, secretary to the Foundation, and to Jack Conroy, the American novelist, attests.[3]

A Life: From British Guiana to Roundway

In his biographical sketch "From British Guiana to Roundway" (1952), Walrond called it a "big jump" from the various places he had lived to Wiltshire, England, and from the Broad Street Hospital, where he worked in New York as a telephone operator, to Roundway Hospital. Walrond goes on to say, "The jump, for a 'depression casualty' in the years following the Wall Street crash of 1929, is almost frightening. It is as though I'd entered a new world, a compact, almost self-contained community set in surroundings of rare beauty."

Making big jumps, however, was the essence of Walrond's life, which was always marked by being an outsider beginning with his birth on December 18, 1898, in Georgetown, British Guiana, to two Barbadian-born parents. Financial necessity, triggered by his father's abandonment of the family when he sought work in the Panama Canal Zone, drove the family to Barbados and Panama. In both places, he was again an outsider, a foreign-born "Mudhead" (a term denigrating the natives of British Guiana, which is below sea level) in Barbados and a *chombo* (a black West Indian, or, more vulgarly, a "nigger") in Panama. Seeking his fortune, Walrond migrated to the United States on June 30, 1918, where again he was an outsider. Despite the prejudice he encountered as a black and as a West Indian, a "monkey chaser" (Reid 113–16), Walrond experienced his greatest literary success in the United States as an author of numerous essays, reviews, and stories and as an editor of Marcus Garvey's *Negro World* (1921–23) and *Opportunity*, an organ of the National Urban League (1925–27). During his time with the latter journal, Walrond published his most significant work, the short story collection *Tropic Death,* one of the most important volumes of the Harlem Renaissance.

The generally favorable response of the critics to *Tropic Death* prompted Walrond's publisher, Boni and Liveright, to provide an advance for another book on the French involvement in the building of the Panama Canal. Walrond's success as an author may also be measured by three major awards he received in 1927–28: a Harmon Award in literature, a Zona Gale scholarship to attend the University of Wisconsin, and a Guggenheim Award (later renewed for an additional six months) to complete fiction on Caribbean life. After traveling to several countries in Central America and the Caribbean, he arrived in London in June 1929 and departed for France the next month ostensibly to complete his project on the canal and, as he wrote in a letter to Henry Moe, to "settle down to a siege of writing" (Apr. 2, 1929, Guggenheim files). He remained there off and on in Paris, Bandol, and Avignon until the summer of 1932 when he moved to London where he lived intermittently until 1939 (Fabre 138–39).

Time in France

When Walrond arrived in Paris in 1929, there was a small but established group of blacks already living there. About 200,000 African Americans had served in France during World War I, some staying and many more returning to the United States and telling of the experience of living in a non-segregated society. Black artists in particular thought of France as a haven from U.S. racism. Those who stayed, for varying lengths of time, included musicians Louis Mitchell, Ada "Bricktop" Smith, and Josephine Baker and writers, Claude McKay, Countee Cullen, Walter White, Gwendolyn Bennett, James Weldon Johnson, Jessie Fauset, Alain Locke, J. A. Rogers, and Nella Larsen (Edwards 1–15; Stovall 25–129 passim). Walrond immediately fit into this circle. He enjoyed especially the Left Bank, saying that "[i]ts traditions and literary associations stimulate the best efforts in one. Here one can find variety or peace" (quoted in Bald 4). There were lively cafes in Montmartre and Montparnasse where African Americans and West Indians and Africans could revel. Life in these areas of Paris was "passionate, joyous, outrageous, dangerous, and at times tragic, but never dull" (Stovall 43). One club in particular was the lively Bal Nègre, described as "the French Harlem," that Walrond reportedly frequented and where he was befriended by the artists Augusta Savage, Palmer Hayden, and Hale Woodruff (Fabre 83, 141). Walrond, in fact, may well be one of the card players in Hayden's painting "Nous Quatre à Paris" (ca. 1928–30) (Leininger-Miller 84–85, 128). He also met playwright Shirley Graham, later to become the wife of W.E.B. Du Bois, offering her dubious advice on how to win a Guggenheim Award. She rewarded him by providing "niggerati gossip" from back home, and sending him money after she returned to North America (Horne 53–54).[4] In addition, Walrond met up with the American literary couple Marjorie Worthington and Willie Seabrook who lived in France from 1930 to 1933. Walrond had known Seabrook, author of several popular "exotic" travel books, while living in America and had requested that he write him a recommendation for a Guggenheim fellowship.

The two most important connections Walrond made or reestablished, however, were with Countee Cullen and Nancy Cunard. In the spring of 1930 Walrond lived for a time with Cullen in an apartment they rented in Paris, about the same time as Cullen's disastrous two-year marriage to Yolande Du Bois ended. Walrond had been close friends with Cullen (perhaps even lovers briefly) when they were in the United States and both worked for *Opportunity* magazine.[5] He had favorably reviewed Cullen's book *Color* in the *New Republic* (Mar. 31, 1926) while Cullen, in turn, dedicated one of his most famous poems, "Incident," to the West Indian. It is entirely appropriate that what is perhaps Cullen's most racialized poem is dedicated to Walrond, for as Blanche E. Ferguson points out, Walrond's "militant outgoing personality was a helpful contrast to Cullen's introspection" (120–21). In May 1931 Walrond also met shipping heiress Nancy Cunard who scandalized her wealthy socialite family with her radical politics and her interest in black causes. Walrond soon became a member of her entourage and, in all probability, one of her several black lovers (Chisholm 177). Cunard would be someone with whom he would remain in close contact for the remainder of his life.[6]

It is unfortunate that what little is written about Walrond's time in France focuses not on his work itself but more on his time spent in the social scene. Walrond did not, however, devote all of this time to revelry. First, as a member of the National Committee for the Defense of Political Prisoners headed by American novelist Theodore Dreiser, he became involved in the campaign to free the Scottsboro Boys (letter from Dreiser to Walrond, Jan. 6, 1932, in Walrond Papers).[7] Second, upon his arrival in Europe, he immediately wrote several reviews that he published in a monthly London Socialist magazine, the *Clarion*. Two of these, reprinted in this anthology, focus on his Renaissance compatriots, Cullen and Claude McKay. Not surprisingly, his review of Cullen's volume The *Black Christ and Other Poems* (January 1930) praises "a young Negro poet of undisputed talent." Walrond especially admires the title poem depicting the lynching of a young black man.

The review of McKay's novel *Banjo* ("The Negro Renaissance," July 1929) is more mixed. Walrond opens the review by providing a brief overview of Harlem Renaissance authors, McKay in particular, for his British audience. Walrond had had an increasingly testy association with McKay. While he wrote favorably of the Jamaican's early work, their relationship gradually soured.[8] This is evident in letters between the two when McKay was seeking assistance from Walrond in placing his work while the latter was working for *Opportunity* and also in a letter Walrond sent to Arthur Schomburg on December 24, 1925 (Schomburg file, Schomburg Center). In his review, Walrond maintained that McKay had been gone from the United States too long to be able to write authoritatively of black life in America in novels such as *Home to Harlem* (1928). In particular, he was of the opinion that the novelist was unable "to reproduce accurately the nuances of Negro speech." Walrond had long believed in the importance of capturing the language of those that he was writing of, whether the Caribbean natives in the stories of *Tropic Death* or in his later Roundway pieces. He was convinced, however, that in *Banjo*, set on the docks of Marseilles, France, McKay was on somewhat surer ground and was able to create black migrant lifelike characters.

Ultimately, Walrond maintained that the power of the "bleak and sad" portrayal of black diasporic life by McKay was enough "to commend his book."

Walrond, was, in fact, compared with McKay in an article written by French journalist Andre Levinson, "De Harlem à la Cannebière," criticizing the episodic, ultimately pointless nature of *Banjo*. In contrast *Tropic Death* was praised for its accurate use of Caribbean Creole, lush descriptions, seriousness of purpose, and objective narrative style. Walrond was also interviewed by Jacques Lebar ("Avec Eric Walrond") in the French language paper, *Lectures du Soir* (Jan. 14, 1933) where he sets forth the clearest expression of his writing philosophy: "My duty and my *raison d'être* is to give an accurate portrayal of my race, its history, its sufferings, its hopes and its rebellions. Therein lies a rich source of emotion and pain. It is there that I draw the essence of my work, and I will dedicate my energy as a writer to serving the black race."[9] This emphasis on black life is reiterated in an undated letter to African American poet Melvin Tolson from a chateau near Paris, where Walrond had gone in order to "secure a better perspective for the portrayal of Negro character in the Americas" (cited in Tolson, *The Harlem Group* 86).

Perhaps Walrond's most significant writing during this time was published not in English, but in French and Spanish periodicals, enhancing the transnational character of his work. "Harlem," published in *Lectures du Soir* (Feb. 4, 1933), a Parisian weekly newspaper, is a vivid piece written from Walrond's memories of the black capital. The Harlem described is a lawless place filled with violence, alcohol, stolen merchandise, and lascivious women that is nonetheless exotic, exciting, and teeming with life. Initially seen as a paradise, it was corrupted by the encroachment of whites.[10] "El Negro, Expulsado del Cabaret, Vuelve a Labrar la Tierra," published in the communist, antifascist newspaper *Ahora* (Madrid), June 21, 1934, an indication of his increasingly Marxist perspective, is a much more sober text, examining post-Depression Harlem. Unlike the city in its heyday of the previous sketch, the Harlem portrayed here is one in which the economic bubble has burst. Unemployment and inflation have caused blacks to desert it, returning to their native homes in the South or the Antilles. Harlem is a bleak place symbolizing the false promises Walrond believed North America holds for blacks. He had clearly made up his mind never to live in America again. In a brief visit to New York in 1931, the last time he returned to the United States, "he experienced no thrill of homecoming," indicating that "[o]nly urgent business brought me back to this country" (*Amsterdam News* [New York], Sept. 9, 1931).

While Walrond, like many others, believed that France presented the black artist with opportunities unattainable in America, his own years in France were not without their troubles. This is corroborated by his friend Ethel Ray Nance (Williams), who recalled that he wrote her "quite some long letters telling me about his experiences in going to France and living on the Riviera, of accidents he's had and his life being very turbulent" (15). Walrond was also afflicted with bad health, which is confirmed by his former literary agent, Edna Worthley Underwood, who speaks of his having been hospitalized "for a long time" in the American Hospital in Paris (67). What put him there and for how long remains another of the many mysteries of Walrond's life, since hospital records for him are not available. But it may well have been psychological turmoil exacerbated by alcoholism, problems that had long plagued him and would continue to bedevil him in his later years.[11]

Life in England

West Indians had been brought up to think of Britain as their homeland and to see themselves as British citizens. So it seems somewhat natural for Walrond to imagine he would gain acceptance in England. He was not the first West Indian émigré to think along these lines. McKay, for example, had written early verse extolling the virtues of the colonial motherland. However, major rioting against blacks in Cardiff, Liverpool, and other British cities in 1919, shortly after McKay's arrival, would quickly shatter his early idealism. Eventually, McKay would arrive at the conclusion "that prejudice against Negroes had become almost congenital among [the British]" (76).[12] Walrond, too, approached England with optimism, "reared on the belief that England was the one country where the black man was sure of getting a square deal" ("White Man, What Now?"). He would, however, eventually arrive at the same painful conclusion as McKay.

After settling in England in 1932, Walrond immediately plunged into the small black community living in London. He published several short stories in English (or West Indian) periodicals, including "Inciting to Riot" (*Evening Standard,* July 26, 1934; first published as "Sur les Chantiers de Panama" in *Lectures du Soir,* Jan. 7, 1933); "Tai Sing" (*Spectator,* Apr. 20, 1934); "Harlem Nights," *Star* (London) (Sept. 26, 1935); and "Morning in Colon" (*West*

Indian Review, Apr. 1940). "Inciting to Riot" and "Tai Sing" both explore violence, racial tension, and unequal justice in Colón. The matter-of-fact depiction of violence, use of vernacular language, and objective representation of interracial tensions are typical of Walrond's writing. In "Inciting to Riot" Juan Poveda, a Basque grocer transplanted to Panama, hates the *chombos* who frequent his store. Eventually he kills one of his West Indian customers and is escorted into exile by Panamanian police. In "Tai Sing," the eponymous Chinese storekeeper shoots and kills a black man while trying out his new pistol. Tai Sing is able to buy his freedom and after re-establishing himself, shoots another black who refuses to pay him for watching over a bag left at his store.

Violence is also evidenced in "Harlem Nights," which recalls the earlier "Harlem," particularly the section on Jim Rawlins, in its language and portrayal of a wild, violent, hard partying African American locale. The tale relates the two nightspots owned by Tim Jim, "[a] small black man with a loud bass voice and a laborious shuffling gait." The first, the Red Moon, changed from an all-black cabaret into one that catered to whites out slumming until a riot broke out one night. Jim then opened a second venue, the Club Vodeo.

"Morning in Colon," set in Panama, is a charming piece of dialect prose that describes the transplanted cultural traditions as well as the social and economic realities of migrant life in the Canal Zone. Writing for a primarily West Indian audience, Walrond was free to indulge himself in his use of Creole. Indeed, the work succeeds because of Walrond's spot-on use of the vernacular. "Yo' must wahn me fi' t'ief [to steal], eh! Where yo' t'ink me gwine get eighty cents fi' pay fi' a scrawny, yallah-leg fowl cock? Off a ackee bush?" Walrond never lost his skill in utilizing dialect. As Langston Hughes has said about the stories in *Tropic Death,* "the ease and accuracy of Mr. Walrond's West Indian dialects support one in the belief that he knows very well the people of whom he writes." Yet, ironically, as Louis Chude-Sokei notes, "it is possible that his literary voice may have been marginalized in part for being too overtly laden with black languages and vernaculars, as well as for being too experimental with multiple black dialects and modes of register" (111). Dohra Ahmad and Shondel Nero point out how writers such as Walrond are often unfairly stigmatized because of misunderstood or condescending notions of the vernacular. They argue that, in fact, vernacular literature is very carefully crafted, reflecting the skill and acute linguistic sensibility of the writer.[13]

In addition to his creative writing, Walrond continued to contribute non-fictional articles to journals. He also made contacts with members of the integrationist League of Coloured Peoples in England headed by Dr. Harold Moody and including Jamaican-born author Una Marson (Jarrett-Macauley 81, 84). Walrond, at Marson's invitation, contributed brief book reviews on fiction by his old Harlem Renaissance friends Zora Neale Hurston (the novel, *Jonah's Gourd Vine*) and Langston Hughes (the short story collection, *Ways of White Folks*) to the league's organ, the *Keys*.[14]

Walrond's more radical impulses, however, would soon come to the fore. These beliefs had been demonstrated while he was still living in the United States. For example, "The Black City," published in the leftist periodical the *Messenger* (Jan. 1924, 13–14) vividly dissects the contradictions in Harlem, "a sociological *el dorado*" of vibrant creativity and crushing poverty. Walrond also served as a contributing editor for the communist journal *New Masses* from 1926 to 1930. "White Man, What Now?" (1935) demonstrates his constant outsider status, whether in the Anglophone Caribbean, Panama, Haiti, the Dominican Republic, or the United States. Having been brought up in a British colony, he was raised to believe that "there is no difference between ourselves and white folk." Therefore, he does not expect to find a color bar.[15] Deftly told, as James Davis, observes, "through ironic understatement," Walrond, with tongue firmly in cheek, manages to flaunt the hypocrisy of the British system, and, amazingly, does so in a mainstream journal. Written in the context of an increasingly antiblack atmosphere in England, "what's remarkable about the *Spectator* essay is its restraint. It sounds an ameliorative note, emphasizing the common ground between white Britons and colonials" (Davis), disguising the author's real intent.

Walrond's increasing disenchantment with England is clearly chronicled in his writings for Marcus Garvey's *Black Man*, his steadiest source of publication in the 1930s. Garvey, who had been deported from the United States after being released from jail in 1927, had, like Walrond, settled in England in the mid-1930s. Their reconciliation is not surprising despite some earlier acrimony. Although Walrond's increasingly leftist political views were sometimes at odds with Garvey's black nationalist agenda, he was still attracted to the Jamaican's fighting spirit and his emphasis on black pride. Walrond published several pieces in *Black Man*; in fact, other than Garvey himself, he was the chief contributor, and even received a small retainer from the editor (Grant 438). "A Fugitive from Dixie" (May/June 1936) is a sketch about a Southern black who was driven off his land by whites and has resettled in Saint Louis with no intention of ever returning to his home. The work may in some ways reflect Walrond's own desire to escape America, despite the prejudice he witnessed in England. It particularly recalls his trip to the American South, via Jim Crow rail cars, while doing research for an article for *Forbes Magazine* in 1924. Nance alleges that Walrond "was never very anxious to return to the United States. He could find fault with the United States, he could tell you in a very few words, its short comings and they always made sense" (15).

As Robert Hill observes, Walrond's writings in *Black Man* show him "to have been moving towards an explicit adoption of the theory of historical materialism and its then stylistic accompaniment in literature, proletarian realism" (19). His writing took an increasingly leftist stance, perhaps in response to the tide of fascism sweeping Europe and criticized in such essays as "Fascism and the Negro" (*Black Man,* Mar.–Apr. 1937). This leftist tendency is evidenced in the essay "On England" (July 1938), a scathing indictment of the colonial motherland. Walrond attacks the British class system, saying that "any suave, gilt-edged rascal may be a gentleman" provided he is "of gentle birth." He also criticizes the entire concept of liberty and democracy in England, concluding that an Empire that will not allow its subjects any representative voice cannot truly lay claim to such ideals.

When the *Black Man* ceased publication in 1939, Walrond was hard-pressed for work. He wrote to John Lehmann, editor of the annual volume *New Writing* published by Penguin, about authoring "a short story of about 3,500 words in length which deals with life in the West Indian slum quarter of Brooklyn, N.Y." (letter July 14, 1939, Walrond Papers). He corresponded with George Orwell about the possibility of writing reviews for the London *Tribune* (Walrond Papers) and also applied for a Rosenwald Fellowship in 1939–40. Nothing came of these ventures, and in desperation, he turned for support to his old friends, including Charles S. Johnson and his secretary Ethel Ray Nance. The two tried to help place his writings, but with little success, probably because, as Johnson suspected, many publishers had forgotten Walrond in his years of silence. He did, however, contribute several works to Johnson's *A Monthly Summary of Events and Trends in Race Relations* from 1944–46. It is difficult to determine his exact contributions since the articles were unsigned, but an essay such as "Education and Training of Negroes and Indians in Britain" (Dec. 1944) was clearly by Walrond since it was also published under his name in the *People's Voice* (Dec. 30, 1944). While this material shows the enormous scholarship and attention to detail that Walrond put into his journalistic work, unfortunately, it brought in very little revenue.[16] It is also revealing that he was able to publish the same piece in such vastly different journals as those edited by the integrationist Charles S. Johnson and the more radical Adam Clayton Powell Jr.

Walrond, in fact, became the overseas correspondent for the charismatic minister and political activist Powell Jr.'s progressive African American newspaper, the *People's Voice*. It is quite possible that he obtained the position through the influence of his ex-girlfriend Marvel Cooke from his years in Harlem.[17] Walrond was always skillful at gaining favors from those in his past such as Garvey, Johnson, and Cunard. Between 1944–46, he published several essays expressing his anticolonial beliefs in the *People's Voice*, including the two-part "The Men of the Cibao," one of his strongest journalistic writings despite its somewhat clumsy narrative structure. The blurring of journalistic and fictional boundaries was, in fact, typical of many of Walrond's writings going back to such works as "On Being a Domestic" (*Opportunity*, Aug. 1923) and "On Being Black" (*New Republic*, Nov. 1, 1922). Its strength probably originates from his own memories of the U.S. Occupation of the Dominican Republic from 1916 to 1924, the effects of which he later witnessed firsthand during his Guggenheim travels. This piece doubtless also reminded him of Panamanian struggles against American control of the Canal Zone, and he saw the brave resistance of the natives as a harbinger of growing resistance to imperialism in southeast Asia. He also seems at this time to have not lost his fighting spirit, which is much in evidence in a letter dated May 22, 1946, to his old college and Harlem Renaissance friend, Gwendolyn Bennett, in which he chastises "some smarmy parvenue of an editor" who had attempted to mislead him (Gwendolyn Bennett Papers, Schomburg Center).

Wiltshire and the Roundway Years

We do not know exactly why Walrond moved from London to Wiltshire, but there were several possible reasons. The years between 1932 and 1939 were generally not good times in his life. His publications declined to a trickle since he had come to Europe, and he had no steady source of income in London. The outbreak of World War II in September 1939 may also have precipitated his relocation. In fact, in the story "Strange Incident" (1956) the narrator (likely Walrond) announced that he had relocated to Wiltshire "from London on the evening of the day Hitler's ultimatum to

Poland expired [September 1, 1939]." A number of Londoners moved to the relative safety of Wiltshire as the bombings of Britain's capital increased. Another, more troubling reason, may also account for Walrond's departure from London. According to an item in the *Times* (London) of September 22, 1938, he had been arrested for allegedly stabbing a man in the neck, "causing grievous bodily harm" (7). While the charges were later dropped, the very incident itself reveals the turbulence he was experiencing at the time. For all these reasons, moving to the countryside may have appealed to him at this juncture in his life.[18]

The town in which he settled from 1939–52, Bradford-on-Avon, about ten miles east of Bath, would seem a perfect writer's retreat. It was picturesque, with narrow streets, medieval architecture (it was founded by the Saxons) and a small chapel, and the River Avon flowing through the midst of the town, which had about 4,000 residents. It promised a tranquil environment which, unfortunately, was not reflected in Walrond's personal life—though it did provide the setting for several of his British writings. Walrond would again have been an outsider as one of only a handful of immigrants and very likely the only black resident. There he lodged in a small stone cottage atop a hill at 9 Ivy Terrace with a married couple who were artists. He seems to have gotten along with his neighbors though they kept some polite distance from him. While they knew he worked as a journalist and recognized his intelligence, none realized the fame he had achieved during the Harlem Renaissance years. During the war years he worked as a laborer for the Avon Rubber company, an important industry at the time, in nearby Melksham.[19]

There is no clear indication of what led Walrond to enter Roundway Hospital. Certainly it was for some sort of mental illness, since Roundway was a psychiatric hospital that admitted only patients with psychological problems.[20] He was, by all reports, a charming, energetic figure, much sought after for companionship during the Harlem Renaissance days when he served as an unofficial conduit "between Uptown and Downtown New York." However, as David Levering Lewis observes, "Walrond also had a brooding side, and was given to bouts of paralyzing self-doubt" (128). This is evident from letters to Alain Locke in the 1920s complaining of fits of depression. In one letter, for example, dated May 5, 1924, he speaks of being in "one of my old shifting, restless, nervous moods." And in a letter one month later, he states that he is unable to visit Locke in Washington due to a "highstrung, unnatural, morbid, discontented state of mind."[21] He felt enormous pressure to follow up on his youthful success and become the significant literary figure that was expected of him. His letters to Henry Moe frequently lament his failures to produce, are filled with guilt, and place responsibility squarely on himself: "No one feels more keenly than I do the inadequacy of my performance up to date" (June 20, 1940). Inevitably, the letters end with a desire that he will one day be able to fulfill his own and others' high hopes for him. His disappointment and regret over his failure to honor his obligations may well have influenced his decision to seek professional help at Roundway. This seems to be confirmed in a letter from his friend Arnold Herman Kamiat, who recounted that Walrond had been experiencing a "spiritual crisis" shortly before entering the hospital,[22] and that this may even have led him to contemplate suicide. This is hinted at when he tells Moe that he had "a moment in Wiltshire when I must have forgotten [a reason for living]" (letter June 11, 1960).

Although Walrond's case history does not seem to have survived, it is possible to reconstruct what life was like for a patient in Roundway Hospital in the 1950s,[23] a large, somewhat sprawling facility spread out over several buildings and housing over 1,300 patients. The hospital, despite its spacious grounds and rural ambience, was far from idyllic. It tended toward overcrowding and did not begin to prescribe new psychotropic drugs until the mid-1950s, several years after many other hospitals. However, reforms were being made there and at other English mental institutions during the 1950s. For example, many of the patients were at Roundway voluntarily. At a similar facility, Claybury, for instance, in 1956, over 84 percent of patients admitted were voluntary (Pryor 104).

Dr. Millar Speer's tenure as Medical Superintendent of Roundway (1948–57) saw many changes come to the hospital including the introduction of major tranquilizing and antidepressant drugs. The most commonly prescribed medications used during the time of Walrond's stay were Largactil and Thorazine, psychotropic drugs administered to treat major depression and violent mood swings. These drugs, though they often merely alleviated symptoms and did not cure the patient, allowed the massive increase in hospital discharges in the late 1950s. Walrond was among those discharged.

Speer also increased the number of social workers, and he encouraged patients to become active within the hospital through recreational therapy and expanded art, music, and sports facilities. Additional measures were taken to prepare patients more fully for their return to the outside world.

In this environment, it is not surprising that the *Roundway Review* was established in 1952. The *Review*, which developed from a crude typescript to a professional looking pamphlet, was published monthly and circulated within and beyond the confines of the hospital. While much of the material, written by patients and staff, focused on Roundway activities, the contributions tended to be of a fairly high caliber (Steele 81). From the very beginning, Walrond was closely involved with the publication, serving as assistant editor and regular contributor. It is probably not coincidental that the periodical's inception coincides with his admission to the hospital and its demise came shortly after his release. If he was not *Roundway Review*'s creator he was, at the least, the driving force behind it. In a note enclosed with his short story "By the River Avon" (*Crisis* January 1947), Walrond indicates that he has a number of stories "under [his] hat." The *Roundway Review* would be the perfect vehicle to showcase these writings.[24]

The Quintessential "Other"

In the narratives published in the *Roundway Review* Walrond re-imagines colonial and metropolitan landscapes as sites of fragmentation, displacement, and alienation. Such emphases are not unexpected in the texts of one of the earliest black literary historians of the diaspora, regarded by critic Robert Bone as the quintessential "other" (176–77). Social realism is the primary mode in these fictions; the experiments with the gothic and naturalistic modes of *Tropic Death* (Wade 417–23) are replaced by a more direct scrutiny of essentialist representations of race and social conflict, although Walrond's exploration of these issues is not without humor and poignancy in the best of these tales.

The *Roundway Review* stories examine social divisiveness, economic inequity, as well as racial anxiety, and tribal identities, although Walrond's language occasionally identifies him as a creature of the times possessing similar obsessions. The writer implies that these resilient images and self-images complicate his vision of a transnational diasporic community. This dream has been intensified through his renewed association with Marcus Garvey, and the Pan-Africanist movement in general during a period, Deborah Rossum notes, when Walrond, along with a number of other black intellectuals living in London, interrogates notions of black identity, as fervently and fearlessly as he had done in a Harlem setting, specifically the orthodox thesis in which "Englishness was conceived as the ultimate measure of civilization and an attribute whose superiority was dependent on the inferiority of its subject gaze" (7). These intellectuals also challenged an "*Alienness* as equated to inferiority [that] became the language of racialist discourse and, as such, was promoted specially in the popular customs and the culture of the time" (7). In challenging the European formulations about persons of African ancestry and their lack of a literary tradition and "presence," Walrond claims Francis Williams, Olaudah Equiano, Alexander Pushkin ("the flowering of the Negro genius at its zenith"), among others, as representatives of the race's potential and achievement.[25] Bone's observation on Walrond's concerns about "race" in the earlier writings therefore remains relevant to a reading of the *Roundway Review* and other European pieces: "What troubles Walrond most about the racist mentality is its relentless categorization. People are judged, so to speak, by the backs of their necks, rather than their faces. They are threatened psychologically with facelessness—with a humiliating loss of individuality. Depersonalization is the essence of the crime" (180–81). The autobiographical flavor of the stories suggests the impact of the author's personal experience of racial antipathy throughout the diaspora.

Walrond's vision of a black global community was shared, as we have suggested, with his Caribbean contemporaries exiled in England, who were disillusioned even further by their experiences in the metropolis and by the geopolitical developments up to and during World War II. In addition, the race riots involving black servicemen that erupted in the 1940s throughout cities in the United Kingdom, the British color bar, and Italy's invasion of Abyssinia (Ethiopia) in 1935 helped galvanize anticolonial sentiment among members of this community, further crystallizing an ideology that had taken root in the United States during the first decades of the century among black male intellectuals such as McKay, Garvey, and C.L.R. James. Michelle Stephens posits that this reimagining of the black state as a single community transcending nationalism was in response to a changing geopolitical and intellectual climate. For as immigrants, Caribbeans "had no easily identifiable national homelands, arriving in America from diverse island colonies whose only bond was, at best, their shared history of colonialism and European exploitation" (*Black Empire* 2). But redefining the black state in ways reimagined by these intellectuals, as Jamaican-born poet Louis Simpson observes, presented the challenge of locating models of black nationality, and of confronting a colonial mentality that hindered cultural self-determination and self-representation, in other words, a sense of their Caribbeaness (cited in Stephens 2).

Walrond himself confronts this legacy in many of the articles published during this period, at the same time revealing the disillusionment of one who, retreating from the racist environment of the United States, had sought to assert an identity as a British colonial. In "On England" (1938) and "White Man, What Now?" (1935), he exposes the hypocrisy and injustice at the core of British society, simultaneously revealing the disillusionment of the alienated colonial. "The Negro in London" (*Black Man* 1936) provides an example: "Viewing the 'Mother Country' with an adoring eye, the Negro in British overseas colonies is obviously at the mercy of a rainbow. He sees England through a romantic and illusive veil. What he affectionately imagines he sees does not always 'square' with the facts" (Parascandola, "Winds" 282).

Walrond also asserts that "The Negro is sometimes made to feel like some species of exotic humanity from another planet, and this despite the presence of 50,000,000 Negroes in the British Empire." He scrutinizes, even dismantles, the colonial construct of England as "home," and "the Empire's centre of gravity" (Ras Makonnen, quoted in Rossum 1). Examining the marginalization of colonial blacks in England, Walrond writes with obvious understatement in "The Negro in London": "[I]t is indeed a paradox that London, the capital of the largest Negro Empire in the world—the cradle of English liberty, justice and fair-play—the city to which Frederick Douglas[s] fled as a fugitive from slavery—should be so extremely inexpert in the matter of interracial relations" (284–85). Walrond's growing recognition of Caribbean colonials, as Louis Simpson put it, "as a remote branch of England" (quoted in Stephens, *Black Empire* 2), contributes substantially to the transnational perspective implicit in the late writings.

The Roundway Fictions (Caribbean Stories)

Diverging somewhat from the principal focus of the narratives is "The Servant Girl" (Jan. 1953), the first published and perhaps the first written tale from the *Roundway* stories. This is an exploration of a young protagonist's coming of age to some of the complexities and mysteries of social interaction in the British Guiana of the author's youth. The story also displays the random violence that characterized so much of Walrond's fictional narratives, whether in most of the stories from *Tropic Death* or later writings such as "Inciting to Riot" and "Harlem Nights."

In addition to facilitating the nostalgic return to childhood memories, as in "The Servant Girl," the British Guiana setting also appealed to the writer because its multicultural society provided an appropriate context for the examination of racial antipathy and cultural displacement, as can be seen in "The Coolie's Wedding" (Aug. 1953) and "A Piece of Hard Tack" (Oct. 1953). In "The Coolie's Wedding" a Hindu's lack of accommodation in Caribbean society is represented by his lodgment in the cellar beneath the young protagonist's house where he has sought refuge in retreat from the plantation world and the animosity of the wider community; by the same token, this character is, in some sense, imprisoned within his own culture and history. The failure of the Hindu community's efforts at cultural assimilation is symbolized by the collapse of the vehicle conveying a bridal party to the Christian wedding, and by their objectification through the anthropological gaze of the Afro-Guyanese characters, in particular, a servant girl.

"A Piece of Hard Tack," a story similar to "Poor Great" (published in a London magazine *Arena*, Sept./Oct. 1950), offers very similar episodes of inter- and intra-racial antipathy in yet another Guyanese setting. Here the generosity of an empathetic observer toward "different" ethnic Caribbean groups—Amerindian "bucks"—is subverted by the hostility initiated by one equally demonized by European ideologies. That the anthropological gaze is directed toward a community marginalized as unprogressive and superstitious despite its status as an indigenous people is the occasion for Walrond's understated but trenchant irony—and an indication that his reimagined community occasionally transcends ethnicity as well becoming, in contrast to Garvey, increasingly anticapitalist and class-based.

The protagonists of "Wind in the Palms" (Sept. 1954), "Bliss" (July 1953), and "The Loan" (Nov. 1953) are all men beset by racial anxieties and self-denial. In "Wind in the Palms" Coolie (the term itself is pejorative) is the "dougla" product of an African and East Indian union whose angst and social suppression of his mother signal his own partial self-erasure. He prides himself on those physical attributes that he has inherited from his unknown East Indian father, yet those attributes alone are not sufficient to make him the equal of the brown men "with their mixture of European blood." It is ironic that Coolie's heavily creolized language confirms his membership in the very group from which he seeks to distance himself. In this tale, as elsewhere, Walrond's subtle narrative strategies function to undermine these constructs of self and of others, and suggest that the possibilities of cross-culturality remain unexplored in postcolonial contexts where such ideologies prevail.

Similar misgivings are also reflected in "Bliss" and "The Loan" where Walrond again dramatizes the antagonistic encounters between different ethnic groups in the diaspora, in these instances the *chombo* and the Spaniard (native Panamanian). The title of the former story ironically alludes to the clichéd maxim "Ignorance is bliss." In the story Boysie, a *chombo*, is seemingly treated with respect by a wealthy white man. But is it Boysie who is naively dreaming that he has achieved a measure of equality because of this unusual treatment in the Canal Zone's racialized system or is the system itself being mocked? Boysie himself hopes that his Spanish Panamanian friend Ramon does not witness the scene so that Ramon may not have his faith in the racial hierarchy challenged. In "The Loan" Curly, Rufus, and Buster, all *chombos*, must deal with their own ambivalence when interacting with Spanish Panamanians, vacillating between pride in their heritage and their internalized sense of inferiority toward the Spaniards. Collectively, "Wind in the Palms," "Bliss," and "The Loan" reveal much about the conflicted, often tortured psychology of West Indians residing in the Canal Zone, as well as the racial tensions of a multiethnic community.

As Rhonda Frederick contends, Walrond's interrogation of some of the many "mythographies" of the West Indian immigration to Panama, reveals dimensions of this enterprise not recorded by other types of narratives. The writer draws on his unique vantage point as an Anglophone Caribbean newspaper reporter (Panama *Star and Herald*) whose beat is the West Indian ghettos to dramatize the travails and trials of the immigrant quest for "Panama gold." Many of the Panama narratives in this collection reiterate the concerns of similar tales in *Tropic Death*, revealing, among other things, as Frederick suggests: "Colón men [and occasionally, in this collection, women] at odds with Panamanians, European and Euro-American laborers, as well as French and North American supervisors whose racial prejudices resulted from xenophobia, racism, religious and language differences, and/or economic competition" (32).[26] As some commentators have pointed out, West Indian workers were further exploited during the years of United States involvement in the building of the canal (1904–14) by their status as "silver" men. The Canal Zone had a notoriously discriminatory system characterized by unequal access to education and social amenities, and in which black laborers were paid in silver whereas white workers were paid in gold (Watkins-Owens 11–18; Newton 104–5, 131–32, 139–52).

An example of the Panama narrative, "The Iceman," which is reminiscent of "Panama Gold" (*Tropic Death*) through its maimed protagonist and its vision of a random and contradictory universe, is an account of the resilience of one of these silver men, Nattie, a former Panama Canal laborer, who endures life's adversities, ever more certain of his indestructibility. But unlike Poyah, the successful returned Colón immigrant from "Panama Gold," Nattie achieves little more beyond a sense of his own insignificance in the larger scheme of things. Perhaps the most poignant of the Roundway stories, "The Iceman," like "Morning in Colon" and "Inciting to Riot," also captures many dimensions of the hardscrabble existence of the West Indian migrant laborer, in particular, the threats posed by the encroachment of capitalism, imperialism, and technology, as well as pervasive poverty. Walrond would frequently rail against the colonial system with "its enforced cruelty, its terrible carceral aspect, its inhumanity and degradation of the human spirit" (Stewart 72). However, in this tale the cultural and other conflicts among West Indians in the Canal Zone are deflected through humor in the protagonist's optimistic and expansive vision of life. Nattie's sardonic work songs integrate tribulation and triumph, disappointment and possibility, transcending adversity in the process.[27]

"Two Sisters" (Mar.–May 1953) incorporates and yet transcends these concerns, in some ways often revisiting the motifs of Walrond's most accomplished fiction: the journey to further alienation and exclusion, creativity in conflict with destructiveness and malice. Set in Barbados at the turn of the twentieth century, this tale also re-creates the barren natural and social landscapes of *Tropic Death*. It is yet another example of Walrond's use of fictional biography, being modeled on the circumstances of his first visit to his parents' ancestral homeland in 1906.[28] One can only conjecture that, at a period of financial, psychological and artistic crisis, the writer's imagination retreats to landscapes of experience and memory, particularly as a child. "Walrond seem[s] to have retained a lifelong sympathy with himself as a boy beset by the adult world" (Stewart 57). Similar to his fellow West Indian, Claude McKay, Walrond would return psychically to his homeland, but "only in flights of imagination" resulting in some of his best, most authentic work (Ramesh and Rani 83). Perhaps Walrond's most accomplished hymn to black matriarchy, "Two Sisters" utilizes the motif of the resourceful and creative mother in company of a devoted son in search of "home" and community. Its secondary protagonist, Phinee, is the pedestalized nurturing maternal figure, inspired by Ruth Walrond, Eric's mother, in whose portraiture the author conflates constructs of femininity from his earlier narratives, especially the short stories "Tropic Death" and "The Black Pin."

"Two Sisters" is the tale of Phinee's return to her native Barbados when her Guyanese husband joins the Caribbean exodus to the Panama Canal Zone, only to encounter hostility and alienation from her relatives and the wider community on account of her marital and religious choices.[29] This narrative develops around several major ironies: that Phinee's quest for temporary tenancy is frustrated in spite of her legitimate claims to an ancestral space; that the threat to her enterprise emanates from her own relatives; and that it is the resourceful mother figure who demolishes her own creation. The tale's most tragic irony, that the woman's most powerful experience of dislocation occurs at the site identified as "home," is a recurring theme throughout Walrond's fictions. The marginalization resulting from Phinee's religious and marital choices, and Henry's exclusion on the basis of his ascribed status as "Mudhead," therefore unites them with the remaining protagonists in the *Roundway Review* narratives.[30]

"Success Story"

In "Success Story" (Feb.–June 1954), a semiautobiographical six-part work, we witness a more complex reenactment of the struggle that occupied Walrond in both his fictional and nonfictional texts during this period, and which is more fully developed in "The Second Battle" and other narratives. This narrative resumes the threads of some of the Caribbean tales, specifically "Two Sisters," reprising characters, incidents, and settings in addressing the intersection between familial and communal discord in the immigrant community in the United States and Central America. In deconstructing the black West Indian version of the American dream, it develops the themes of the earlier New York tales such as "City Love" (1927). The intragenerational tensions that we have come to associate with the work of author Paule Marshall in *Brown Girl, Brown Stones* (1959) and *The Fisher King* (2000), among other texts, links Walrond's work to a major tradition of Caribbean American writing.

Nevertheless, as the New York scenes especially illustrate, this is essentially a tale about the quest to redefine and validate self outside the paradigms and parameters of colonial ideology. At times the story offers a tense and complex negotiation of spaces and identities in the multiracial setting of the Isthmus, enriched by the author's experiments with narrative viewpoints. Walrond probably reworked elements of the narrative from the unpublished "Shadow in the Sun," especially the shooting down of the transplanted Bodie Prout, father of the ostensible narrator, Jim Prout, by his colleague, the white American policeman Rowde (ironically, the name of a village in Wiltshire). Prout's fate in some ways prefigures that of his son and recalls a similar incident in "Subjection," from *Tropic Death*, and may also communicate a belief about the invalidity of West Indian racial and class distinctions in the wider world, not least of all, the Panama Canal Zone. Through the relationship between the policemen, one a mixed race West Indian, the other, a white American, Walrond captures, once again, the racial tensions and anxieties of the Isthmus. Bodie Prout as a West Indian is caught between the prejudice of the Euro-American colleague and the suspicion of the native "rebels," his dilemma complicated further by his job, his apparent class background, his ethnicity, as well as his nationality.

Bodie is implicated in an oppressive oligarchy through his participation in its pastimes, its forms of reference, dress and address, and its rituals. In this role, he is locked in conflict with the "outlaws" who personify a nationalist ideology of resistance, assertion, and subversion. To the rebel, Manuel Fonseca, "a Gringo was a Gringo, whether he was dark or fair, spoke with a Texas drawl or a British Guiana accent." Yet, ironically, it is also Bodie's presumptions about privilege that culminate in his death at the hands of the white American policeman.

As is so often the case in Walrond's writings, "Success Story" takes liberties with the facts of family history to strengthen the fictional illusion. For example, "Prout" was the name of Walrond's maternal rather than paternal ancestors, as is suggested. Some elements of Bodie Prout's portraiture may also signal the writer's subconscious repudiation of the maternal branch of his family on the grounds that the ethnic composition and social standing of the Prouts implicated them in a system of dominance and oppression that Walrond himself encountered, especially in the United States and Britain. In this regard, it is significant that in "Success Story" and "The Vampire Bat," the Prout name is assigned to culturally remote authority figures with pronounced European ethnic characteristics. The latter, a gothic tale from *Tropic Death*, recounts the fate of Bellon Prout, a white soldier returning home to Barbados after the Boer War, who is linked with oppression and death (Parascandola 27–28) through his ethnicity. Prout suffers a mysterious death resulting from a conspiracy of supernatural and human (native black) agency, a fate that is in some ways repeated in "Success Story." "The Vampire Bat" is a moral fable about the consequences of racial pride and blindness. The fact that none of the attributes associated with the Prout characters in Walrond's fiction such as occupation, social status, and ethnicity, apply to William Walrond (Eric Walrond's biological father) substantiates the view that in "Success Story" and "The Vampire Bat" Walrond is looking beyond the historical father-son relationship explicated by Bone in *Down Home*, to exorcise some other private demons.[31]

Jim Prout's vision develops and deepens in the New York episodes when centered as narrator-protagonist, and resisting his own liminal status as West Indian and black, he embarks on a mission to secure employment commensurate with his achievement and sense of self. In contrast, Walrond targets the West Indian immigrant community's renunciation of its cultural heritage, and its capitulation to essentialist constructs of black identity, implicit in its socioeconomic marginalization.

The narrator-protagonist's sarcastic representation of the typical hard-working immigrant family invokes a still somewhat prevalent American stereotype of West Indian immigrant life where all members of the household are limited to what he considers menial occupations. Jim Prout's resistance to this imposed identity is linked to the rejection of such social roles as prescribed by American society, and accepted as ideal by some members of the West Indian community. However, through the fate of Bodie Prout in Central America and the protagonist's discovery of the futility of his own quest for revisionary self-definition in the United States, as confirmed in the closing episode, the ironic title "Success Story" directs the reader to the inevitability of black "invisibility." Even if, which is doubtful, Jim is eventually assimilated into American society, at what price has this been achieved? Is it worth renouncing one's racial or ethnic identity in order to be considered a success? In earlier pieces such as "Vignettes of the Dusk" (*Opportunity*, Jan. 1924), Walrond warns of the lurking dangers, "the vanilla temptation," for black foreigners trying to assimilate into America. Inevitably it is an unattainable and self-destructive quest, and this story may well be reiterating that warning. In this semiautobiographical piece, he may also, ironically, be reflecting on his own life, considering whether his own story has been a success. Though Walrond's letters from the 1950s show a dogged perseverance and optimism, the fact that he, a middle-aged and almost forgotten figure, is writing this piece from a psychiatric hospital could not have been lost on him. Thus, the whole concept of "success" and what it means has been called into play.

British Stories

Some of the narratives set in England, for example, "Strange Incident" (Jan. 1956) and "The Lieutenant's Dilemma" (May 1955), develop the concerns of the nonfiction published in *Black Man* and other journals. "Strange Incident" and "The Lieutenant's Dilemma" dramatize the exacerbation of these tensions by the presence of black and white American soldiers in wartime Britain. One of the most polemical of the British narratives, "Strange Incident," another seemingly autobiographical piece this time set in the Wiltshire region where Walrond was institutionalized, develops the theme of racial exoticizing introduced in its opening statement: "Even as transients non-whites of whatever variety—colonial war workers, English mulatto evacuees or West Indians in the R.A.F.—were such a novelty I had a feeling that when they did put in an occasional appearance they possessed for the local folk all the interest of an exotic, war-time phenomenon."[32] The unnamed first person narrator's self-constructed identity as an intellectual and literary man—no doubt drawn on Walrond himself—comes into conflict with more entrenched images of people of African ancestry.[33] Similarly set in Wiltshire, "The Lieutenant's Dilemma" also examines the predicament confronting the black characters, African American as well as West Indian, that, as in the former tale, derive from the confluence of British and American racist discourses.[34]

"The Second Battle"

W.E.B. Du Bois in a letter dated January 20, 1942, recalled Walrond, who "once planned and partially finished a study called *The Big Ditch* which treated the Panama Canal and the various West Indian Negroes who worked upon it." Du Bois said he "often wondered what became of that manuscript" (2: 308). His puzzlement over "The Big Ditch," a work that was listed as forthcoming in the 1927 Boni and Liveright catalog and as a published text by critic Elizabeth Lay Green (1928)—but whose fate remains a mystery, is one that has been shared by many literary historians.[35] The work had progressed to the point that Walrond had been given an advance of $1,000 even though Horace Liveright had never seen the manuscript (letter to Liveright from fellow publisher Julian Messner, July 27, 1928, University of Pennsylvania Library). Signs of trouble were already brewing in 1927, however, when Walrond was unable to get any of it serialized (letter to Moe, Dec. 17, 1927).

Despite the uncertainties about "The Big Ditch," we do get tantalizing glimpses of Walrond's work on the Panama Canal in "The Second Battle," published in fifteen installments, totaling about ninety printed pages, between April 1956 and July 1957 in the *Roundway Review*. The manuscript breaks off abruptly, obviously incomplete, perhaps because of Walrond's impending release from the hospital in September 1957, but it never seems to have been resumed. Despite its weaknesses, the manuscript is important for its continued focus on themes that had dominated Walrond's early writings, including his empathy for oppressed peoples. This subtext manifests itself, in particular, in the anticolonial (especially anti-American) view that pervades the work.

The problems with "The Second Battle" are largely ones of purpose, audience, and style. In several letters between Walrond and Erica Marx, editor of the Hand and Flower Press, Walrond's intent in writing the manuscript is clear. He saw it as "an experiment in presenting in a new form the story of Ferdinand de Lesseps' failure in Panama," and he particularly hopes to dispute the claim "that the failure of M. de Lesseps in Panama was due to the decimation of his workers by yellow fever" (Walrond to Erica Marx, June 28, 1957). In her letter from June 25, 1957, Marx had warned Walrond of the chief problem with the manuscript, its highly specialized nature. Marx also attempted, in as gentle a manner as she could, to get him to loosen up his writing, particularly in the opening chapters, which are filled with abstruse footnotes and details about the building of the canal. Walrond does agree, in fact, "that the first two or three chapters [are] cramped and taut" and that he needs to "introduce a little air into them." However, he was never quite able to do this. Walrond himself acknowledges his failure in a letter to Moe, from June 11, 1960, when he apologizes for having "inflicted upon" him a "poorly conceived [manuscript—perhaps both 'The Big Ditch' and 'The Second Battle'] based upon inadequate research and hurriedly produced."

The title of the work suggests that Walrond's focus would be on Ferdinand de Lesseps, the Frenchman whose "second battle" (the "first" was the completion of the Suez Canal) was the struggle to build a canal connecting the Caribbean Sea and the Pacific Ocean between 1880–89. However, it is obvious early on that the real intent of the work is to chronicle the machinations of the American government in the planning of the canal. The narrative, in fact, gains power when Walrond digresses from de Lesseps, a representative of the imperialist forces, and takes up the tale of Pedro Prestan, the mixed-race proletarian leader of the rebel band. Though the rebellion was quickly suppressed by Americans and Prestan hanged in 1885, he is portrayed as a folk hero resisting the colonial authorities. His plight is similar to that of the protagonist who bravely stands up to American oppression in the story "Subjection" (the most overtly political tale in *Tropic Death*) and is brutally murdered for his defiance. In Walrond's narrative, Prestan and his chief lieutenants Antoine Portuzal, a Haitian mulatto, and George Davis, a black man from Jamaica, are seen as martyrs who burn Colón down, in an almost cathartic ritual, before finally being stopped, an incident he had earlier fictionalized in the story "The Godless City" (*Success,* Jan. 1924). It is the most powerful scene in the work and serves as the climax of the story.[36]

In order to understand why the author depicted the anti-American, anti-Colombian rebels as heroes, we must understand Walrond's feelings toward his adopted country. While living in the United States between 1918–28, he was witness to many shocking instances of discrimination. These are depicted in such early works as "On Being a Domestic" (*Opportunity,* Aug. 1923) and "On Being Black" (1922). Walrond also was well aware of the growing imperialistic tendencies of the United States in the Caribbean as demonstrated in "Subjection." Despite these feelings, however, he did not leave the United States on September 20, 1928, with the intention of never residing in the country again. He had, in fact, only recently applied for naturalization by putting in his first papers, an important step toward becoming a citizen, but a process that he would never complete.

At some point during his travels throughout the Caribbean in 1928–29, he began to change his views toward the United States. It is a shift that is clear by 1931, when Walrond acknowledges in a newspaper article, "I feel different. There has been an inward change" ("Eric Walrond, Back in City"). One important occurrence was his visit to the island of Hispaniola. He reports in a letter to Henry Moe that "In the three months that I spent on the island I had exceptional opportunity to study the Occupation from both the American and the Haytian side, and I have decided, out of the welter of material I have acquired, to address myself to the *Revolt of the Cacos.*" The Cacos, according to Walrond, were merely "peaceful peasant farmers" acting in self-defense (Apr. 2, 1929). Although Walrond never wrote this book, he did later write forcefully of the U.S. occupation of the Dominican Republic in "The Men of the Cibao." As Walrond researched further into the

U.S. involvement in the building of the Panama Canal, he became more and more disenchanted with America.

In reflecting on "The Second Battle" (and by extension "The Big Ditch") one wonders why Walrond maintained an interest for so many years in the Panama Canal and the lives of those involved in its construction. Michelle Stephens posits that with the canal "the United States was building a bridge between the European imperialist past and a new, modern imperialism of international trade and capitalist development for the future" (*Prospero's Isles* 172). Walrond was certainly politically astute enough to see the transnational nature of the canal as a force that would wrenchingly transform the rural Caribbean folk and "create a modern, mobile, emergent, third world proletariat" (173). It demonstrated "the crowning achievement of American civilization and engineering genius," yet it also represented "an edifice of racial categories and hierarchies, a micro-economy of subjection" (Stewart 67).

There was also a highly personal reason for this interest at play for Walrond. The building of the canal, in many ways, was a dominating factor in his life. Its promise of wealth lured his father, as it did so many other Caribbean immigrants, and helped trigger Walrond's lifetime of migration. Its completion in 1914, which considerably curtailed new migration to the region, helped prompt Walrond's own departure to the United States in 1918. His experiences while in the Canal Zone, where he was an outsider ethnically, racially, religiously, linguistically, and culturally, helped frame his alienation and contributed to his never-ending search for home, the major concern both in his writing and in his life. The canal, in fact, may serve as a metaphor for his sojourn in Panama, a time linking his Caribbean and American/European years. Unfortunately, Walrond never seemed able to bridge this gap successfully, and in many ways remained a permanent migrant, someone perpetually "mid-Atlantic." His struggle to finish "The Second Battle" (and perhaps "The Big Ditch") marks the fragmentary nature of his own life, one caught between two often disparate worlds.

Beyond Roundway

The work with *Roundway Review* was an important part of Walrond's therapy, and it was a job he took seriously, possibly being one of the reasons he stayed in the hospital so long. His writings in the *Review*, not just his literary work but in essays on the catering facilities, laundry, and farm, demonstrate how much he was involved with all aspects of the hospital.[37] Over time, however, Walrond pursued more and more projects that took him out of the hospital and began to reintegrate him into the wider community. He visited the British Museum and the Wallace Collection in London, for example, when identifying photographs of African sculpture for a book on African art by Boris de Rachewiltz published in Italian in 1959. His major project, though, was selecting poems for a program on African American poetry presented at the Royal Court Theatre in London on October 5, 1958. The program featured an excellent cast. Gordon Heath produced the program and wrote the introduction to the playbill as well as starring in it (along with Cleo Laine and Earle Hyman).[38] The poems were published as a book entitled, like the program, *Black and Unknown Bards*, by the Hand and Flower Press in 1958.

Research for these projects started while Walrond was still hospitalized. The letters written between the press' editor, Erica Marx, who had been introduced to Walrond by Nancy Cunard, and Walrond in 1957–58 (available at Atlanta University) provide a telling commentary on this period of his life. *Black and Unknown Bards* was a project he threw himself into completely, spending countless hours on research. In all probability, he was relieved to escape the hospital temporarily and engage in an intellectual pursuit. He saw his assignment as a means to introduce some lesser known black artists, including those from Africa and the Caribbean, for example, to the English public. Unfortunately, however, the press took a more conservative approach, selecting largely familiar names such as Countee Cullen, Langston Hughes, and James Weldon Johnson. The result, as Walrond admits in a letter to his friend Harold Jackman, from December 28, 1958 (at Atlanta University), is that "it does not quite reflect the immense amount of labour that has been put into the project that I have been working on."

Walrond's ability to do sustained work and to move beyond the hospital's environs undoubtedly gave him the confidence to leave the facility. While the world of Wiltshire and Roundway Hospital had provided needed solace and revitalized his writing, he was quite anxious to change his life (letter to Erica Marx, Aug. 27, 1957). He was ready to participate again in a wider circle of society and attempt to resuscitate his literary reputation. As a result, he returned to London upon his release from the hospital. While in the hospital, he was reticent to mention details in letters to Marx, Moe, and Jackman about his confinement. He clearly did not want to dwell on this period of his life, simply telling Moe after his release, "I would rather not talk about the Devizes interlude" (letter June 11, 1960).

Unfortunately, the 1950s was a lost decade in terms of Walrond's reputation. His time spent in Wiltshire and especially at Roundway had prevented him from being a vital part of the vibrant postwar London literary scene, in which West Indians played an important part (Kalliney 89–104). Walrond, instead, took what was probably a clerical position to pay expenses, but, despite his disappointments and poor health, as his letters to Conroy and Moe as well as publisher Paul Bremen indicate, he never abandoned his literary projects.[39] He was discussing writing the introduction to a work by Amy Ashwood Garvey, Marcus's first wife, who was equally in need of assistance (Martin 279).[40] As he told Moe in a letter from 1960, "in spite of age and years of silence I have not lost sight of my objectives, or the high aims with which I set out as a Guggenheim Fellow such a long time ago" (quoted in Ramchand 75). Even in the 1960s, he was negotiating with Henry Pell, an editor at Liveright Publishers, for a reissue of *Tropic Death*, complete with some stylistic revisions he had made to it and plans to add three other stories. Unfortunately, however, Walrond did not live long enough to complete these projects. He died of coronary thrombosis at Saint Bartholomew's Hospital, Smithfield, London, on August 8, 1966, and is buried in a pauper's grave in Abney Park Cemetery, Stoke Newington, in the London Borough of Hackney. A copy of the text of *Tropic Death* with his handwritten corrections still remains at the Liveright offices in New York City.[41]

Unpublished Writings

The previously unpublished works contained here, all from the Walrond Papers, help to flesh out Walrond's oeuvre. They were written at various stages of his life, from his college days in New York through the 1930s, '40s, and '50s. Together, they help to provide us with a sense of his writing process and supply us with a glimpse into projects that he had been working on for many years.

Fiction

We have included two examples of Walrond's unpublished fiction, the short story "Shadow in the Sun" and two excerpts from his fragmentary novel "Brine." "Shadow in the Sun" fuses elements of both "Success Story" and

"The Iceman," but it is impossible to determine the precise order in which these narratives were written. It may be, however, that Walrond saw in the simple incident of the workman run over by the train in "Shadow in the Sun" the inspiration and the idea for "The Iceman," reinforcing his ongoing resistance to the forces of technology, capitalism, and imperialism in the region imposed by America and Britain, and sought in "Success Story" to develop some conflicts from "Shadow in the Sun," particularly those involving the West Indian policeman and his American counterpart. Indeed, whole sections of "Shadow in the Sun" appear verbatim in "Success Story." Like the latter, "Shadow in the Sun" addresses some of the socio-cultural dynamics of the postcolonial world, specifically the inequalities of a transplanted Jim Crow system and their impact on the Caribbean immigrant society in the Canal Zone setting. As with "Poor Great" (1950), which is reshaped into the more appealing "The Coolie's Wedding" and "A Piece of Hard Tack," this narrative furnishes further evidence of the diligence and imagination with which Walrond often reworked his fiction.

While we do not know exactly when "Shadow in the Sun" was written, it is possible to date Walrond's fragmentary novel, "Brine," fairly precisely. Notes appearing on pages of the manuscript suggest that this story was developed for an extension class through Columbia University in 1925, specifically Techniques of the Novel, a course taught by Dorothy Scarborough (1878–1935), a Texas-born author best known for the novel *The Wind* (1925), later made into a film starring Lillian Gish (1928).[42]

Our selections from "Brine" recount the marriage of a Caribbean couple, their conflicts and their physical separation culminating in the wife's return to the land of her birth. Given what we know of the author's own troubled marriage to Edith Melita Cadogan (see notes to the introduction 1 below), and on the basis of other details of family history), "Brine" may safely be read, at least in part, as autobiography, and in this regard, the fragment shows the author's early attraction to this genre. It also introduces some of the staple figures found in the *Roundway* fiction especially and elsewhere in his work: the religious mother and the ineffectual father.

The story is undoubtedly a fictional reworking and expansion of an episode from "On Being Black," a vignette published in 1922. In the earlier piece, the author uses the occasion of his wife's planned return to Jamaica to rail against American racism which is the major purpose of his text. But while racial antagonism surfaces in "Brine" as well, it is less pervasive than in "On Being Black." What may be most interesting about "Brine" is Walrond's (through the protagonist Jim's) own unsympathetic actions toward his wife. Apparently, Walrond's guilt in repeating the actions of his father and abandoning his young family was already beginning to take shape.

It is highly possible that "Brine" is a version of the novel Walrond refers to in a letter written to Alain Locke, dated June 4, 1924, and revised for his class at Columbia. Walrond describes the "novel" he was working on as being "loosely constructed" and "baldly unadorned" and he considered the time spent in this endeavor as being profitless. He informs Locke of his eagerness to enroll in Columbia University in the fall of that year, most certainly to improve his expertise in the craft of writing. The corrections on the manuscript might suggest that he used the advice from his instructors at Columbia to revise the manuscript; however, despite these changes, the manuscript never jelled enough to find its way to publication. Still, "Brine" may ultimately be valuable as a benchmark for measuring the experience at Columbia. The benefits are manifested in the stylistic experiments of *Tropic Death* in general, and the ability of the author to transcend the limits of fictional biography in his most accomplished narrative. As such, "Brine" serves as another important piece, as did some of his earlier fiction, in Walrond's apprenticeship, one that would culminate in the more mature writing of *Tropic Death*.

Non-Fiction

"The Panama Scandal" is not truly an unpublished piece. It is essentially the English version of the essay "Como de Hizo el Canal de Panama," which was published in *Ahora* (Aug. 19, 1934). The work is significant for several reasons. First of all, although it (and the Spanish version of it as well) are essentially unknown to scholars, it supplies us the first, and perhaps the finest, glimpse of the material that Walrond was collecting for "The Big Ditch." This essay provides an overview of the initial involvement of Ferdinand de Lesseps with the project until his eventual fall over the sale of stocks. Though the details of the Panama scandal may be lost for most current readers, the roguish behavior of the participants will likely still resonate with those knowledgeable of Enron and Bernard Madoff. The essay has added significance for its parallels to the eventual undermining of Marcus Garvey over a similar incident, his alleged mail fraud over the sale of Black Star Shipping Line certificates. Walrond could not fail to see a connection between his former (and eventually future) employer and de Lesseps. Both were strong-willed, visionary leaders who were in all likelihood not guilty of embezzlement but rather of gross mishandling of funds. The personal, as well as national, tragedies involved played out on an epic scale. The result in "The Panama Scandal" is a coherent, engaging narrative that, if he were able to sustain it throughout an entire manuscript, might have created the master text that Walrond had long promised in "The Big Ditch."

Epilogue

In the *Roundway Review* stories and his other late European writings, Eric Walrond captures the socio-cultural conflicts of the diaspora, especially those experienced by Caribbean immigrant communities. These narratives also show the writer transcending the Pan-Africanist creed he once shared with Marcus Garvey and other contemporaries to articulate—with increasing skepticism—a more inclusive vision. In utilizing the imaginative text to delineate and confront colonial ideologies, the author anticipates contemporary traditions of Caribbean and postcolonial writing. Moreover, the most accomplished of these late narratives confirm that despite the personal crises that contributed to his institutionalization in Roundway Hospital, Walrond still possessed those creative talents exhibited especially in *Tropic Death* and celebrated in the Harlem Renaissance.

Notes to the Introduction

1. Being a voluntary patient, Walrond admitted himself and had some control over when he could leave the hospital. The *Roundway Review* stories form part of the Countee Cullen/Harold Jackman Collection (see especially box 37, folder 2) at the Robert Woodruff Library of the Clark Atlanta University Center, which generously permitted access to these tales. Thanks to librarians Meredith Raiford and Karen Jefferson for their help. Many of the stories and "The Second Battle" may also be accessed at the Wiltshire Heritage Museum and Library in Devizes, Wiltshire, England. The authors are indebted to Lorna Haycock, Robert Moody, and Chris Cox (formerly of Green Lane Hospital, Wiltshire) for making some of the narratives available and for providing other useful information on Eric Walrond. The Walrond Papers are in the possession of Eric's daughter Dorothy Stewart and her daughter Joan Stewart. We thank them for access to this material and permission to publish from it and from Walrond's correspondence. Walrond had three children, Jean (Campbell), Dorothy, and (Dr.) Lucille (Mathurin Mair) before divorcing his Jamaican-born wife, Edith Melita Cadogan about 1923. Walrond had met Edith in Panama, and they married in New York in 1920. After the divorce, he never saw the children again until he was in

his fifties. Writer John Hearne recalls hearing Lucille say that her mother was so upset over Walrond's actions that she burned all the copies of *Tropic Death* that she could get her hands on (cited in Daryl Cumber Dance, *New World Adams: Conversations with Contemporary West Indian Writers* [Leeds, United Kingdom: Peepal Tree, 1992], 105–6). We found no evidence, despite the claims of critics such as Enid Bogle, that Walrond had married again while in England (476). Thanks also to the late Robert Bone, who provided us with copies of several pieces and passed on a number of useful leads.

2. *Tropic Death* (New York: Boni and Liveright, 1926) remains Walrond's only major published text. It consists of ten stories set in the then British West Indies and Panama. The publication of this collection was hailed as one of the highlights of the Harlem or New Negro Renaissance. For listings of early reviews of *Tropic Death*, see John E. Bassett, *Harlem in Review: Critical Reactions to Black American Writers, 1917–1939* (Selinsgrove, Pa.: Susquehanna University Press, 1992), 65–67.

3. Walrond had been contracted to the publishers of his first text to complete "The Big Ditch," described in documents submitted as part of the application for the Guggenheim Fellowship as "a story of the French attempt to construct a canal through Nicaragua," and "a human interest account of the Canal from the arrival of the French on the Isthmus in 1880 to the opening of the Canal in 1914." This correspondence was made available to us courtesy of the Guggenheim Foundation, as were other documents concerning Walrond's relationship with the foundation.

One of Walrond's reliable correspondents in the 1960s, Conroy (1898–1990), the author of *The Disinherited* (1933), is considered an exponent of proletarian literature. Copies of the correspondence with Conroy were made available at the Liveright (W. W. Norton and Co.) offices in New York. Thanks to Stephen King for access to this material. Conroy recounts his and Arna Bontemps's attempted intervention on Walrond's behalf in "Memories of Arna Bontemps: Friend and Collaborator," *Negro American Literature Forum* 10.2 (Summer 1976): 53–57.

4. Walrond's letters to Graham clearly detail his financial distress while in France and his difficulties in finding a publisher for "The Big Ditch." Letters are in the Shirley Graham Du Bois Collection, Schlessinger Library, Harvard University. Thanks to James Davis for supplying copies.

5. Cullen's correspondence with Walrond during the 1920s is available at Tulane University in New Orleans. The two may have had a sexual relationship. See A. B. Christa Schwarz, *Gay Voices of the Harlem Renaissance* (Bloomington: Indiana University Press, 2003), 57, and Alden Reimonenq, "Countee Cullen's Uranian 'Soul Windows,'" in *Critical Essays: Gay and Lesbian Writers of Color,* edited by Emmanuel S. Nelson (Binghamton, N.Y.: Haworth Press, 1993), 152. Seth Clark Silberman also provides a gay reading of Walrond's "Adventures of Kit Skyhead and Mistah Beauty" in

"'Youse Awful Queer, Chappie': Reading Black Queer Vernacular in Black Literatures of the Americas, 1903–1967." Ph.D. Diss., University of Maryland (2005), 190–99.

6. See also Henry Crowder with Hugo Speck, *As Wonderful As All That?: Henry Crowder's Memoir of His Affair with Nancy Cunard, 1928–1935* (Navarro, Calif.: Wild Trees Press, 1987); Lois G. Gordon's *Nancy Cunard: Heiress, Muse, Political Idealist* (New York: Columbia University Press, 2007); Laura A. Winkiel's "Nancy Cunard's *Negro* and the Transnational Politics of Race" *Modernism/Modernity* 13 (2006): 507–30; and Jane Marcus's *Hearts of Darkness: White Women Write Race* (New Brunswick: Rutgers University Press, 2004). The Cunard books, though, provide little direct information on Walrond. There are several letters between Walrond and Cunard in the Walrond Papers and in Cunard's correspondence at the Harry Ransom Humanities Research Center at the University of Texas, Austin. Cunard frequently tried to assist Walrond financially or by connecting him with publishers. Despite her assistance, Walrond did not contribute to Cunard's massive anthology, *Negro* (1934). Walrond, like Claude McKay, withheld material because Cunard did not provide financial remuneration for contributions (Lewis 303).

7. The Scottsboro Boys were a group of black youths unfairly accused of raping two white women in Alabama in 1931. For more on the Scottsboro Boys, see Dan T. Carter, *Scottsboro: A Tragedy of the American South,* rev. ed. (Baton Rouge: Louisiana State University Press, 2007); James Haskins, *The Scottsboro Boys* (New York: Henry Holt, 1994); and James A. Miller, Susan D. Pennybacker, and Eve Rosenhaft, "Mother Ada Wright and the International Campaign to Free the Scottsboro Boys, 1931–1934," *American Historical Review* 106.2 (Apr. 2001): 387–430.

8. Walrond's favorable review of McKay's *Harlem Shadows* was published in *Negro World* (May 6, 1922). The two had been introduced by Hubert Harrison, a mutual friend of the writers who had once worked for *Negro World* before his leftist politics caused him to leave the paper. The deterioration of McKay's relationship with Walrond is fully documented in a letter from McKay to Nancy Cunard, while he was in Tangier, Morocco, dated September 18, 1932, where he describes Walrond as a "very pretentious lightweight" (letter at the Harry Ransom Humanities Research Center University of Texas at Austin. Reprinted in Cary Wintz, ed., *The Harlem Renaissance 1920–1940: The Politics and Aesthetics of 'New Negro' Literature* [New York: Garland Publishing, 1996], 317–18).

9. "Mon devoir et ma raison d'être sont de peindre l'existence de ma race, son histoire, ses souffrances, ses espoirs et ses révoltes. Il y a là une source féconde d'émotions et de peines. C'est là que je puise les éléments de mon œuvre et c'est au service de la race noire que je consacrerai mon activité d'écrivain." Thanks to Shondel Nero for her help with the translation into English.

10. It is ironic that Walrond was one of the chief conductors for whites who wanted

to explore Harlem. While he worked for *Opportunity*, Walrond served as an unofficial ambassador to Harlem. The translator for Walrond's French writings was Mathilde Camhi, a well known translator of such authors as John Dos Passos, B. Traven, and Heinrich Boll into French.

11. E-mail to Louis Parascandola from Sylvie Marquer at the hospital, indicating that files are destroyed after thirty years (July 12, 2006). Underwood, who had served as Walrond's agent in his Harlem years, republished several of his works in the *West Indian Review* (Jamaica) while she was on the editorial staff of that periodical.

12. For more on blacks in England during this period, see Peter Fryer, *Staying Power: The History of Black People in Britain* (London: Pluto, 1984), 298–337.

13. Thanks to the authors for allowing us to make references from their unpublished manuscript on vernacular use in education and literature.

14. A reprint of the *Keys* is available (Millwood, N.Y.: Kraus-Thomson Organization, 1976). For more on the league and Moody, see Roderick J. Macdonald, "Introduction to the *Keys*," and David Killingray, "'To Do Something for the Race': Harold Moody and the League of Coloured Peoples," in *West Indian Intellectuals in Britain*, edited by Bill Schwartz, 51–70. See also Delia Jarrett-Macauley's book on Marson in our works cited. One intellectual gathering in London in which Walrond participated is described by Vera Brittain in *Testament of Friendship: The Story of Winifred Holtby* (New York: Macmillan, 1940), 355–56.

15. Walrond also had several other ventures. In 1935, for example, he was employed as a publicist for a traveling vaudeville company that visited Ireland. While resurrecting West Indian melodies was in keeping with his desire to help preserve West Indian heritage, it is a measure of how far Walrond's stock had fallen that this award-winning author, who only a few years earlier had written for "sophisticated journals," was now reduced to "penning publicity about the traveling vaudeville troupe" ("Mr. Eric Walrond in Dublin," *Daily Gleaner*, Apr. 5, 1935; "Waldrond [*sic*], Harmon Winner, Travels with Troupe," *Afro-American*, Apr. 27, 1935). See also "West Indian Culture," *Irish News* (Mar. 13, 1935).

16. The material is located in a Walrond folder in the Charles S. Johnson file at Fisk University in Nashville. Thanks to archivist Beth Howse at Fisk for her assistance in locating this file and the Ethel Ray Nance (Williams) transcript. Letters between Johnson and Nance discussing Walrond are located at the Bancroft Library, University of California, Berkeley. Thanks to librarian David Kessler for his help in locating this material.

17. Cooke (1903–2000) was a journalist and assistant manager for the paper. She discusses her relationship with Walrond in an interview with Kathleen Currie for the Washington Press Club Foundation oral history project "Women in Journalism" http:wpcf.org/oralhistory/cook.html (accessed Aug. 20, 2008). See especially sessions one, two, and three. There is no mention of Walrond, however, when Cooke

recalls her years with the *People's Voice*. For more on Cooke, see *Notable Black American Women, Book 3* (Detroit: Gale, 2002).

18. For more on this incident see "Coloured Men's Quarrel," *Westminster and Pimlico News* (Sept. 9, 1938): 6. The Westminster article reports that Walrond was on remand (in custody) between August 26 and September 2, when he was committed to West London Sessions.

19. Thanks to James Davis who provided some of this information on Walrond's life in Bradford-on-Avon culled from several interviews with those who recalled Walrond. For more on Bradford during these years, see Margaret Dobson, *Bradford Voices: A Study of Bradford on Avon through the Twentieth Century* (Bradford on Avon: Ex Libris Press, 1997), 112–41.

20. See the *Hospitals' Directory: England and Wales 1955* (London: Ministry of Health, 1956) and *The Medical Directory 1954* (London: J. A. Churchill, 1954). There are two brief firsthand accounts of Walrond's time in Roundway. Reginald Turner, a guard employed at the hospital, who knew Walrond for several years, states that he "always found Eric a very nice fellow during his time in Hospital, he was never confined to ward, he was very helpful in everyway and was well liked by his fellow patients and by all the staff" (letter to Robert Bone, Sept. 15, 1987). Letter in the possession of the editors. Don Cox, first editor of the *Roundway Review*, describes Walrond as "a very well educated, up-market man." Quoted by Chris Cox in an e-mail message to Carl A. Wade dated Feb. 8, 1999.

21. See Alain Locke correspondence, Moorland-Spingarn Collection, Howard University.

22. Letters available in the Walrond Papers. Kamiat, who lived in Brooklyn, was the author of a number of philosophical works including *Social Forces in Personality Stunting* (1939), *Feminine Superiority, and Other Myths* (1960), and *Ethics of Civilization* (1954).

23. E-mail message to Louis Parascandola from Martyn Henderson, archive information assistant, Wiltshire and Swindon Record Office, June 23, 2004, indicating that hospital records for patients have not survived "after the late 1940s."

24. For more on Roundway and other British mental hospitals at this time, see Steele 77–89; Pryor 1–38; Courtney Dainton, *The Story of England's Hospitals* (London: Museum Press Limited, 1961), 165–75; and Liam Clarke, "The Opening of Doors in British Mental Hospitals in the 1950s," in *History of Psychiatry* 4 (1993): 127–51.

25. "Can the Negro Measure Up?" *Black Man* (Aug. 1937): 10.

26. For more on the historical quest for Panama gold, see Bonham Richardson, *Panama Money in Barbados, 1900–1920* (Knoxville: University of Tennessee Press, 1985).

27. For examples of the Colón-Man figure demonstrated in Walrond's writing, see Frederick's "*Colón Man a Come*," 147–63.

28. Ruth Walrond and her children returned to Barbados, her native country, when her husband, William—a tailor—migrated to the Panama Canal Zone, before joining him there later. The exact date of their own journey to Panama is unknown, but although some critics place it around 1910 or 1911, Walrond himself suggests in "Footnotes to Good Books, 1929" (Walrond vertical file, Schomburg Collection) that he spent three or four years in Barbados. However, in "From British Guiana to Roundway" he writes that "[t]he interlude in Barbados lasted about two years," a point that is later reiterated: "Four years after the Canal was open to traffic [1914] and *ten* years after my arrival in Colon, I pulled up stakes and moved north. . . . It was June, 1918" [emphasis ours]. The later date seems more accurate. The only other visit Walrond is known to have paid to Barbados occurred in 1929, on his way to Europe from Central America.

29. The General Register Office in Georgetown, Guyana, where Eric Walrond's birth was recorded on January 10, 1899, lists both Ruth and William Waldron [*sic*] as "natives of Barbados," thus seeming to dispel the persistent belief that William was born in British Guiana. Winston James, who states that William was indeed born in Barbados, suggests that he might have been one of scores of Barbadians migrating to this British South American colony in the late nineteenth century to work on sugar plantations. (See *Holding Aloft the Banner of Ethiopia: Caribbean Radicalism in Early-Twentieth-Century America*, [New York: Verso, 1998], 118.) However, some of the stories from the *Roundway Review* suggest a more intimate connection between William and the South American territory—that he may have had close relatives in this country, and may have regarded it as his adopted home. It is important to note also that Ellis Island records from 1920 list Georgetown, British Guiana, as William's place of birth.

Although in respect of the nationality of the fictional father, Walrond takes some liberties with history, the account of the fictional mother's religious affiliation and its consequences, repeated throughout his stories, appears to be accurate. Ruth Walrond was a member of the Plymouth Brethren, a religious sect that demanded from its members strict doctrinal conforming extending to the ostracism of nonbelievers, whether family members or not. (See the stories "Tropic Death" and "Success Story," in particular.) Ironically, in a different way, Ruth's religion promoted its own brand of "otherness." The Brethren, begun in Plymouth, England, in the early 1800s, has had a complicated history with numerous divisions. They established their first church in Barbados in the 1880s. Basic beliefs include aggressive evangelism, a literal interpretation of the Bible, frequent assemblies, severe aestheticism, the need to be born again, predestination of the Elect, and a priesthood of all believers. Services could last for several hours, and prayers were not recited but said extemporaneously. In Panama, belief in the Brethren was one way by which West Indians could establish a difference between themselves and the Catholic majority.

30. Ruth Ellen Ambrozine Walrond (née Prout) was born in Saint George, Barbados, in 1873 (Certificate of Naturalization, number 3733467), reputedly the granddaughter of Joseph Benjamin Prout, a "mulatto" shopkeeper and landowner who owned the "Mess House" in Flat Rock, Saint George, and "Arise," in the neighboring parish of Saint Thomas, now known as Prout's Village. Although there is no evidence to confirm that the property in dispute in "Two Sisters" was ever formally willed to Ruth Walrond, official rate books from that era confirm that a J. B. Prout paid taxes for a plot of land located in the Saint Stephens, Black Rock, Saint Michael district described in this story during the first decade of the twentieth century when the Walronds resided there. Jim's Aunt Josephine and Uncle Seafort in "Success Story" either appear or are mentioned in "Two Sisters." However, Walrond seldom attempts strict correspondence between life and art. The Seafort family in "Success Story" may be very loosely modeled on the family of Ruth's sister Julia King-Nichol(l)s who migrated to New York from Barbados early in the last century and with whom Walrond boarded after his arrival from Panama in 1918. The late Professor Charles Nichols of Brown University, son of Julia and first cousin of Walrond, confirmed that the fictional family matches his own relatives (e-mail message from his wife Mildred T. Nichols to Carl A. Wade, June 7, 2002). See also "Charles Nichols" by Mildred T. Nichols, *African American National Biography* (On-line)http://www.oxfordaasc.com/article.

31. Walrond's father did not die in Panama during Eric's adolescence. He signed Walrond's marriage certificate in 1920, and Eric was said to have visited him in New York in 1931. Rowde's actions may also represent the psychic killing off of Walrond's West Indian self by white British Wiltshire.

32. There were rumors that Walrond had been lost in a German air raid while serving in the Royal Air Force ("Eric Walron [*sic*], Novelist, Lost in Air Raid," *Chicago Defender,* April 29, 1944). The report was unfounded. Walrond did take an interest in the RAF (perhaps because many Caribbean immigrants served in it), but there is no evidence that anyone named Eric Walrond (or Walron or Waldron) served in it (letter to Louis Parascandola from P.L. Stafford from the Personnel Management of the RAF, July 13, 1999).

33. It is worth noting that in the original version of the story (contained at Fisk University), it is simply titled "Incident." Walrond no doubt wished to emphasize his own position as well as the incident itself by adding the adjective, "Strange."

34. Walrond records a similar event in his essay, "White Airmen in England Protest Treatment of Negro Comrades," *People's Voice* (Dec. 9, 1944): 16.

35. Du Bois inquired about the manuscript when he and Walrond had a brief encounter in London in 1959 (letter to Moe, June 11, 1960). Perhaps using the Boni and Liveright catalog as her reference, Green, wife of American dramatist Paul Green, even provides the cost and the actual number of pages found in the text. See *The Negro*

in American Literature: An Outline for Individual and Group Study (College Park, Md.: McGrath, 1928), 50–53.

36. Prestan may be the model for the rebel Fonseca in "Success Story." The editors are indebted to conversations with Robert Bone for some of the ideas expressed on Prestan. For more on him, see David McCullough, *The Path Between the Seas: The Creation of the Panama Canal 1870–1914* (New York: Simon and Schuster, 1977), 175–79, and Andrew Parkin's *Flames of Panama: The True Story of a Forgotten Hero, Pedro Préstan* (Leicester, United Kingdom: Matador, 2006). For further discussion of Walrond's anti-imperialism see George Hutchinson, *The Harlem Renaissance in Black and White* (Cambridge: Belknap Press of Harvard Press, 1995), 409–10; Robert Phillipson, "The Harlem Renaissance as Postcolonial Phenomenon," *African American Review* 40.1 (2006): 145–60. See also Stephens's works listed in our works cited.

37. "The Catering Department," *Roundway Review* (Nov. 1953); "The Laundry," *Roundway Review* (Jan. 1954); "On the Farm," *Roundway Review* (Sept. 1953).

38. Gordon Heath—birth name Seifield Gordon Heath (1918–91), African American-born actor, musician, director, and producer. He founded the Studio Theater of Paris and was co-owner of the L'Abbaye nightclub. For more, see his *Deep Are the Roots: Memoirs of a Black Expatriate* (Amherst: University of Massachusetts Press, 1992); Cleo Laine—birth name Clementina Dinah Campbell (1927)—born in the London suburb of Southall to a black Jamaican father and a white English mother, Laine is an actor and jazz singer best known for her scat style singing. She has won several Grammy Awards and as an actor has been nominated for a Tony nomination (1985) for her role as Princess Puffer in the musical *The Mystery of Edwin Drood*. She was appointed the title of Dame in 1997; Earle Hyman (1926–) is an African American-born actor. He has had a distinguished career as a film and stage actor, and is best known for his role as Russell Huxtable on *The Cosby Show*.

39. Walrond worked for the now-defunct firm of F.W.N. Hornsby, likely as a bookkeeper, from 1960 until his death. Hornsby wrote a letter to Jean Campbell, Eric's oldest daughter, shortly after Walrond's death, praising him for the work that he did for the firm. He reported that Eric had several heart attacks prior to his death, and that the final attack was in a train station while Walrond was on his way to a lunch appointment (Walrond Papers). According to a letter to Paul Bremen (Oct. 10, 1963), Walrond was earlier hospitalized in the Metropolitan Convalescent Home in Cooden, probably from a heart attack (Walrond Papers).

40. Letters exchanged between the two suggest a close, possibly intimate relationship (Walrond Papers). Walrond may also have been the ghostwriter for Amy's often revised but never published biography of Marcus Garvey. Walrond in earlier years likely frequented Ashwood's establishment, the International Afro Restaurant, a mecca for London's black population. Trinidadians C.L.R. James, George Padmore,

and Eric Williams and Africans Jomo Kenyatta and Kwame Nkrumah were regulars at the café as was African American Paul Robeson, an acquaintance of Walrond's while both were in America. Walrond had long had connections with left-leaning groups and would have fit comfortably with the radical politics of the London group. Walrond was, in fact, close enough to Padmore to feel his death deeply (letter to Paul Bremen, Sept. 29, 1959, Walrond Papers) and he attended his funeral that year.

41. Thanks to Charles Egleston who informed us of this copy. Egleston edited the volume *The House of Boni and Liveright 1917–1933: A Documentary Volume*. In *Dictionary of Literary Biography*, vol. 288 (Detroit: Gale, 2003). See especially pages 404–8. Also thanks to Stephen King of Liveright for access to Walrond's copy. Many of Walrond's revisions de-Creolize his language, obviously in an attempt to make his writing more accessible to a general audience. These changes, in some cases, weaken the authenticity of the stories.

Abney Park was once a parkland converted into a cemetery to honor the poet and hymn writer Isaac Watts, author of "Joy to the World," who wrote a number of his verses and hymns on the park grounds. But the site fell into disrepair in the 1940s and '50s and was no longer used as a cemetery beginning in 1976 except for some family interments. By 1966, when Walrond was buried, the poor conditions were evident. Walrond was buried in grave number 81538. Between September 14 and October 24, 1966, some fourteen indigent people were buried in this same gravesite, which is now covered in thick undergrowth. Thanks to Mark Andrew Pardoe, a freelance researcher at Hackney Council, who provided this information in his letter of June 27, 2007. The cemetery is now being redesigned as a local research and arts center, and a marker has finally been erected for Walrond. Perhaps this same renaissance will happen for Walrond's writings, which, like his gravesite, have been largely forgotten for too many years. Thanks to Lisa Hook and David Solman of the Abbey Park Cemetery Trust for providing much of this information and for assisting us in erecting the marker. For more on Abney Park, see Paul Joyce's *Guide to Abney Park* published by the Trust and see their website: www.abney-park.org.uk.

42. Scarborough completed her doctoral dissertation at Columbia on "The Supernatural in Modern English Fiction" (1917) and also edited collections of ghost stories and African American folklore. Her attention to these subjects may have spurred Walrond's budding interest in such topics as well as his experimental writing as manifested in *Tropic Death*.

Walrond also took a course at Columbia on the technique of short story writing taught by Blanche Colton Williams (1879–1944). Although Williams expressed little interest in modernism and the avant-garde writing that was Walrond's bent, her workmanlike teaching of the conventions of the short story genre, as reflected in her *Handbook on Story Writing* (1917), likely helped him to hone his craft. Perhaps this is best seen when comparing the early version of "The Palm Porch," published in *The New Negro* (1925) with the one that appeared in *Tropic Death* a year later. This growth is also apparent in comparing *Tropic Death* with "Brine."

The story can also be dated by a letter from Carl Van Vechten to Walrond dated November 8, 1924. In the letter, Van Vechten praises the portion of "Brine" Walrond had sent him, saying "you are exactly on the right track; you have the inside dope on material that any novelist would give his soul to possess and you know how to treat it." This is similar to advice Van Vechten gave to black writers in general, to utilize the material of their people before white writers (such as himself in *Nigger Heaven*, 1926), beat them to it. Walrond himself referred to "Brine" as "claptrap" in a letter to Van Vechten (Mar. 4, 1925; letter contained in the Van Veehten Papers, Box 10, New York Public Library). Walrond wrote a favorable review of *Nigger Heaven* ("The Epic of a Mood," *Saturday Review of Literature,* Oct. 2, 1926).

Works Cited

Bald, Wambly. *On the Left Bank 1929–1933.* Edited by Benjamin Franklin. Athens: Ohio University Press, 1987.

Bogle, Enid. E. "Eric Walrond." In *Fifty Caribbean Writers: A Bio-Bibliographical Critical Sourcebook*, edited by Daryl Cumber Dance, 474–82. Westport, Conn.: Greenwood Press, 1986.

Bone, Robert. *Down Home: Origins of the Afro-American Short Story.* New York: Columbia University Press, 1988.

Chisholm, Anne. *Nancy Cunard: A Biography.* New York: Knopf, 1979.

Chude-Sokei, Louis. *The Last "Darky": Bert Williams, Black-on-Black Minstrelsy, and the African Diaspora.* Durham, N.C.: Duke University Press, 2006.

Davis, James. "Anticolonial on the River Avon: Eric Walrond's Black British Writing." Paper delivered at the American Studies Association conference, Oct. 15, 2006.

Du Bois, W.E.B. *The Correspondence of W.E.B. Du Bois.* Edited by Herbert Aptheker. 3 vols. Amherst: University of Massachusetts Press, 1973–78.

Edwards, Brent Hayes. *The Practice of Diaspora: Literature, Translation, and the Rise of Black Internationalism.* Cambridge: Harvard University Press, 2003.

"Eric Walrond, Back in City, Feels No Homecoming Thrill." *Amsterdam News* (New York). Sept. 9, 1931: 11.

Fabre, Michel. *From Harlem to Paris: Black American Writers in France, 1840–1980.* Urbana: University of Illinois Press, 1991.

Ferguson, Blanche E. *Countee Cullen and the Negro Renaissance.* New York: Dodd, Mead and Co., 1966.

Frederick, Rhonda D. *"Colón Man a Come": Mythographies of Panamá Canal Migration.* Latham, Md.: Lexington Books, 2005.

Grant, Colin. *Negro with a Hat: The Rise and Fall of Marcus Garvey.* Oxford: Oxford University Press, 2008.

Hill, Robert, comp. and ed. *Black Man: A Monthly Magazine of Negro Thought and Opin-ion*. Millwood, N.Y.: Kraus-Thomson, 1975.

Horne, Gerald. *Race Woman: The Lives of Shirley Graham Du Bois*. New York: New York University Press, 2000.

Hughes, Langston. "Marl-Dust and West Indian Sun." *New York Herald Tribune*. Dec. 5, 1926: 9.

Jarrett-Macauley, Delia. *The Life of Una Marson, 1905–65*. Manchester: Manchester University Press, 1998.

Kalliney, Peter. "Metropolitan Modernism and Its West Indian Interlocutors: 1950s London and the Emergence of Postcolonial Literature." *PMLA* 122 (Jan. 2007): 89–104.

Leininger-Miller, Theresa. *New Negro Artists in Paris: African American Painters and Sculptors in the City of Light, 1922–1934*. New Brunswick: Rutgers University Press, 2001.

Levinson, Andre. "De Harlem a la Cannebière." *Nouvelles Littéraires* (Sept. 1929).

Lewis, David Levering. *When Harlem Was in Vogue*. New York: Penguin, 1997.

McKay, Claude. *A Long Way from Home*. 1937. New York: Harcourt Brace, 1970.

Martin, Tony. *Amy Ashwood Garvey: Pan-Africanist, Feminist and Mrs. Marcus Garvey No. 1, Or, A Tale Of Two Amies*. Dover, Mass.: Majority Press, 2007.

Nance, Ethel Ray. Transcript of Oral History Interview with Ann Allen Shockley. Nov. 18, 1970, and Dec. 23, 1970. Fisk University Library.

Newton, Velma. *The Silver Men: West Indian Labour Migration to Panama, 1850–1914*. Kingston, Jamaica: Institute of Economic and Social Research, University of the West Indies, 1984.

Parascandola, Louis J., ed. *"Winds Can Wake Up the Dead": An Eric Walrond Reader*. Detroit: Wayne State University Press, 1998.

Pryor, Eric H. *Claybury 1893–1993: A Century of Caring*. Laventhan, United Kingdom: Mental Health Care Group, 1993.

Ramchand, Kenneth. "The Writer Who Ran Away: Eric Walrond and *Tropic Death*." *Savacou* 2 (Sept. 1970): 67–75.

Ramesh, Kotti Sree, and Kandula Niruda Rani. *Claude McKay: The Literary Identity from Jamaica to Harlem and Beyond*. Jefferson, N.C.: McFarland, 2006.

Reid, Ira De A. *The Negro Immigrant, His Background, Characteristics and Social Adjustment, 1899–1937*. 1939. New York: AMS Press, 1970.

Rossum, Deborah J. "A Vision of Black Englishness: Black Intellectuals in London, 1910–1940." *Stanford Electronic Humanities Review* 5.2 (1997): 1–21.

Steele, Philip. *Down Pans Lane: The History of Roundway Hospital, Devizes 1851–1995*. Bradford-on-Avon, United Kingdom: Redwood Books, 2000.

Stephens, Michelle. *Black Empire: The Masculine Global Imaginary of Caribbean Intellectuals in the United States, 1914–1962*. Durham: Duke University Press, 2005.

———. "Eric Walrond's *Tropic Death* and the Discontents of American Modernity." In *Prospero's Isles: The Presence of the Caribbean in the American Imaginary*, edited by Diane Accaria-Zavala and Rodolfo Popelnik, 167–78. London: Macmillan 2004.

Stewart, Frank E. L. "Eric Walrond, *Tropic Death* and the Predicament of the Colonial Expatriate Writer." *Studies in the Humanities and Sciences* 38.2 (1998): 29–88.

Stovall, Tyler. *Paris Noir: African Americans in the City of Light.* Boston: Houghton Mifflin, 1996.

Tolson, Melvin B. *The Harlem Group of Negro Writers.* Edited by Edward J. Mullen. Westport, Conn.: Greenwood Press, 2001.

Underwood, Edna Worthley. "West Indian Literature: Some Negro Poets of Panama." *West Indian Review* (Mar. 1936): 36–37, 57.

Wade, Carl A. "African American Aesthetic and the Short Fiction of Eric Walrond: *Tropic Death* and the Harlem Renaissance." *CLA Journal* 42 (1999): 403–29.

Wade, Carl A, and Louis J. Parascandola. "In Search of Asylum: Eric Walrond's *Roundway Review* Writings, 1952–1957." *Journal of Caribbean Studies* 19.1&2 (2004–5): 21–42.

Watkins-Owens, Irma. *Blood Relations: Caribbean Immigrants and the Harlem Community, 1900–1930.* Bloomington: Indiana University Press, 1996.

◇
◇
◇ **THE LATER WRITINGS**
◇
◇
◇ **OF ERIC WALROND**
◇
◇

Figure 1. Eric Walrond, by Winold Reiss, pastel on board, ca. 1925. Fisk University Galleries, Nashville, Tenn.

Figure 2. Photograph of Eric Walrond, Atlanta University Photographs—Individuals, Robert W. Woodruff Library of the Atlanta University Center.

Figure 3. Walrond's home in Bradford-on-Avon, Wiltshire, England. Photograph by James Davis. By permission of James Davis.

Figure 4. Walrond's gravestone in Abney Park Cemetery, London, England. By permission of Abney Park Cemetery Trust.

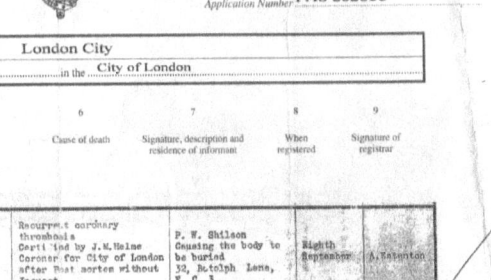

REGISTRATION DISTRICT					London City			
1966 DEATH in the Sub-district of London City					in the City of London			

Columns:-	1	2	3	4	5	6	7	8	9
No.	When and where died	Name and surname	Sex	Age	Occupation	Cause of death	Signature, description and residence of informant	When registered	Signature of registrar
50	Eighth September(3) August 1966, Found dead on arrival at St. Bartholomews Hospital, Smithfield	Eric D------ WALROND	Male	6 2 Years	of 8, Blyth Road, Hornsey, Accountant	Recurrent cordnary thrombosis Certified by J.N.Helme Coroner for City of London after Post mortem without Inquest	P. W. Shilson Causing the body to be buried 32, Butolph Lane, E. C. 3.	Eighth September 1966	A.Ta..nton Registrar

Figure 5. Walrond's death certificate. General Register Office, City of London, England.

◇◇◇ HARLEM ON MY MIND

"The Negro Renaissance"

Review of *Banjo* by Claude McKay, *Clarion* (London), July 1929

Banjo is Mr. McKay's second novel. His first—the chronicle of the return of a prodigal son of ebony hue from a "spell of seafaring" to the fleshpots of Harlem, that Babel of exotic Negro tongues situated in the heart of New York City—was the product of the poet's initial venture in fiction. Prior to that, Mr. McKay had earned a reputation for himself as a poet of protest and propaganda. His poem, "If We Must Die," was designed to stir the blacks to revolt against the crimes of lynching and mob violence. Coming at the height of a post-war wave of mob terror, the poem drew widespread attention to the polemical gifts of the writer. McKay was asked to join the editorial board of the *Liberator*, a radical monthly, edited by Max Eastman. Shortly after that, his first volume of verse to appear in America *Harlem Shadows* (issued in England under the title of *Spring in New Hampshire*,* was brought out and scored an instant success. Some years before, while still a member of the island constabulary, McKay had brought out *Songs of Jamaica*—narratives and folk-myths done in the dialect of the Jamaica lower classes. On the *Liberator* staff McKay's working-class sympathies, which seemed to have possessed him always, ripened, took a more positive turn. He was invited to visit Russia as the guest of the Soviet Government and he set forth, sundering all ties with America.

A Rebirth

Nearly ten years passed. In the meantime there had occurred in the "Black belts" of the North rumblings of a "cultural re-birth"—a re-birth founded on the indigenous *motif* of the Irish and Mexican Renaissances. The movement began feebly; met with skepticism and apathy on both sides of the racial fence. Jean Toomer broke the ice with *Cane*, a book of poems, sketches and brief tales of a rare and exhausting beauty. Cast in an experimental mould, *Cane* bespoke a high and lofty promise. Miss Jessie Fauset followed up *Cane* with a novel, *There is Confusion*. Walter White, drawing upon the lore of lynchings and race riots and the phenomena of the mulatto who is light enough in skin to pass as white, compounded a sturdy brace of novels, *Fire in the Flint* and *Flight*. The young poets, Countee Cullen and Langston Hughes, entered the fray with books of verse built upon a scale of folk values ranging from the exploitation of the spontaneous "blues" rhythms of the melancholy plantation blacks to lyric poetry of a Housmanic order.*

"The Negro Renaissance" was on, at full tilt. In the midst of the clamour Claude McKay emerged from the shadows of his European exile with the manuscript of *Home to Harlem*. As a novel of the Negro quarter, the book had a certain historical interest, but as a picture of present-day Harlem, it was reminiscent of a decade that had long since died. And if the poet's memory of old haunts and dives played him comical tricks, his rendering of the dialects suffusing the polyglot district was as monstrous as it was monotonous. The truth of the matter is the poet's stay in the United States was too brief to enable him to absorb with any degree of purity the language of the lower classes of American Negroes.

In *Banjo*, the action of which is pivoted on the Marseilles waterfront, the dialect is only slightly varied. It is important to reproduce accurately the nuances of Negro speech, for the impetus to present the Negro as he is and not as others fancy him to be was the seed from which the renaissance sprang. When T. S. Stribling* in *Birthright*, made Peter Siner, educated at Harvard, "revert to type"; when Octavus Roy Cohen* insisted on putting into the mouths of his "darky" creations a lingo which no one in heaven or hell has ever heard spoken—well, the young Negro writers saw red. It was to correct these errors in psychology and race-logic, in folk-speech and folk-ways that they took up the cudgels of self-defence.

Life-like Creations

Like sargasso cast upon a Caribbean reef, Lincoln Agrippa Daily, black and broke, arrives in Marseilles. Lincoln's assets are a golden smile, a gift at repartee, a tolerance of all broken humanity, a lordly zest for life, and a rattling banjo. Banjo sets the wretched cadavers of Bum Square and the Ditch shuffling to the tune of *Shake That Thing.** He is no Homeric creator of blue rhythms, however, as was the black in Howard Odum's *Rainbow Round My Shoulder** with whom he invites comparison. Nevertheless, Banjo is a life-like creation—a type authentically observed. No less real is the wistful Arab girl, Latnah, habitué of a Boody Lane* stall. Seemingly unconsciously Mr. McKay has created in Latnah a nostalgia for peace and "an honest man's love," which is sustained all through the book. In this respect she is the only decent person in that cess-pool of bums, coke sniffers, perverts, wharf rats and jobless seamen. Whenever Banjo is down on the heel Latnah is the one who contrives to raise him up. But no sooner is he on his feet again than he deserts her; at the close of the narrative they go their separate ways, Banjo back to America, Latnah back to Boody Lane. But it was not Mr. McKay's plan to unite the lovers. In bringing Malty, Bugsy, Ginger and Ray under the roof of Marseilles the design—that of showing how average Negroes, "the shock troops of democracy," fare on this side of the Atlantic—is quite apparent. The pool produces results that are terribly illuminating. One learns that blacks are not especially wanted in Britain, that the equality they enjoy in France is but skin-deep and that after all the best place for the black man is America! One learns also that amongst the blacks there is violent inter-tribal feeling. The high-toned mulattoes of Martinique are scornful of association with the Senegalese on the ground that they are savages; the Senegalese stand aghast at the impudent assumptions of these descendants of slave ancestors. The Arabs of North Africa despise the blacks of the Madagascar archipelago and there is no love lost between Banjo and his cronies from the Caribbean! All of which from the pen of a man hipped on the universalization of the Negroes, must be rather bleak and sad; and which, if for no other reason, ought to commend his book.

"Recent Negro Literature"

Clarion (London), January 1930

Of the outstanding poets of the younger generation in America there is none who ranks higher than Countee Cullen. Although he has just turned twenty-six, Cullen has been famous for nearly a decade. His fame rests on the fact that he is primarily a poet, whose racial origin is of secondary import. From the very beginning Cullen has refused to follow in the tradition of the dialect poets, although he has by no means eschewed the utilization of Negro themes. His "Ballad of the Brown Girl"—the poem on which he rode to fame—"The Shroud of Colour" and "Heritage" testify to the intense racial quality of his work. These poems, unfortunately are not included in The Black Christ, Cullen's fourth volume of verse. The book represents the results of a year's residence in France on a fellowship awarded by the John Simon Guggenheim Memorial Foundation. The title poem is a narrative of profound beauty and intensity and centres upon the lynching of a young Negro in one of the former slave states. It serves to depict a situation that is a sorry reflection on the state of white civilization and to introduce to the English reading public a young Negro poet of undisputed talent.

In "Black Magic," the prolific author of "Open All Night" deserts the nocturnal gaieties of Europe for the provocative state of Negro affairs in Africa, America and the West Indies. It is a large, ambitious order and Mr. Morand* fulfills it creditably. He writes with grace, ease, humour and that economy of words which has made the French the masters of the short story. And he brings to the subject of Negro life a viewpoint that has enabled him to get, if not at the black man's soul, then certainly at the forces conditioning his existence. [. . . .]

Sometimes in his zeal in depicting the exotic Mr. Morand becomes far-fetched and lurid, as in "Congo"—a voodoo ceremony gotten up by the Louisiana blacks in Montmartre! Similarly, in the case of "Charleston"— the story of a Negro saxophone player in a Juan-les-Pins* cabaret who is prevented by a Ku Klux ambuscade from carrying out a rendezvous with an admiring patron of the opposite sex and race.

Goodness knows, despite the expressed attitude of the French government, there is enough of the Ku Klux spirit in those quarters of France overrun by Americans, but to use the mythical existence of the Klan to motivate a racial murder is highly questionable artistically. The Klan is certainly no

Camorra,* Fascisti or Chinese Tong; on foreign soil the best—or worst—it can do is to agitate against the admission of Negroes into hotels and public places of amusement, and to strive to prove how "savage" and "inferior" they are. But it is to be hoped that Mr. Morand will be persuaded to let his bucket down on the "lighter tragedies" of the spirit in which blacks, both native and foreign, are subject in France.

"Harlem"

(*Lectures du Soir*) February 4, 1933 (translated from the French by Debora Bone)

Harlem, the black quarter of New York, is an agglomeration of 250,000 souls which could be considered the African epicenter of the New World, the black capital of the universe.

At the corner of 135th Street and Lenox Avenue a handsome Negro cop, over six feet tall, directs traffic with large white-gloved hands, and the arbitrary gestures of an Ethiopian despot. Suddenly we find ourselves amidst the noise and bustle of an exclusively black world, proud of its independence, for whom the white man, to all appearances, has very little importance. Throughout Harlem, deep and strong, beats a pulse deriving from the primitive rhythms of the African jungle. During the ten years I lived there, I never lost that impression.

Let's imagine we are walking through Harlem on a warm, sunny Thursday. Thursday is often called "pot wrestler's day," as it is the day off for domestic servants. Maids, valets, porters, and elevator boys are free to seek their pleasure. A long line of black men and women wearing loud colors and Sunday finery wait in front of the Lincoln Theater.* Further along, in a small tobacco shop filled with thick clouds of smoke, a sporty crowd of colored youth gather together. Several lean carelessly on the counter, others drop coins in a gum machine, or spar playfully with each other. They all wear bright ties and are laughing that unique Negro laugh, like the cackling of a barnyard gone berserk—a sound that must be heard to understand the true nature of the Negro soul. Beneath the brassy insolence of their humor lies an intense mockery. There is a deep skepticism of the hypocrisy and absurd pretentiousness of mankind, and an understanding that life must be taken lightly.

The sidewalk is crowded with customers in front of a hot dog stand. They are sleek and prosperous, wearing light colors, with felt hats pushed back on their foreheads. Feet planted in a firm stance, thumbs linked in the armholes of a brocade vest laced with silver embroidery, their shiny white teeth chew hot dogs on seeded rolls, while they gulp down large cups of foaming root beer, for lack of anything better to drink.

Next we see the window of a shoeshine parlor. The shoemaker is busy with on the spot repairs for those who have but one pair of shoes. Two shoeshine boys, like Siamese twins, brush and polish the shoes of their dark clientele, humming the latest blues: "My Baby Loves Shortening."

In front of a chop house, two men stand picking their teeth and digesting their meal. One is stocky, short, and black in color; the other is tall and thin, very light brown, and with sad eyes. They are two musicians, outdoors in evening dress. The light one has a saxophone under his arm, while the dark man holds a shiny trombone. They are chatting.

—You're doing pretty well, says the high brown.

—No complaints from the ladies!

Silence, then his envious companion implores

—Introduce me to these chicks, won't you?

—What? replies the black man, indignant. You know white women don't like café au lait* men like you. And he saunters off, his legs a bit twisted, his feet a bit flat, but with an air of infinite self-satisfaction.

Strivers' Row,* on 139th Street, is the exclusive residential section for Harlem's aristocrats. This neighborhood, dominated by the Negro "top brass," sets the tone for the whole of Harlem. Harlem's elite is governed by nebulous and ill-defined ideals which include a certain savage and disheveled hedonism. And so, side by side, we see the most curious and whimsical incongruities.

Harry Wills,* the boxing champion, is one of the well-known personalities of this elite. He and Mrs. Wills, who is fair and blond enough to pass for white, live in one of the elegant stone-carved homes which are the pride of Strivers' Row.

Two doors down from Harry's house is the residence of Jim Rawlins. Stocky and overweight, with nutmeg-colored skin, Jim was the congenial owner of "Rawlins' Paradise,"* Harlem's most famous night club.

During the early postwar years Jim ran a shady honky-tonk bar down by the river, Harlem's most sinister neighborhood. The "Bucket of Blood," appropriately named, was located on the corner of 135th Street in the basement of a building belonging to the Workers' Association of the Silver Leaf, which dealt in Cuban tobacco.

At first Jim wasn't overly ambitious, just a respectable Harlem proprietor. The "Bucket of Blood" didn't put on airs, it was just a humble cabaret, whose popularity and prestige came from the spontaneity of its clientele and its trouble-free environment. Maids, grooms, dishwashers, and local stevedores were the usuals at Jim's. Every night a dense crowd packed into the humid basement, suffocating under its low ceiling. The floor was covered with a thick layer of sawdust. A stark light from a fat yellow lamp on the ceiling turned the dark Negro faces a sickly green.

Everything went fine at Rawlins' place until the day when gaudy Park Avenue beauties, tipped off by writer Carl Van Vechten, began to invade the "Bucket of Blood." Decked out in diamonds and mink, wearing silver and gold spangled dresses, they took on the condescending and languorous air of affronted goddesses. Their escorts were "big butter and egg men"— opulent businessmen from the middle West with fat wallets, and themselves swollen with self-importance.

Jim was dazzled by the splendor and luxury of these ladies. Suddenly his daily takings far surpassed his wildest dreams. He felt himself riding a new wave of success. Gradually the night club was transformed. His old customers accused him of preferring white patrons, saying he had a bad case of "white fever." Some said he tried to pass for white. Negroes began to boycott. The word spread across Harlem: "Hey, he wants to compete with the Cotton Club and Connie's Inn.* We pay plenty for his booze, but it's an ofay* hangout. It's not our 'Bucket of Blood' anymore."

One night, Lady W., a famous English novelist, left her corset in the cloakroom, grabbed a glistening young "honeyback" or gigolo, that she didn't know from Adam, and began dancing an extravagant "bump the bump."* Compared to this exotic step, the wildest bellydance would seem designed for a debutante's ball. The Negroes watching began to nod their heads in disapproval. As "her majesty" began to feel better and better, she commenced to shout "Oh, sweet papa, give me more." Open-mouthed, the Negroes watched the scene, totally scandalized. Then they whispered to each other "Look at that, man. These white folks are acting more and more like niggers all the time. . . ."

One night Barney Googles (they all had nicknames) arrived at Rawlins' cabaret. A huge black man from Georgia with club-like fists and brawny arms, he was extremely sensitive to insult, like blacks in general. The stylish waiters, eager to humor the delicate feelings of the white beauties spread out in a semi-circle under the brilliant yellow light, tried to lead him to a table off to one side, in an obscure corner of the room.

"Wait a minute, papa," roared Barney, "my money is just as good as anybody else's. Put me near those charmers over there, so the light shines on my face." The boss signaled to the waiter to do nothing. The Negro responded by lunging at the unsuspecting man. Suddenly everyone was fighting in an incredible free-for-all.

The cops arrived and closed the cabaret. The next morning at ten o'clock Jim was handcuffed and taken to see the police commissioner.

Two weeks later, much to the surprise of those who don't understand the connections between the police and the underworld, Jim prepared ceremoniously for his re-opening. This time he opened under the name "Rawlins' Paradise," on Seventh Avenue, for a chic and exclusively white clientele. Jim's secret, from lowly policeman to the head of Tammany Hall,* was to pay, and to pay generously.

Despite Negro hostility Jim's "Paradise" continued to prosper. He himself left the slum behind and moved into a luxurious penthouse on Strivers' Row. He bought a magnificent Italian motor-car equipped it with a uniformed, Japanese chauffeur, and the envy of Harlem, supported two mistresses, one white and one black. Cautiously he set them up in sumptuous apartments on opposite sides of town, keeping a key to each door for himself. Rumor has it that he would love to arrive, unannounced, at a time when they would least expect it. But Jim was cheerful and easy-going, and never stingy. He gave them each $50 a week spending money and sent them separately to spend two weeks by the sea at Atlantic City, the favorite resort of the black elite.

Jazzbo Brown,* a well-known figure of Harlem's underworld, had an elegant home built for himself down the street from Jim Rawlins on Strivers' Row. Jazzbo's café, on 133rd Street, was the center of organized crime in the black ghetto. Along with the sale of alcohol and drugs, Jazzbo's most profitable business was to receive and resell "hot stuff," or stolen goods. The response of his neighbors is indicative of the economic realities within the black city. Sale of stolen goods was extremely widespread. Thousands of honest, law-abiding citizens, in no way part of the underworld, saw this simply as a divine favor which helped keep down the cost of living.

In America, blacks are the last hired and first fired; they occupy the bottom rung of the country's economic ladder. They pay higher rent than whites for comparable lodgings, and so, naturally, in an effort to build a comfortable life, and acquire the same material possessions as white people, blacks often fall prey to installment buying. The American way of "one dollar down, and a dollar a week" traps them into buying all sorts of things at exorbitant prices.

In addition, a universal scorn for the law flourishes among blacks as well as whites, and this explains in part why "hot stuff" is so popular in Harlem. One consequence, remarked by a knowledgeable black man, not without some sarcasm, is that Harlem Negroes are the best dressed people in the world.

I can remember watching a modeling show, with its parade of black mannequins at the Manhattan Casino.* M. Lucien Lelong, a famous designer, visiting New York at the time, joined Harlem's elite for this fashion gala.

It was one of the season's most glamorous evenings. The men wore dress suits, and the women were in elegant evening gowns, generously displaying bare arms, necklines, and open backs. Happy Rhone's* fifty hot-jazz musicians kept couples dancing before and after the parade. The models were chosen for their grace and beauty and their curvaceous gait. In their private lives all of these beautiful girls were gold diggers, or high class call girls, most often kept by rich white men. They were dazzling with skins of ebony or burnished gold, while the dresses they displayed were equally enchanting.

M. Lelong would have been surprised and amused to discover the origin of most of the expensive cloth used to create these luxurious gowns. Almost all of it came from vast stores of hot stuff belonging to Jazzbo Brown—the flowered Spanish shawls, the sequined pumps, the pearl necklaces and the silk underwear glimpsed at dawn as these beauties drunkenly danced the Charleston, the Black Bottom, the Lindy Hop in the arms of their equally inebriated partners.

In any case, it became standard practice—everyone got what they needed from the stolen goods dealers, and in such reliable quantities that not one of Strivers' Row matrons would ever think to use anything else but hot stuff for their clothing or furniture. To be sure, they would occasionally give in to the temptation to go window shopping along Fifth Avenue, making imaginary purchases from each store's elaborate displays. But as soon as it came to the real business of buying a purse, a dress, or a phonograph, they would invariably turn to the local dealer.

The men were no different. Everyone from the honest worker, always short of money, to the Seventh Avenue dandy, had caught the hot-stuff fever. Simple jackets, rose-colored silk shirts, long fur coats, flat silver gin bottles, and even automobiles were obtained in the same manner.

Where did all the merchandise come from? The demand far exceeded the supply until Jazzbo got to work. Before him, the arrivals were scarce and unpredictable. The embryonic hot stuff industry lacked control, central organization, and a common distribution point. But once Jazzbo became the hot stuff dictator this racket grew to extraordinary proportions. Jazzbo systematically organized the theft and sale of everything imaginable. Before him, occasional Negroes working in delivery or shipping or as elevator boys in several of the large white department stores, brought modest booty back to Harlem. To supplement the work of these amateurs, Jazzbo added a team of pick-up men who rode around in delivery trucks gathering stolen goods at strategic spots throughout the city. He strengthened his operations by having some of his best burglars get jobs at factories and warehouses. Some of his men worked as stevedores on the docks or as warehouse clerks in order to turn over large loads of merchandise.

Thanks to the Puritan founders of the United States, legal prostitution, like everywhere in the country, is unknown in Harlem. "Houses of tolerance" are simply not to be found in Anglo-Saxon countries. But despite the Puritanism and respectability of its legislators, America is an unruly nation, and its citizens have managed to bypass laws forbidding the world's oldest profession.

To this end, many buffet flats can be found in Harlem. These variations of the luxury bordello, furnished to suit the most refined taste, look like elegant speakeasies and operate under the benevolent and protective eye of the police.

The buffet flats belonging to Jazzbo's organization, opulently furnished in rococo style, were the fanciest black "houses" in town. A uniformed lackey stood guard at the door, and there was always a well equipped kitchen and bar. There was ample choice of beautiful girls ranging from black to chestnut to light brown and near white, attracting mainly white men and catering to their taste for exotic women. Most often these establishments were run by an aging prostitute who, after a rich life of pleasure and adventure could put on the haughty and detached airs of an authentic Madam.

One such Madam, hostess of the most exclusive and well frequented buffet, was well deserving of her nickname, "the Duchess." She wore little makeup on her broad face, she was tall and her vast bosom inspired, above all, respect. She had a remarkable gift of determining at first glance, the exact financial status of each of her clients. While she was married, in a real wedding, to a black man, she couldn't stand to have colored men as clients. But mostly she abhorred those, white, yellow, or black, who didn't know how to "let go."

Harlem, African epicenter, black capital of the universe! Do your tumultuous streets contain more immorality than the city of luxury that surrounds you?

"The Negro, Sent from the Cabaret, Returns to Labor in the Fields"

["El Negro, Expulsado del Cabaret, Vuelve a Labrar la Tierra"], *Ahora* (Madrid), June 21, 1934

During the last six months, Harlem, the famous district of New York, has been the center of a continuous exodus of Negroes. The rising cost of rentals and the ever increasing difficulty of earning a decent wage has forced thousands of colored people to flee towards the suburbs, towards Brooklyn, Long Island and New Jersey, leaving their comfortable homes on Sugar Hill* and Strivers' Row and seeking lodgings at a lower price. Some, like rats leaving a sinking ship, are heading for the Antilles, their original homes, hoping for a rebirth through primitive means of production, simple forms left from an era of prosperity already fading for some time.

Others, by far the majority, are emigrating in ever increasing numbers towards the Southern plantations of cane, rice and cotton.

One well informed observer has said regarding the significance of this displacement "Harlem's bubble has burst"; "the crow's nest has collapsed." "This Negro return to the land is like a child running back to the arms of its mother. There is no other alternative for a self-respecting people."

It had been possible to make all kinds of sacrifice and to have recourse of hope and enthusiasm, to become a part of urban life as the Negroes did when they came to New York during the prosperous times. But in these days of misery, hunger and uncertainty, the Negro cannot go running after empty ideals which don't satisfy his hunger and can't even pay his rent.

Now the colored man seeks at the very least to ensure his material existence, arms to fight against death. For him, knowing that the best opportunities are to be found in the South, despite the low daily wage paid to workers, despite the proportion of the harvest that must be shared with the landowners, under the constant danger of lynching, Negroes set off anxiously in this direction. Upon returning to agriculture, the Afro-American feels a solid and familiar ground under his feet . . . and, the whites offer a warm welcome, as long as he is a necessary part of the production team.

Four years of economic depression have been enough to undermine profoundly the proud notions of self-sufficiency of the "black belt" of New York. This self-sufficiency was, in reality, no more than a mirage brought about by the quicksand of credit and excessive confidence based on speculation.

This fact can be illustrated no better than by the phenomenon of ownership of real estate in Harlem. Only a very small proportion of the buildings having both stores and private homes, which occupy an area of 100 blocks, were held by Negro ownership. Almost all of the buildings belong to whites or are mortgaged to white financing.

In addition, Negro porters, bell boys and waiters, earning $18–22 a week, must pay rents of 90 dollars a month for an apartment with 5 or 6 rooms. Many times 3 or 4 of these rooms would be sublet for 5 dollars a week or they were designated as clandestine nightly lodgings.

Of course the red velvet furniture, the mechanical piano, the radio and kitchen items provided in each apartment were bought on installment, following the American method of "a dollar down, and a dollar a week."

In spite of countless difficulties, overpopulation, high mortality rate, racial prejudice which is constantly felt, including even in the search for employment, despite exorbitant rents and low wages, the large majority of Negroes have lived in Harlem more or less content with their lot. They succeeded, to an unbelievable extent, if not to cover all vital necessities, at least to give the impression of a comfortable and solvent life.

This is how Harlem, capital of the Negro world, came to be the symbol of the promised land, of the fortitude, independence and unity of the race.

For whites, on the other hand, this section of New York was no more than a great center of extravagant and exotic amusements.

"Beer barons" (dealers in contraband liquor) and their well-dressed lady friends would come to listen to the deep voices of Negro singers, to admire the sculptural shapes of the bronze colored dancers and to participate in the birth of "hot jazz."

As early as the beginning of the depression, Negroes had a forewarning of the sharp hatchet of the enemy. The contractors of Negro workers had adopted in practice the following axiom: "take Negro workers on as a last resort, let them go at the first opportunity."

Skilled workers employed in factories were the first to go. Tobacco plants in Connecticut laid off more than 300 workers in one week. In some industries, a policy was instituted to substitute white workers for blacks, so much that by the end of 1931, Negro workers ceased to compete with white workers for skilled jobs. If, thanks to their efforts and tenacity, they managed to keep a hold of their present jobs, they were crushed by the cruel reality of decreasing salaries.

In the area of domestic services, traditional monopoly of colored people, a new form of competition arose. For the first time in Negro history, large groups of young, college-educated people were forced to look for work as stewards, waiters and porters in train stations.

Some of these young people, with recent diplomas, sought in this way the means to set up as doctors, lawyers, or dentists. Others, in spite of being experienced professionals had to close their practices for lack of clients, and join the ranks of servants, as a last resort.

As the depression expanded to terrifying proportions, hungry bands of Negroes roamed the streets of New York fruitlessly seeking work. If there was no help in his determination to survive, he had to fall back on his own ingenuity.

For example, bankrupt tenants found a pleasant way to pay their rent by organizing "rent parties" in their homes which came to replace the fashionable cabarets. 25 cents was the price of admission, and gallons of extremely bad contraband liquor would be available at the gathering.

Excited by dance and alcohol, the young people were willing to take a passionate chance with their last pennies playing dice.

At the end of the evening, the impromptu entrepreneur almost always attained the necessary amount to pay his rent.

There's a crisis in Harlem. . . .

"Harlem Nights"

Star (London), September 26, 1935

The Club Vodeo in Harlem was the nightly storm-centre of the jaded swells of Park-avenue.

It was the haunt of butter-and-egg men and their orchidaceous femininity.

It was a large, airy, subterranean place with soft refined jazz music and a fine dance floor. There was a "buffet service," an elaborate revue at midnight and a "cover charge" high enough to keep out the canaille.*

The owner of the Vodeo, Tim Jim, was a small black man with a loud bass voice and a laborious shuffling gait.

Tim was a remorseless stickler for "class." He made it a rule to admit no pauperised ebony scum in his place. "If you can't pay six bits for a cigar, or a dollar and a half for a bottle of ginger ale," said Tim, "then make way for the folks that will."

Tim, without a doubt, was on the uprise. Nor was he going to let sentiment or "race pride" stand in his way.

Varsity Men

The waiters, drawn from amongst the red-capped porters at Grand Central Station, were black university men who had just taken their degrees. Self-made fellows, they had seized upon the quickest way of earning the money necessary to set up as doctors, dentists and lawyers.

No finer type of involuntary domestic could have been picked to give Park-avenue a gently reassuring notion of Nordic superiority, largesse and "class."

But Tim hadn't been always like that. There was a time, in the far away and long ago before Harlem's reputation had soared beyond the Colour Line, when Tim wasn't so infernally high-hat, when he hadn't such an agile eye to raking in the shekels.

In those days Tim was proprietor of the Red Moon Cabaret, situated in a seedy corner of the "Black Belt."

The Red Moon was a stuffy, low-ceiled cellar and there was always sawdust on the floor. It was a plain honky tonk, or low type of cabaret, catering almost wholly to porters, ladies' maids, "pearl divers"* and stevedores.

Its patrons were required on entering to check their knuckledusters, razors and gin flasks at the cloak room, or else be forcibly relieved of them.

One evening a mixed party of whites, on an avowed voyage of discovery, dropped in. With a simulated lack of effort they set out to put their dusky hosts at their ease and ended, before daylight began trickling through, by being accepted on terms of easy familiarity.

Night after night they returned, drawn by the hot, tingling music, the nostalgia of the blacks for the warm, sunlit fields of Dixie, the savage tomfoolery and hilarity.

But their persistence and rapidly increasing numbers went to Tim Jim's head. His nightly intake soared. He visualized an impending wave of prosperity.

He began catering to the white man's tastes by setting up a Colour Bar.

The tables forming a half-circle round the dance floor, in front of the orchestra, were reserved for the whites. The dancing, always indecently close and foetid as the air, was to be toned down, soft-pedalled.

The waiters and the chuckers-out were hustled into dinner-jackets, and a swallow-tailed tout was parked outside to usher in the "slummers."

Even Lola, the phlegmatic, sickle-faced yellow girl who did the "split" dance, was forced to put on a long evening gown over her spangled tights.

Tim's old Negro customers threw a fit. The mixing of whites and blacks to them had always seemed a trifle off-colour, but they had not expected to see the Red Moon turned overnight, as it were, from a "honky tonk" into a butter-and-egg man's paradise.

The Colour Bar was in itself an act of treachery, but to see Tim taken down so heavily with the "white fever" was nauseating in the extreme.

One evening Sol Lucas, who played his own game in a local racket, sauntered in.

Sol was a little hammered-down runt of a mulatto who always carried a razor carefully held up his sleeve. He was soft-spoken, well-dressed and slow to fly off the handle. But once aroused Sol was a cage of apes.

As he suavely entered, a waiter eyeing the butter-and-egg men and their orchid lilies, tried to steer him off into a dark corner.

"Go easy there, fellah," cried Sol. "A ring-side seat, you know. Nothing on the Q.T., see? Somewhere where the dames can *lamp** me." There wasn't the faintest obscurity of meaning in Sol's crisp tones.

Police Arrive

Tim Jim, standing nearby, winked at the waiter, and the waiter took on a puzzled look and began scratching his head; but Sol with no more palaver slashed into Tim Jim and the waiter.

In a twinkle the place was engulfed in a riotous melée.

The police descended on the Red Moon and quietly obliged Tim, one arm in a sling, to talk it over with the Captain of the Police Precinct.

The Red Moon went into permanent eclipse; but not long after the Vodeo on the strength of the notoriety attending the "black and tan"* near-riot, opened its doors.

And Tim Jim prospered, despite the open hostility of the porters, ladies' maids and stevedores.

He moved out of the end wing of the "centre of African gravity" into the smart set of Strivers' Row. He bought an expensive Italian motor-car and hired a uniformed Japanese chauffeur to drive it.

He took unto himself the luxury of two wives—one "high yellow" and the other "fast black"* whom he prudently installed in elegant flats at opposite ends of the "Black Belt."

His pin money to each was fifty dollars a week and during the sweltering summer months he would send them alternately to the seashore for two weeks.

No strings were attached to the trip; the girls were free to amuse themselves as they chose—until they got back to Harlem and the tyranny of Tim Jim.

"Tai Sing"

Spectator, April 20, 1934

Beneath an exterior of rustic simplicity Tai Sing was a man of roving fancy and tender heart. He was capable of long sustained passion and ingratiating naivety. But like most true sons of the soil he was wholly lacking in imagination and powers of reflection.

When 'Fo 'Day Morning stepped inside the doorway he was standing before the ironing board sprinkling drops of water from a calabash on the rose-festooned neck of a *pollera** frock.

"John,"* cried 'Fo 'Day, "keep this suit-case for me till I come back—I jess gwine down the road."

'Fo 'Day had just had a pay day, but he had no fixed abode. His bare feet and trousers legs were spattered with the brick-red clay of Gatun Valley. 'Fo 'Day was one of a gang of Jamaica Negroes employed on the *déboisement** on the slopes across the river. Once a month, barring a touch of the black vomit,* he got back to Gatun and "civilization," and then only for a brief, two-day spree in the village bars and canteens.

Tai Sing had never seen 'Fo 'Day before. He gave him a sidelong glance and with an acquiescent nod answered: "Put 'im over there; me keep you come back."

'Fo 'Day put the wobbly old straw valise on the counter. It contained all the worldly belongings he possessed. "Don't let nobody carry it 'way fo' me yo' hear?" he cautioned, going out, "I gwine soon come back. I jess gwine down the road."

As he heard 'Fo 'Day patter down the steps and leap across the open ditch to the muddy hedge, Tai Sing stood the flaming iron up on end and tiptoed to the window overlooking the old *camino real** of the town. He eased up the jalousies,* and peering through the flowering bougainvillea vines saw 'Fo 'Day turn off the hedge and swagger down a by-path to the *Shark! Shark!* café.

He slowly finished ironing out the *pollera*, laid it safely away in a basket, then crossed the room to the coal stove. He threw a handful of coals on the dying fire, picked up a fresh iron and clogged back to the ironing board. As he shook out the silken slip of that symmetrical Zamba* beauty who danced nightly on the "point of a nail" at the *Shark! Shark!* café, Tai Sing commenced to chant in slow, dirge-like fashion a melancholy love lyric of the Orient.

Some months before Tai Sing had owned a grocery shop at Bal Singe, a *chantier** on the Obispo River. One day a Gringo peddler of firearms unceremoniously walked in and offered to sell him a revolver. It was a big ugly .44 with a flashy pearl handle.

"You can't go wrong on this proposition, John," said the peddler. "It is guaranteed not to rust, clog, or go off when it ain't supposed to."

"How much you ask for him?" said Tai Sing, giving the weapon a close and rapturous scrutiny.

"Three thousand pesos," replied the peddler.

Tai Sing came to a rapid decision. "Me tek," he cried, "Me tek." He peeled off from a wad of New Grenadine bank notes the equivalent of fifteen shillings and handed them to the peddler. "Me like," he repeated, fascinated, "Me like."

A small boy with a toy gun, or a monkey with a peanut, could hardly have been happier than was Tai Sing with the revolver. He flicked open the gun, gazed with one eye quivering through the empty chambers, then snapped it shut again. He cracked open the gun once more and slowly inserted a round of bullets. How thrilling it would be to see the gun go off!

Tai Sing moved out on the veranda in search of a target. He wanted, in a sudden impish upsurge, to hit something that could *feel*. He wanted to strike nothing inanimate, dead—else how could he assure himself on the weapon's exalted claims?

He glimpsed out of the corner of one eye a big scaly lizard running up the bark of a cocoanut tree. He turned round swiftly with the revolver cocked, but it was too late. The lizard was safely aloft. Perhaps it were better to go behind the shop to the lagoon and ferret out one of the crocodiles swarming in the reeds. But no, the river was still at high tide; he would have to put out in the canoe and. . . .

Tai Sing was distracted suddenly by the motion of a Decauville car,* full of smoky blue chunks of stone and clodded earth, crawling up the small gauge track which ran from the railroad yards down to the river bank. As the car slowly came on he saw that it was being pushed with one hand by a Negro in overalls.

With a curious inner agitation Tai Sing took a step forward. He knelt down beside the veranda's slatted wooden railing and cocked the revolver.

The bullet struck the Negro full in the stomach. He doubled up and with a despairing cry fell across the railway tracks. The Decauville car, freed of propulsion, continued upgrade until, at the end of its momentum, it receded towards the dead man.

The shooting was traced to Tai Sing, and the Negroes in the section, armed with dirt shovels, pick axes and machetes, began a march upon the grocery. Tai Sing hid behind the door like a cornered rat. A hanging was averted by the timely arrival of a cavalry detail of Guards, just as the mob started battering in the door. The leader of the column dismounted, and upon being apprised of the killing threw a cordon of men round the house and soon secured Tai Sing's surrender. The Chinaman, half-dazed and shivering with fright, was manacled, amidst the mob's jeers and threats, and led off to the cuartel* in an adjacent village.

Two days later, however, Tai Sing returned to Bal Singe. He was escorted by the Alcalde* of the section and a retinue of young men of assafoetida* complexion in white drill suits. These were the *tinterillos** of the Town Hall, the pettifoggers of parasitic elegance and parokeet-like volubility, who trailed in His Honour's wake wherever he went like a flock of carrion crows.

The Guard retired at a gesture from the Alcalde, and the party, led by Tai Sing, who wore an expansive grin, entered the dingy shop. There was a torrent of talk, in a patois of broken French, Spanish and pidgin English, followed by the emptying of Tai Sing's coffers. Store, gun and liberty were restored to him and a quinine* cocktail mixed to seal the bargain.

But the amity of the Cabildo* was no immunity against the Negro boycott, or pot shots in the dark. Tai Sing gradually felt the necessity of moving on, if he would stave off an unequal clash with the blacks.

By the purest hazard he was enabled through a compatriot to trade the shop, at a heart-breaking loss, for a laundry in Gatun. It meant that he had to begin all over again, in a new line of business and in a locality where he was unknown.

⁞

'Fo 'Day had a Spaniard's unearthly time-sense. He returned for his valise three days later.

"John," he said, "yo' got that suit case I lef' here wit' yo' Monday? Yo' best don't tell me yo' give it to somebody by mistake."

Tai Sing hadn't given it to anybody by mistake. After 'Fo 'Day had not come to recover it by Monday evening, he had stored it safely under the counter. He took it out and began wiping off the dust with a rag.

"Why, man," cried 'Fo 'Day," elated at the sight of the suit case. "I taught you wuz gwine tell me you couldn't find it—that somebody break in yo' place an' carry it 'way. Why, man, that is my bag. Lemme see um heah—"

He stretched forward to seize the bag. But Tai Sing's grip on the suit case tightened. 'Fo 'Day looked up, wide-eyed, startled.

"Man, leggo!" he cried, tugging the suit case out of the Chinaman's grasp. "Leggo my bag."

A volley of hot, liquid words tumbled in short, quick gasps out of Tai Sing's mouth.

"You pay Chinaman," he said, visibly agitated, "pay Chinaman, else yo' no can have bag."

"Pay yo' for keepin' my bag?" cried 'Fo 'Day incredulously.

He paused, and Tai Sing nodded in the affirmative.

"Pay yo' fo' lettin' my bag stan' here while I jess go down to the *Shark!* and get a few drinks and say howdy do to Zamba?"

Again the Chinaman nodded. His yellow skin was turning paler and paler.

"Man, yo' must be drunk!" declared 'Fo 'Day, starting for the door. "Somebody must be bewitch' yo'."

"You no pay?" repeated Tai Sing, "you no pay Chinaman?"

"Man, pay yo' for what!" cried 'Fo 'Day, casting the words over his shoulder, "pay you jess fo' keepin' my bag three teeny weeny days. . . ."

Suddenly a pistol shot rang out. A trailing puff of smoke invaded the doorway; once—twice—the pistol barked.

"Inciting to Riot"

Evening Standard (London), July 26, 1934. Reprinted by permission of Solo Syndication.

[I]

Neither the mestizo lad, face clouded beneath a palm leaf hat, nor the one-eyed Basque grocer, Juan Poveda, turned a hair. The boy was engrossed in a dazzling new toy. He was juggling with a bolero—spinning in the air the leashed, vari-hued ball, tunnelled half-way to the core, and then trying to settle the revolving spherical shape upon the polished end of a wooden stump. More often than not he failed.

Son of a Culebra peon and eight years old, the boy had trailed in behind the two negresses. He was the first served. The act was characteristic of a mental bias which the grocer possessed regarding the merits and "rights of priority" of non-Latin blacks and mestizos, respectively. For the boy was a Panameno—already he seemed to possess all the exuberant self-esteem of the Panama mongrel which so warmed the cockles of Juan Poveda's heart—while the women were only *chombos*—"savages" from the British West Indies.

The distinction in itself was sufficiently explicit. It was, more directly, the result of Juan Poveda's persistent effort to even up the score. It was due to his blind, ungovernable way of showing that he had not ceased, though the occasion was fast dimming, to brood over the loss of his eye.

"Five cents worth of salted cod," cried the boy.

"Like a body ain't got nutton else fo'* do but stan' yah," cried Miss Fashion.

She was large, black and barefooted. Gold and silver bangles jingled on her huge chocolate-coloured arms. Her headkerchief of red, green and yellow was like a clump of gaudy autumn crotons. She wore a peony-coloured shawl and a white calico skirt, gathered up from just beneath the hips by a girdle of banana shags.

"My Joey," cried Mrs. Piggott, "will be home tereckly* the whistle blow fo' knock-off."

A small wizened creature with a squeaky voice and a mottled nutmeg hue, Mrs. Piggott, like Miss Fashion, shared with an ebony *comado** a one-room flat in a box car lying on a shunting in the Culebra foothills. She was newly shod and wore a deep-crowned straw hat. Her dress of spotless white drill was stiffly starched.

"Shut up!" snarled Poveda, glaring.

Delving in a crate beneath the counter, the grocer extracted the codfish, spread it across the redwood slab, and cut off a thick slice. He weighed and wrapped it up and shoved the parcel before the boy.

"Dime of spuds."

Fastening the bolero in his belt as he would a redskin's scalp, the boy seized up the parcel and began unfolding it. "Then when he carry it home to he murrer," murmured Miss Fashion, "he'll swear to Gawd the dog snatch it out o' he hand."*

"Lil' forced-ripe brat!"*

Poveda weighed out two pounds of Irish potatoes and poured them in a sack which the boy extended to him.

"Hurry up an' give me a chopine* o' black-eyed peas," cried Miss Fashion, "me is next."

"Yo' don't got no black puddin' an' souse,* me?" cried a squeaky voice.

The boy paid the bill and strolled out.

Sweeping the coins in the cash drawer, Poveda proceeded to measure out two pints of the speckled grain.

"Pound o'corn' pork," added Miss Fashion.

Mrs. Piggott's inquiries might be ignored, but she was determined not to be silenced by the grocer's predilection to curry favour. "The las' souse I got heah," she said, "was so hard it musta come from the sow gran'murrer.* Hard no rock stone. The bone was so hard, chile, an' de seasonin' taste so wishy washy, an' de cucumber water wuz so sour, ah must needs tell yo', Mistah Poveda, dat it berry nearly aggle* me stomach."

With a preoccupied air Juan Poveda fetched up from the pork barrel a slab of meat and laid it before Miss Fashion.

"That's too fat," cried that elegant lady, turning up her lips, "don't give me that, man. Ain't yo' got no lean?"

Poveda held the leg high up before her gaze. The fast encrusting brine twinkled on it like silver spangles. "Yo' don't like fat," cried Poveda in aston-ishment, "but every people like fat."

"No," sulked Miss Fashion, "yo' bes' lemme have de salt beef. When de pork fat so, it stan' pon me stomach an' giv' me de krolick."*

Poveda slipped the leg of corned pork back into the cask of brine.

"An' tree cents worth o' yucca."

"Yo' tek," cried Poveda, wrapping up the corned beef, "when yo' go out." He nodded toward a medley of fruits and vegetables lying beside the door.

"How much is the yucca?" asked Miss Fashion, counting out her coppers.*

"Two fo tree cents."

"Lahd, yo' dear wid yo' tings though, eh?"

Packing her purchases carefully in her basket, she turned and moved away from the counter.

"Come now, Mistah Poveda," cried Mrs. Piggott, "lemme get out o' yah. My Joey gwine soon come home now. Gimme a gill* o' ripe plantains."

There was a big bunch of plantains hanging overhead. Poveda reached up and twisted off two ripe, deeply-dyed ones. As he started to wrap them up, he turned and glimpsed Miss Fashion lifting from the vegetable heap something which she had neither asked nor paid for.

"*Trampo!*"* cried Poveda, running from behind the counter.

Mrs. Piggott turned and observed, scandalised: "Hey, look 'pon she though, teefin' the man red pepper."

"'Clare to Heaven," vowed Miss Fashion, lamely. "A body can't even tek up a pepper fo' look 'pon it beout all yo' tink me gwine teef it."*

Poveda's swarthy face turned purple with fulsome rage.

"To look 'pon dis yah man," continued Miss Fashion, "yo' would a tink me gwine run 'way wid him dutty ole red pepper. The man go on so like me nebber see a lil' red pepper in me life befo." With an affected air of injured pride and exalted self-righteousness, Miss Fashion scornfully tossed the in-criminating object back upon the vegetable heap and, throwing up her chin, strutted out.

"*Tramposa!*" cried Poveda, gazing after her.

"Some people can teef an' got so much mout' besides," ruminated Mrs. Piggott.

Bending down over the pyramid of yams, eddoes and cassavas,* Poveda shuffled the basket containing the peppers, thyme, okras and watercress; tore a russet leaf off a cluster of sapodillas,* then, growling savagely, returned to the counter. He was entirely unprepared for the tirade which greeted him:

"Look yah, Mistah Poveda, wha' dis yo' give' me? Me ax yo' fo' ripe plantains, yes, but yo' don't oblige fo' giv' me nutton as sawf as dis. Ain't yo' got no harder ones? Pick them from up top yonder," she cried, pointing to a cluster of green ones nearer the stem. "Why man, these is sawf as pap."* She sank her fingers in them to convince him of their softness.

Poveda stood petrified. Suddenly he seized the plantains and flung them upon the vegetable heap. "Go!" he spluttered in a violent rage. "*Allez . . . allez . . . zut!** You savvy?" he leered at her angrily, his one blueish grey eye aflame. "You shameless *chombos,* you *sacrè negras jamaicanos* me no like you! Go to the Chinaman next door—he please you! Don't come again my store."

Alarmed at the grocer's sudden explosive manner, the negress turned and swiftly walked out the door.

II

If Pelota y Gracios had not been a *contre-maître** in Egypt, Juan Poveda would never have had the pluck to leave Oracq and a job in a blacksmith's shop to join the French in Panama. A chubby weasel of a man with rosy cheeks, a walrus moustache and mocking blue eyes, Pelota y Gracios was the richest peasant in Oracq. He was held on a pedestal by the peasants in the small Pyrenees village as a model deserving of emulation.

The path which Pelota y Gracios had trodden to fame and fortune lay paved with the bottomless mud silting sands of the Nile delta. As an overseer at Lake Timsah during the excavating of the Suez Canal, Pelota y Gracios had had supervision of a gang of Arab *fellahs.** He early got on to the ways of overseers and was not slow in mastering the art of padding the payroll. When, after an absence of five years, Pelota y Gracios returned to Oracq he was wealthy enough to buy up half the farming properties in the valley and the big seignorial mansion on the ramparts.

One day Pelota y Gracios met Juan Poveda in the street and quietly said to him:

"Juan, my boy, take my advice and go to Panama."

"Panama?" cried the blacksmith's apprentice.

"Yes, Panama," declared the crafty *contre-maître*. Then drawing Juan by the lapel of his blue velvet jacket, Pelota y Gracios added: "The same syndicate I worked for in Egypt is now in Panama, cutting a canal there. This is the chance of a lifetime, Juan. It's idiotic to be frittering away your life in a place like Oracq earning wages no Arab *fellah* would spit on, in a blacksmith's shop. Get out and try your luck in Panama."

"Panama!" cried Juan Poveda, dreamily, "Panama. . . ."

⋮

Dusk deepened into night.

With a splash the propellers started vibrating and the steamer again got under way. The lights of Cartagena, growing steadily dimmer, flickered along the invisible shore.

Lying in a hammock on the poop deck, Juan Poveda experienced a twinge of joy. Only one more night at sea and then Colon, gateway to the Promised Land! It was a far cry now from Oracq, slumbering at the feet of a Pyrenees altitude.

He was riding on the voluptuous bosom of the Sea of Darkness! He was nearing, at last, the *chantiers* of Panama!

Landing at Colon, Juan Poveda was given the rank of *contre-maître* and sent with a batch of Jamaica negroes and Chinese coolies to a settlement on the Cruces River. Tons of cement and a quantity of high-powered machinery were to be brought in, the jungle cleared and a reservoir built. It was all part of a vast engineering project to harness the Chagres and its numerous tributaries.

One day in a dispute with one of the negroes a scuffle ensued and the big muscular *contre-maître* was seized by the back of the neck and butted into unconsciousness. One eye shut up instantly, never to open again. Juan Poveda was taken to the clinic on Buccaneer Hill and the eye was removed. He wore a piece of crêpe, like a blinker, over the hollow and from then onward hated the very sight of a West Indian negro.

He gave up the Cruces job and settled down in San Felipe, a pueblo outside Panama City, as a vendor of celery, white cheese and strips of meat dried in the sun. Still a good Oracq peasant as regards frugality—still a disciple of Pelota y Gracios—Juan Poveda, at the end of two years, was ready to join the mad rush to Culebra, the centre of the canal excavations, and set up as a retail grocer.

III

A negro labourer entered the shop.

"Poveda," he said, "gimme a pound o' corn meal."

The grocer scooped up a ladle of the bright yellow dust, poured it out upon a sheet of brown paper and wrapped it up.

"A dime o' okras," cried the man.

"Take," gestured Poveda, "yonder—when you go out."

"Got any lard oil?"

"Yes, how much you want?"

Producing an empty olive oil bottle, the negro answered: "Oh, fill it half full."

"Anything else?" asked Poveda.

"Tree cents worth o' fat pork."

Poveda's forearm sank in the adjacent cask of brine. He drew up a leg of pork and spread it upon the redwood slab. He sliced off a large portion, stuck it upon a piece of paper and placed it in the scales. Just then the negro intervened.

"Wait there, Mistah Poveda," he said, "lemme see dat piece o' meat yo' got there."

Poveda tossed it over at him: whereupon the negro examined it as might a veterinary surgeon the tick-infested flank of a pedigree cow.

"Why, man, this pork is nothin' but fat," drawled the labourer, "it ain't got a bit o' lean. Ain't you got no mo' lean? Go look in the barrel yonder an' see if yo' can't find a piece with a bit mo' lean 'pon it fo' me."

With a snarl and a volcanic burst of rage, Poveda leaped upon the counter and kicked the negro full in the chest. Reeling across the room, the negro fell at the foot of the pyramid of fruits and vegetables, lying in a half-dazed condition.

"You *sacré negroes jamaicanos*!" cried Poveda, striding with a machete toward the fallen man. "Don't any o' you cross my doorway again! Stay out! *Chombos negros*!"

Slowly the labourer rose to his feet. Red as a beet and puffing furiously, Poveda stood above him with the machete twirled high in the air.

"Is fight yo' want, fight?" cried the negro. "Tell me, is fight yo' want fight?"*

"Aw, what you want?" growled Juan Poveda, uncertainly.

"Knock me, no," teased the negro, advancing to meet the machete. "See me here—why don't yo' knock me?"

Poveda wavered. He was seized by a strange indecision. Somehow the negro's unexpected bravado disarmed him.

The tension slackened and the labourer stepped out calmly from beneath the menacing machete. "Wait!" he cried, shaking a finger under Juan Poveda's nose. "You wait till I come back and see if yo' ain't gwine have to buss open my head wit' yo' machete."

He turned and slowly walked out the shop.

Plagued by the rising suspicion that the negro in some way had triumphed in the fray, Poveda returned behind the counter in a black, angry mood.

⁝

A shrill warning cry—someone shouting his name—roused the grocer. Rushing to the door, Juan Poveda went out upon the veranda and stood gazing across the ravine. On the edge of the railway embankment stood Coloradillo, a squat Napacundi albino, employed as a *vigilante* in the native constabulary.

"The Jamaicans!" cried Coloradillo, breathlessly, "they are coming to attack you! A hundred of them—"

Poveda fled to the dark interior of the shop. He took down from a shelf a long carbine and rammed it full of shells. In case of attack he had certain decisive factors on his side. A person entering the shop by the veranda was like a spot upon a disc, a silhouette against the sky. With a gun at his elbow he would always have the better of the invader.

Someone was crossing the plank lying across the swampy ravine from the edge of the railway embankment to the veranda. An impression of swagger was conveyed by the person's long free strides.

Above the sound of the approaching footsteps Juan Poveda also heard the murmurings of a mob. The blacks were talking: saying how—if and when they caught him—they were going to mince his meat.

Suddenly the doorway darkened.

"See me here now," cried the negro, "why don't yo' knock me now?"

Juan Poveda, crouching beside an oil drum, resolved to take the negro at his word. Quickly bringing the carbine to his shoulder, he fired. The negro fell bleeding like a stuck pig.

The shot quickened the mob's advance. Poveda crept deeper in the shop. Another negro, flying to the side of the fallen man, darted within Poveda's range and the carbine again blazed forth.

Poveda flicked out the smoking shell and again cocked the carbine. But no more blacks advanced to satisfy the grocer's avenging passion.

Above the confusion of flaming tongues and the wheeling movement of the mob, Poveda recognized the voice of the chief of the Culebra *chantier*:

"If you men don't get back to your barracks, I'll set the Federal cavalry on you, too."

Poveda heaved a deep sigh. His ears tingled with the memory of the negroes' threats. He heard them shuffle down the veranda, file across the plank and go up to the railway embankment like a flock of sheep.

He drew courage and straightened up, and three men, in the blue tunics and cork helmets of the French, entered the shop.

"Come on, Poveda," said one of them. "We can't let you stay here. You incite the labourers to riot. Hurry up—you leave for Panama* at once."

A constable with the granulated eyelids of a San Blas albino was delegated by the chief of the *chantier* to escort Juan Poveda into exile.

"A Fugitive from Dixie"

Black Man, May/June 1936

It was Fred Boykin's first day in St Louis. Newly arrived in town, Fred was a Negro emigrant from Dixie. He was thirty-seven years of age and had a wife and three kids.

Our "contact man" had seen Fred wandering about the railway station, trying to get his bearings. He had no difficulty in persuading Fred to come in and gratuitously avail himself of the services of our organisation.

Fred talked with a wheezy Southern drawl. Sitting there before me, he still wore that forlorn and bewildered look of the Negro tenderfoot "up North." Fred was in dire need of a job, and was in a mood to accept anything we might be in a position to offer him.

"Where did you work last?" we asked.

"Arkansas."

"For whom were you working?"

"Myself."

"What kind of work were you doing?"

"Farmin'."

"Why did you leave?"

"The white folks run me 'way."

Up to this point there had been nothing unusual in Fred's story, but now that he had been "driven away" we gave him a closer look.

"Why did they run you away?"

"Well, I had a good bottom land farm down in Arkansas," said Fred. "I was gettin' a good yield of long staple cotton every year. I didn't raise much corn, jes' enough to feed my hogs over winter. I never had any schoolin', but my brother, who lived in the next county, was kinda educated, so I got him to do all my business for me. I had jes' cleared by 150 acres of mortgage and was ready to save some money when the trouble began.

"One evenin' when me and my family went home, there was a piece of paper tacked on the door. One of my boys read it, and it said for us niggers to leave there in five days if we knowed what was good for us.

"I didn't pay it no mind 'cause all the white folks in town 'tended to like us.

"On the third day while me and my boys was choppin' cotton, three stray white men come up to me; my boys was choppin' from the other end of the row. One white man asked me if I got that notice on my door. I told him I did. He asked me what I was go'na do, and I told him I was go'na keep on tending to my own business as I had been doin' for the last seventeen years. They left and didn't say no more.

"I planned to do some plowin' the next day, so I left the field early so I could take my turn plow to the shop to be fixed up. It was after seven o'clock when I got away from the shop. The moon was wastin' and it was plum dark on the road. I drove in through the field and unloaded my plow where I was goin' to use it the next day.

"When I started to get back on my wagin somebody hollered at me and said, 'Wait there, nigger!' I stopped and three white men took me down on the big road, and down there was a crowd of them, and one had a big bright light strapped over his jumper. They turned the light in my face so it blinded me. They searched me and my wagin. They didn't take my money, but they did take my knife. After talkin' in a low voice for a while, they told me they ought to kill me.

"Then they asked me if I was going to leave there, and I said 'Yes' so they told me not to let another sun set on my black face there. Then they turned me loose. One hit me over the head with a green corn stalk, and another kicked me and told me not to look back.

"The next day I tried to sell my stuff so I could leave. I couldn't sell a thing. Jes' about sundown me and my family started in the wagin for the station, which was nine miles away. Jes' before we got in town my old lady grabbed the lines and stopped the mules; then I looked, and on the bridge ahead of us was two automobiles. I had my rifle and my oldest boy the shot gun. I hollered and told them to clear that bridge, and that if they didn't I'd clear it. The men on the bridge lit up the two automobiles and moved on.

"When we got to the station them two automobiles was right there. One man got out of one and three out of the other. They asked me where I was headed, and I said 'North.' They told me I wasn't goin' a damn place. I was still holdin' on to my rifle and wasn't a bit scared. Me and my folk went in the station and tried to buy some tickets, and one of the men in the crowd, which had gathered, told him if he sold that nigger any tickets they would kill him. My old lady told me to stop talkin', and I did. My boys had pulled the trunk down on the groun' and my wife and baby was sittin' on it. Most of the crowd left, all but about ten. They told me I was not goin' to leave. I tried to explain why I was leavin', but they jes' said, 'Well, that's all right, you ain't goin'.' I jes' kept my rifle in the crook of my left arm with my right hand on the trigger.

When the train came up they all started movin' roun', and I felt sure they would get some of us because two of them kept their hands in their hip pockets. When the train stopped they told us not to move. I knowed the white conductor, so I looked at him 'till I caught his eye, then I gave him a lodge sign. He came back at me, and I gave him the distress sign. He came over and asked what the trouble was. When one of the white men told him I was gettin' too smart for them parts and that they had jes' about decided to stretch my neck, the conductor then grabbed my rifle which was then leanin' ag'in the trunk, and told me and my folk to get on that train. We all got on, my old lady, my three boys, my baby gal and then me, leavin' every-thing I had in the world, my 160 [sic] acres of rich bottom dirt, a five-room house, four mules, a new spring wagin, fourteen pigs and a cow. All I had was $137.00 and my folks."

We fixed Fred up with a porter job in an iron foundry. It didn't pay much, but it temporarily kept the wolf from the door. But the change of work—the dust and the close factory air—were unsuited to a man accustomed to life on a farm, and Fred fell ill. On the advice of the doctor at the foundry clinic he was shifted from portering to the yard—loading iron rails on to railway cars. He picked up steadily after that, and within a month was fully restored to health.

Sometime after that Fred came in to see us, joy oozing out of every pore. His brother back in Arkansas had liquidated the farm for $750, and had sent him the money. Fred now felt he was sitting on top of the world. Thinking to add to Fred's store of joy and happiness we told him that at last we had found him a job that was more suited to him than the one he had in the foundry yard. Fred, all eyes and ears, displayed a lively interest in it. We told him that a white gentleman from Louisiana had been in trying to get twenty-five Negro families to settle on his Baton Rouge plantation to pick cotton at $1.60 per hundred.

"Well, I can pick three hundred any day," said Fred, with a chuckle, "and a dollar and sixty cents a hundred ain't half bad, but you tell that gentleman if he brings that cotton field to St. Louis I'll pick it."

"Morning in Colon"

West Indian Review, August 1940

The sun, coming up over the swamp, silvered the roof of the baker shop where the zinc was not yellowed with rust. A hen cackled. In the shop there was a burst of flame. There was a lazy swish and a prolonged jingle outside the door of a ground-floor room in the Ants' Nest.* A small Spanish boy had darted out of the room in haste. Up the alley he fled to the refuse yard behind the baker shop. Stepping over old rags, craters of dust and pieces of broken glass he came upon a white shining egg under a cochineal clump. "Mama!" he cried, "it's a big one, a big one." He ran back with the egg, full of excitement.

> "Yo' buy ten cents yo' get nutting
> Yo' buy de fifty cents yo' get napa*
> Say! me no wahn nutton but yo' money."

It was a piece of mockery, not a street-cry. The tenants in the Ants' Nest all occupying one-room flats, were sated with it; none of them was in a position to exploit the promise of a baker's dozen. All this Natty Gumbs knew quite well. Opening the door he recoiled from the tongues of flame licking the rose pink roof of the oven's mouth. His muscles bulged in his dirty singlet.* His perspiring face and arms were a gleaming purple in the glowing heat and darkness.

"Wahn nutton but yo' money
Say! me no—"

Back at the trough under the window he oiled and greased a row of baking pans; tore off, kneaded and patted hunks of dough, all in a mood of sultry unhurrying.

A child's cries floated down from the verandah of the Ants' Nest as if to offset the distant wail of a Moorish survival and the chatter of parokeets in the fustic tree in the yard. The child was sitting on a straw mat. Its brown virgin body lay on the fast encroaching line of the sun. At the sink a tall adz-faced woman* in whom the blood of Castile, the Guinea Coast and the Cholo* aborigine was softly blended was brewing a cup of hot milk, passing it in a vertical flow from cup to cup until it cooled.

A woman, black and buxom, emerged from a bead-curtained door on the verandah peeling a ripe banana. She threw the skin on the roof of the baker shop and fed the banana to a macaw perched on the verandah rail.

"Eggs! Pullets! Fowls!"

The Negress leaned over the rail. "Senora!" she cried. "How yo' sell de fowl eggs?"

The vendor, saddled with a tray of poultry and a basket of eggs, paused. "One for five cents," she said.

"How much?"

"Two fo' ten cents."

"Tell me something," cried the Negress, "Is rob you want rob me, eh?"

The vendor shrugged. "If you don't like my price," she said, "you no can buy."

"But no mo'n de yadda* day," declared the Negress, "me did got four fo' ten cents!"

"Yes," replied the vendor, "but the hens don't lay so much now." Her upturned gaze fell. She started to pick up the basket which she had put down on the ground.

"An' de fowl cock*—him is not fi' sale, eh?"

"Which one?"

"The one up top yonder wid him comb red no cherry an' de blue feathers spread out' pon him neck like yo' country uman *pollera*."

The vendor ran her fingers along the edge of the tray upon her head. Bound by the legs and lying aslant the cock fluttered at her touch.

"This one?"

"Yes, how much the pound?"

"Eighty cents."

"Yo' must wahn me fi' t'ief, eh? Where yo' t'ink me gwine get eighty cents fi' pay fi' a scrawny, yallah-leg fowl cock? Off a ackee bush?"*

"Oh," murmured the vendor. "You Yamaica women no good."

"Why, only de yadda day," cried the Negress for the edification of all and sundry, "me buy a five pound fowl—fomembah* when me did got the gunga peas* an' coconut rice, Miss Flamenco?" Sitting in a hammock gently rocking her baby, now pacified and half-asleep, Miss Flamenco stared at her icily. "An' all me did pay farrim* was turty cents a pound. Now de dyam t'ievin' wretch wahn charge me eighty cents a pound fo' a lil' half-starve', kiss-me-ears* fowl cock."

She drew aside the curtain of glass beads and gazed at her white even teeth in the mirror hanging on the room door.

"Get yo' pullets," cried the vendor, vanishing down the alley. "Fowls! Eggs!"

Jogging under the curving shadow of the verandah the donkey cart almost grazed the side of Rufus Nig's ice barrow.

"Why yo' don't look where yo' gwine?" shouted Rufus at the turbanned Babu* driver, "Yo' t'ink yo' own de road, eh?"

He removed the crocus bag from the ice and wiped the sawdust off the top. He unhooked the pincers from under the shaft and worked a chink between the frozen blocks.

"Lahd, it hot though, eh?" cried Rufus, mopping his brow.

He stood up, inhaling a whiff of something that smelt like water in a lily-crested tayche* in an old sugar mill with the decomposing body of a bullfrog hidden in it. It was the swamp. The snipes flew low over it. The east wind had shifted. Clouds of egrets—silver specks in the tender azure of the sky—dipped and wheeled. A boy was exercising a horse in front of the stables. To-morrow was carnival. It was a rakish, toil-worn nag with a bandaged knee and a sore-razor-edged back. To-morrow there would be dancers on stilts and dark-eyed girls on floats and whirls of confetti and a Negro admiral with a land ship* and rag-tailed urchins crying, "Aye, aye, conoce!"* and, to crown all, horse races in the streets.

"Ice!" cried Rufus, "Ice!"

A Chinese half-caste girl at the canteen door hailed the ice man.

"Eh, eh," cried Rufus. "Is dat you 'New Dress'?"

Wheedling a new dress out of every man she met was the least of Rosie's accomplishments. "Hey!" she protested. "A body speak to one o' you neygurs an' the first thing all-yo' do is lose all-yo' place. Man, yo' bes' show yo' respect fo' me an' fomembah yo' ain't talkin' to none o' yo' low-class neygur women."

Rufus managed a wry smile. He bent down to the piazza and gazing past Rosie's gauzy knee-high skirt and bare legs glimpsed the white trousered legs of a couple of sailors.

"Yo' ridin' 'pon yo' high horse, eh?" he cried straightening up. "Well, tek care yo' don't fall down an' brek yo' neck."

He started chipping the ice with a hatchet.

"Hey!" cried Rosie. "Anybody hear this red-lip, chigger-foot* neygur man talkin' would t'ink me ah live wit' him."

With a goblet* in her hand she crossed the piazza and came and stood near him. "Quattie* worth o' ice," she said.

Rufus demurred. "Me don't sell quattie worth o' ice," he said.

"Look, yaw, don't form fool!"*

"Me don't sell quattie worth!"

"Lahd! Wha' come over yo'?" asked Rosie, arms akimbo. "Mek say yo' don't want sell me quattie worth o' ice?"

"Dis mornin'," answered Rufus, laying down the hatchet, "when me went down to the Ice House yo' know wha' dem say to me? Dem say, 'Rufus, me boy, me 'fraid say me can't give yo' mo' dan fifty pound* o' ice dis mornin'.' 'How day, Mistah Bombley boss,' me say, 'Yo' can't do dat, man! Didn't me pay yo' in exvance fo' seventy five pound?' 'Yes,' him say, 'dat are a fact, but since yo' was 'ere the Yankee fleet come in an' the captain leave a order so big, yo' see, de plant skasely big enough fi' hold it.'"

"Lahd!" cried Rosie. "What dis place a come to! Ev'ry blind t'ing a go up! Yo' know how much de Chinaman want fo' de macaroni now? Ten cents fo' two sprig! Imajing! Two sprig o' macaroni wit' de cobweb dust an' de worrum crawling'over dem—two fo' ten cents. It are a dyam shame."

"Tell me something—yo' go down the market yet?"

"No, me jes' get up."

"Yo' don't do* down to the market yet?"

"No, me jes' get up. Afta' yo' went way dis fo'day mornin' Beryl come call me meet some friends at the Ants' Nest."

"Well, wait till yo' go down to the market. Yo' know what de t'ievin' Spaniard want fi turtle now? One whole dollar! An' as fo' fresh fish an' seasonin'—gal, dere is some patois men wha' want fifteen cents a pound fo' bobo fish.* Tink o' it! An' as for the baker—Natty Gumbs ah mek pappy show!* How long yo' tink him gwine go on askin' ten cents fo' a teeny weeny loaf o' French bread?"

"Yes, me know, Rufus. An' don't tink it confine to things fi' nyam* alone. No, don't tink dat. A man in the Ants' Nest was jes' tellin' me 'bout him properties. Him was tipsy, yo' see, an' him mout' run like fire. Seem like him own a bottle works in Chorillo an' next door to the bottle works is an empty lot an' the owner o' de empty lot is one o' dem craven Gatun contractors. Well, anyway, him need the lot fi' put up a next* bottle works, yo' see, but him play shrewd an' wouldn't give the man the price him ask for it."

"How much him want fi' de yard?"

"A tous'n dollah."

"Pshaw! Him ah mek joke."

"Well, him hold out an' hold out, yo' see, tinkin' dat in time him will mek him sell fo' lil' or nutton. But, bwoy, the man run the price up to six tous'n dollah an' him ah run it up ev'ry time yo' turn round."

"No wonder the man come to Colon fo' ram him gut wit' white rum."

"Well, give me quattie worth o' ice an' let me go 'long 'bout me business."

"Me sorry, Rosie, but the smallest me can sell is five cents worth."

"Lahd!" she cried, giving him the goblet, "Yo' stingy wit' yo' ice though eh?"

◇◇◇◇ FUGITIVE JOURNALISM

"White Man, What Now?"

Spectator, April 5, 1935

As a West Indian Negro, I was reared on the belief that England was the one country where the black man was sure of getting a square deal. A square deal from white folk has always seemed so important to us black folk. Our position in the West Indies, in virtue of the ideas instilled into us by our English education, has been one of extreme self-esteem. We were made to believe that in none of the other colonies were the blacks treated as nicely as we were.

We developed an excessive regard for the English. We looked upon them as the most virtuous of the colonizing races. It was to us a source of pride and conceit to be attached to England. We became even a bit truculent about it.

We took on as much of English civilization as lay in our power. In one island, Barbadoes—a British colony since 1605—the natives drifted so far away from the African ideal as to be considered even more English than are the English themselves! Our love of England and our wholehearted acceptance of English life and customs, at the expense of everything African, blinded us to many things. It has even made us seem a trifle absurd and ridiculous in the eyes of our neighbours. But the absurdity of our position—an ostrich-like one—was not revealed to us until we began to travel. . . .

I remember as a small boy going to Panama. In Panama, where thousands of British West Indians had settled, I got my first taste of prejudice—prejudice on the grounds of my British nationality!

The natives were a mongrelized race of Latins with a strong feeling of antipathy toward British Negroes. But their hatred of us, curiously enough, had been engendered by our love of England.

Since the abortive efforts of the French in the '80's to dig the Panama Canal, emigrants from the British West Indies had settled in large numbers on the Isthmus. They kept sternly aloof. This, to the sensitive and explosive Latins, was regarded as a slight. It was interpreted as an affront to *las costumbres del pais.** Reprisals took the shape of epithets such as *chombos negros* and occasional armed incursions into the West Indian colony.

From Panama I went to Hayti, the Negro republic torn from France early in the nineteenth century by the rebellious slaves under the Negro general, Toussaint L'Ouverture. In Hayti I somehow imagined that I would be taken at my face value as a black man. This notion was soon dispelled the moment I entered Port-au-Prince, by the violent prejudices I encountered there against all foreign Negroes, but particularly Negroes from the British West Indies.

Instead of taking flight, I stayed on, fascinated by the beauty of the country and the curious mentality of the people. I found that the Haytians, a proud and long-memoried, but vain and self-conscious folk, bore a grudge against the English. This grudge was loosely extended to Britain's black wards in the Caribbean area. Personally, I was regarded with mixed suspicion and scorn. In the refined sarcasm of the country I was a *vieux anglais:** someone on whom to take revenge for the reports about cannibalism, insanitation, witchcraft and political instability spread by Froude, Spenser St. John* *et al.*

In the northern part of Hayti I crossed the frontier into Santo Domingo. It was as if I was again in Panama. A Spanish country with a hybrid mixture of Indians, Negroes and Gallegos.* Only the terms of endearment, the epithets slyly hurled at me, were not the same. I suddenly found that instead of a *Chombo* I was called a *Cocolo.** I scratched my head, mystified.

At last, venturing down to the sugar-cane delta of San Pedro de Macoris, I found the revealing clue. *Cocolo*, a rabid term of dislike, was a corruption

of the word Tortola, the name of a nearby British isle, whence came thousands of Negroes annually to work in the sugar mills and cane fields of Santo
Domingo.

I went on to New York. I settled in the Harlem Negro quarter. I found
the community fairly evenly dominated by Southern Negroes and West Indian emigrants. A wide cleavage existed between the two groups. The West
Indian with his Scottish, Irish or Devonshire accent, was to the native Black
who has still retained a measure of his African folk-culture, uproariously
funny. He was joked at on street corners, burlesqued on the stage and dis-
criminated against in business and social life. His pride in his British heritage
and lack of racial consciousness were contemptuously put down to "airs."

The white man in America, strangely, does not consider the West Indian
a "nigger." He is to him a "foreigner."

Now, on coming to England, West Indians invariably do so somewhat in
the spirit of chickens coming home to roost. We possess the undying certainty that in England we shall be on the equivalent of native soil. Trained
to believe "there is nothing in race," and that there is no difference between
ourselves and white folk, we expect to be treated on that basis. We do not
suspect the existence of a Colour Bar. And so thorough has been our British
upbringing that if, in the event, we did find a Colour Bar, we would consider
it "bad form" openly to admit its existence.

"On England"

Black Man, July 1938

When I first came to England I stayed with a family in a London suburb, not
far from the Crystal Palace. An Indian medical student, a retired civil engineer and I were the only "paying guests" in the house. A Tory of the deepest
dye, the engineer struck me at the time as being a kind of museum-piece. He
was one of those dyspeptic chauvinists who, in the normal course of events,
winds up in a big job in the colonies. An obsession that he had was to foist
upon the Government a plan to change the North Sea into the British Sea,
as a gesture to the men who had died at Jutland!* But to out-Herod Herod,
to swallow hook, line and sinker all the Pukka Sahib* nonsense of the British Raj seemed to be the Indian's peculiar failing.

One day at dinner I was asked to sum up the thing which had struck me
most about England. "The love and worship of tradition," I replied. My host,

a Cambridge man, who secretly indulged a taste for Wild Western tales, took that as a compliment, which was not at all my intention. But later on I was able to square accounts, I believe, by asking for a definition of a gentleman. After a long and puzzled silence I was told that "Anybody who is well-dressed is a gentleman." "A gentleman," spoke up the engineer, "is one who is not intentionally rude."

In short, any person of gentle birth, any unborn candidate for the playing fields of Eton,* any suave, gilt-edged rascal may be a gentleman. He may be a jewel thief, a blackmailer or one who lives by his wits, and yet be one.

This definition, which is fairly common in Britain, is consistent with the class basis of English society. It has nothing to do with morality in the abstract. No bloke of a Cockney, however decent or upright, may aspire to that lofty estate. Purity of mind or heart is not enough. If he manages by sheer merit to emerge from the ruck and carve out a career for himself say, in diplomacy, like the Chargé d' Affaires who went out to China after the shooting of the Ambassador by the Japanese, he is looked upon at best as a curiosity. Not to be a gentleman is to be a cad or, a "member of the lower classes."

"Gentleman" is nothing but a catch-word; but a catch-word that serves a deadly purpose. It is used to bolster up the social and economic division between the upper and lower classes. It puts a premium on the well-born and serves notice on the under-dog that the line which separates him from his "superiors" is an ineradicable one.

The word has no end of affinities. Two of them whose powers of distortion are difficult to excel are "liberty" and "democracy." More crimes are committed in their name than one would care to enumerate. But it is characteristic of the English, in their hypocrisy and love of deception, loudly to proclaim the existence of that which does not exist or which they do all in their power to suppress.

Some of the things which they point to with unfailing pride [are] the love of law and order that prevails in the land and the liberty which the subject, like the press, enjoys. But so far as one can see the subject has not, like the French of all classes, an innate respect for law, order and discipline which springs from a wide sense of social responsibility; he is merely bowed down with fear of the heavy hand of the law. The press, too, suffers from the same finicky fear. If it is not muzzled by the severity of the libel laws, it is subtly regimented by the powers that be. But in spite of the ubiquitous flag-waving of the Tory Die-Hards the negation of liberty is not a passing phenomenon but a historic condition against which men like Byron and Shelley tilted with all their poetic fervour. [. . . .]

But the grim pretence of liberty can only be matched by the farce of "democracy." According to its apologists the British Empire is a democracy, in contrast with the countries governed by one or another form of dictatorship. Let us examine the truth of that statement.

The Empire is an unwieldy, complex amalgam. At the centre is the monarchy and at the top is the Crown—"the link of Empire."

The monarchy is not absolute—it has not been so since the days of Charles I*—but it is at once constitutional and bourgeois. The king cannot act without the consent of Parliament. All power resides in that body, which is in itself an incarnation of the "democratic" spirit of the Empire.

It is an elected body with a strong middle-class bias. It sits in Westminster on a mandate from the voters of Britain. Were the Empire restricted to the area of the British Isles the term "democracy" in relation to it would not be a meaningless one. It would accurately describe it. But the Empire is not confined to the British Isles; it sprawls over vast territories half-way round the globe and includes among its citizens millions of black, brown and yellow men, women and children in Africa, India, the Far and Near East and the Caribbean area. But these millions of citizens have no voice in the government of the Empire. There is no one at Whitehall or Westminster to plead their case. If as workers they find themselves in conflict with the sugar interests of Jamaica or the oil field owners of Trinidad, there is nothing they can do but submit to the repressive acts of the Colonial Office. They are a crushed, unorganized and completely voiceless mass. Unlike the coloured natives of the French Colonies, who send their own men to represent them in the Chamber of Deputies in Paris, they are utterly at the mercy of a system which even refuses to give them a hearing. Under such conditions can anybody seriously call England a democracy?

"The Men of the Cibao"*

People's Voice, December 29, 1945, and January 5, 1946

The troopship crept through the black, moonless night to a rendezvous in the Ozama River. Not far off, on the horizonless sea, the big guns of the Second Cruiser Squadron covered the entry.

Zero hour was at dawn. Small boats lowered from the transport then slipped off to the shore. No alarm was sounded; no outcry was raised. The Yellow Republic was asleep. The people, basking in the sunlight of the Monroe Doctrine,* were at peace with the world.

One column of marines and bluejackets raced up the hill to storm the Tower of Homage, where the soldiers guarding the capital were quartered. Another column pushed on under the palm trees in Cathedral Plaza to occupy the Government Buildings. Round a wide stretch of the coast, from Samana Bay in the East to Monte Cristy on the Haitian frontier, the operation was carbon-copied. Everything went according to plan. By daybreak all the key points in the island's defense system, all the chief centers of administration, had fallen.

Men now went about in a daze. Foreign bayonets glistened in the tropical sun. Lean young men in khaki with thin red necks and a southern drawl swaggered about with big Colt revolvers dangling from thigh or hip. People now spoke softly in the coffee houses.

"The Yankees try to make out that owing to the Revolution the economic life of the country was "paralyzed." If they believe that? [sic] well, all I can say is that they do not know the very first thing about us. For if there is one thing all classes in the community are agreed upon it is 'Hands off the Yankee sugar properties.'"

"They think this is Mexico."

"Do you think that is an accident?"

"Not altogether. Thanks to Pancho Villa, they've got revolution so much on the brain that the tiniest ripple on the political stream is enough to send them into a panic. Every act that does not square with the Gringo conception of legality is frowned upon as a threat to foreign property."

"Move over, will you . . . ah, that's better. This place is so filled with the eyes and ears of the Occupation that one cannot be too careful nowadays."

"Do you know . . . the net spread for the men who do the dirty work of the Occupation . . . the press censors, the so-called financial experts, the stoolpigeons . . . why, there's no limit to it. Some of the swine come [from] as far afield as Chile, some from Cuba, but, of course, the majority of our secondary foes are our own blood-brothers from across the Mona Passage."

"It's odd, isn't it? Why do you suppose they do it?"

"Aren't you being rather naive? What else can one expect from a colonial population under Gringo rule?"

"By the way, what has become of Ramirez?"

"Rotting away like so many others in the '27 de Febrero.'"

"Our ancestors would turn over in their graves if they knew what crimes were being committed in the old 'bastion of liberty.'"

"Ah, but let us be reasonable. You know as well as I do that all our troubles today stem directly from the narrow egoism of our forefathers."

"What on earth are you talking about? What do you mean?"

"How long is it since the agitation for the revision of the electoral law has been going on?"

"Oh, let me see . . . from about the time of the revolt of the men of the Cibao."

"Well, anyhow, it's been like a running sore . . . a scandal."

"Oh, I agree that such a law doubtless suited the social ideas and the feudal economy of our ancestors, but we must not forget that in 1844 Santo Domingo was merely the 'Spanish part' of the grotesque empire of Faustin Soulouque* of Haiti, but today I agree that the law serves only one purpose . . . to aggravate the divisions within our society."

"A law which gives a property owner the right to vote as many as seven or eight times is surely too costly a luxury for a young democracy."

"By the way, what was it that Ramirez did to upset the little tin gods of the Occupation?"

"As a keen patriot he thought it right to oppose the curfew."

"Ah, but don't we all?"

"Yes, but he went to the Palace and told them what he thought about martial law."

"Had he had anything to drink?"

"You know he never touches the stuff."

"Poor Ramirez!"

"Well, when they got through with him they threw him into an Army truck and drove off to a prison camp. You should have seen him . . . eyes all blacked up . . . teeth knocked out . . . nose broken. It wasn't a pretty sight."

"Yet, that was nothing to what they did to the old cowman in the Plaza of the Assumption."

"Yes, I heard about that. I was in Puerto Plata at the time. The news somehow got through and created quite a stir in the Cibao."

"An old man of seventy who, while driving a herd of cattle down the muddy cow-path that slopes into Barahona had the ill-grace to refuse with much spirit to join a drunken party of marines at the tail-end of an all-night carousal with some whores. They chained him up bareheaded in the Plaza from 11 o'clock in the morning till 3 o'clock in the afternoon. When they finally released him he collapsed. Have you ever seen a man die of sun-stroke? The blood was oozing from his mouth, his ears, his eyes."

"Tell me. Is that their idea of 'supervising new elections,' 'rebuilding the country's finances' . . . reducing men to a grease spot in the sun?"

"Anyone who'd do what they've done out in the Savannahs . . . round up men, women and children like cattle and put them behind barbed wire as if they were wild beasts . . . well, they'll do anything."

"And yet they talk about coming to restore law and order. That's what beats me. Why, instead of putting down lawlessness, they're creating it."

[Conclusion, January 5, 1946]

"That's exactly what the general told them!"

"Old Baez?"

"Yes! He put on his old army uniform, got on his horse and rode down from his ranch to dine with a friend in town."

"Of course, wearing the uniform of the National Guard is in itself an offense nowadays."

"Oh, I don't know. It depends who wears it. Look at Captain Rafael Trujillo y Molina.* He continues to wear his and nothing happens to him. He is well in with the Occupation, that's why. Well, there was Old Baez talking about how he was beginning to feel the pinch, how the market for horned cattle had dwindled owing to the war and how the preference for Chilean hides was being felt and even here. 'Have you ever been to Chile?' his friend asked. 'No,' said Baez, 'but I've always wanted to. It is still marvelously colonial out there you know.' He then went from the state of depression in the Santo Domingo cattle market to the fine, up-to-date training a soldier gets in the Chilean Army. 'Of course,' he said, 'the credit for that belongs to the drill-master.' At that the Gringoes sitting at the next table cocked their ears and Old Baez either from a sense of senile mischief or perhaps an excess of champagne went on to praise the work of the German drill-master in Chile and to say that from what he had seen of it when he was in Europe the German Army was going to take an awful lot of beating.* One of the Gringoes got up and came over and said, 'Excuse me, but what did you say?' Old Baez [spoke] up. 'The war in Europe,' he said, 'is still five thousand miles away. Your country is neutral and so is mine. As a neutral I have the right to express an opinion—' 'Oh, no you haven't,' said the Gringo officer, bashing him in the face."

"Poor Old Baez! If only he'd see what their game is. They are only trying to provoke us, that's all."

"Exactly!"

"Now you take the case of that priest in Sanchez who was condemned to serve six months in a military prison and at his age, too. A fine good man beloved by everyone but just a trifle too—"

"What did he do?"

"Oh, nothing much. He had the misfortune to get into an argument with a marine about philosophy."

"About what?"

"He told the marine that after a lifetime of study he was quite convinced that the ideas of Immanuel Kant were in no way inferior to those of Plato or Aristotle. 'Who is this fellow Kant?' asked the marine. 'A Jew?' 'He was a great German thinker,' said the priest. At that all the suspicions of the marine flew into his face turning it a deep pink. 'I am sorry, father,' he said, 'but I've got to pull you in. You're talking sedition. Come along, you are under arrest.' When the priest refused to be taken by the arm like a common felon the marine attempted to strike him with his rifle butt. There was a bit of a scuffle and the marine got cut with the bayonet."

"*El Diario! La Prensa!*"

"Hey boy, paper!"

"Yes, sir."

"You do throw your money about. Fancy wasting a perfectly good coin on a journal that tells us nothing but lies."

"*Oh, I don't know. Even in a paper that delights in the virtual restoration of slavery to our country . . . that gloats over the excesses of the marines . . . remember how it tried to whitewash the case of that girl who was de-flowered with a chisel? . . . the rapine* and the tortures . . . the crucifixion of men and the killing of women and children . . . after all, to the Gringo race-purists we may not be 100% white but we are certainly not uncivilized savages . . . I say, even in such a devilish perversion of a sheet a man of patience can find things to give him courage if he knows how to look for them.*"

"Any news from the north?"

"Yes! The men of the Cibao have fled to the mountains and are organizing. It is something in the nature of a silent mass migration from the coastal plains. The hut-dwellers are on the move. At first they lived mostly on army rations stolen from the Gringoes, but you remember, when the enemy landed the military stores in the warehouse at Puerto Plata were somehow overlooked and when General Arias* got back from the capital he turned all the stuff over to the troops who are now with the men of the Cibao. After all, Arias is still Minister of War, even though the Gringoes have put a price on his head, and he and the men of the Cibao whom the Gringoes now speak of as 'bandits' and 'outlaws' have sworn to stand by the Constitution of the Republic to the end. Not just peasants who've put all the precious accumulations of a lifetime into the melting pot, giving up their small tillages and grazing pastures and humble palm-thatched huts to become guerillas, but *the men of the Cibao*! Doesn't that do anything to you?"

"I feel about them just as you do. Well do the Spaniards and the French, the tyrants of the Old and the tyrants of the New World, know it. And the hills of the Cibao form part of the magic, too."

"They have never failed us in the past and I feel certain they will not fail us now."

It was early in June of the year 1924 and up in the wooded hills of Hispaniola, the morning air was fresh and cool. The plumes of sugar canes nodded gently in the windswept fields. Over the remnants of old Spanish and French colonial roads the course of the convoy lay. All during the summer the passage of men and vehicles, horses and stores, down to the shores of the Caribbean Sea or across the frontier into Hayti went on.

The U.S. occupation of Santo Domingo, which had begun simultaneously with that of Hayti in 1915, was at an end. The agony of Hayti was prolonged until 1932 when Franklin D. Roosevelt scrapped the "Big Stick" Latin-American policy* of his predecessors in the White House. The decision to withdraw the marines was made, not only as a concession to liberal and progressive opinion in the U.S. It was made largely as a result of the costly futility of waging a sleepless, night-and-day campaign against a will-o'-the-wisp kind of guerrilla peasantry whose offensive and defensive tactics, at variance with all orthodox military text-book doctrine, baffled the forces of the Occupation to the very end.

Are the peasant masses of Indo-China and Indonesia forged in the metal [sic] of the hardy hut-dwellers of Hispaniola? Are they destined to duplicate the epic stand of the men of the Cibao?

"The Servant Girl"

January 1953

Head cutter at Hendricks', a firm of merchant tailors on Water Street, Son Son's father came home one evening with a large paper bagful of mangoes which he'd bought in town. He opened the bag, selected a big, ripe, purple-skinned mango and gave it to Son Son.

"For me?" cried Son Son, his delight tempered with a feeling of doubt.

"Yes."

"All of it?"

He'd never had more than a slice of a 'turpentine' mango* before. His father didn't say anything. He merely smiled . . . a slow, tender smile.

Son Son held the mango to his nose. He closed his eyes and took a deep breath.

"My, what a nice smell!"

He made a hole in the mango and squeezed some of the juice into his mouth. Then he peeled off the skin and ate the mango down to the white stony seed. What to do with the seed was now the problem. Should he throw it away? No, that would be wasteful. He would *give* the seed to the black and white cow. He didn't know who the cow belonged to, but of an evening at sunset when he had a chance to steal down the stairs to watch the light on the meadow the cow would always be standing (now that the dry season was on) in the tall Guinea grass that filled the water-course* nearby. It was there now, quietly grazing.

"Don't you want it?" asked Son Son, offering the mango seed to the cow. The cow took no notice. "But there is nourishment in it," insisted Son Son, placing the seed on the ground.

Saliva dripped from the cow's mouth as the animal turned lack-lustre eyes upon Son Son, sniffed the seed, snorted, plunged out of the water-course and butted him back whence he'd come.

"Rosetta! Rosetta!"

After a while Son Son came to. He had travelled far . . . clear across the width of the ground under the house, almost up to the logwood fence of the compound next door. Not content with having sent him reeling, the cow had continued after him. It was stamping and heaving and rooting up the ground beside him; but not far away Rosetta, the black servant girl, holding up the tips of her skirt, was dancing from side to side behind one of the piles on which the house stood.

"Shoo, cow!" she cried, "Be off!"

She stooped down and picked up a stone and heaved it *boop* into the cow's ribs. The beast jumped, swung aside and lumbered off.

"Where hurt you, love?" cried Rosetta, gathering up Son Son and pressing him to her bosom, "Where hurt you, nuh?"

Son Son gasped for breath. He had no broken bones, he had not been gored. He was only short of wind. If Rosetta had not responded so quickly to his cry for help the cow might have ripped open his belly or trampled him to death. If he had suffered no serious injury, it was thanks to the speed with which she had come flying down the stairs. And yet he could be so *very* cruel to her. . . .

Even in after years Son Son never understood why he should have wanted to crack Rosetta's coconut. On the day of the attempt it had been raining and Son Son had persuaded himself that by going into the 'drawing room' he could escape from the steady, ear-splitting, drip-drip-drip of the rain on the zinc roof.

Illusion!

The room, deep in the dusk of a November afternoon, was no place to wander in the dark. Stubbing his toe on a conch shell that kept the door ajar, Son Son curled up in a rocking chair and held his foot in his hands. Gently he rocked himself. All about him appeared the dark gleams of polished wood and the sparkle of glass: the arms and legs of chairs (clammy to the touch), the decanter and the wineglasses on the what-not, wall pockets* studded with sea shells, the ornate gilt of a cane-fibred three-legged table with a flower vase on it.

Here on Sunday evenings, lying face down across her swaying knees, Son Son's mother Cora would sing and pat him to sleep—

Trim your lamps and be ready
For 'tis the midnight cry
'Tis the midnight cry
*The midnight cry**

while the mahogany floor was like a mirror in which the white dresses of Cora's Sisters in the Lord appeared and disappeared and the mantle of tin on the kerosene lamp overhead rattled in the cool evening breeze and the day's exertions and delights fused in a sleepy blur: the truant-like escape in the late afternoon along a dusty, tree-fringed road that terminated at the Sea Wall* . . . darting in between one high wave and another to gather up from the foaming sheet of blue water the small iridescent fish that came twinkling over on to the esplanade as the sea pounded the wall . . . vainly trying to remove the fishy smell from his hands with the petals of coxcombs . . . stencilling the patterns on the silver-powdery backs of maidenhair fern against his ebony cheeks to make Rosetta think he was a 'Bush Negro'* with chalk marks on his face. . . .

"No, Baba,* not y'own, mine! Gimme me t'ing, Baba!"

Son Son got up and went out on the gallery. A curtain of rain and mist veiled the little dirt road in front of the house. There was no clang or clatter of buckets, no sign of Negro women with skirts gathered at the hips battling for water. The stand-pipe* opposite was islanded in a sea of mud. Everything was submerged in the drowsy patter of the rain and the croaking of frogs.

He closed the shutters and wandered into a corridor in which a foggy patch of sky appeared through an open window. He drew up a chair, knelt on it and with palms upturned stretched out his hands through the window. Now for the sting and splash of the jewel-bright drops of rain coming down off the roof.

Plop . . . plop . . . plop. . . .

"Come on, what all-yo' waitin' fuh? The rain stop fallin.'"

Beyond the roof of a building below the window, Son Son saw a group of small black boys patter down the verandah steps of a barrack on the opposite side of the compound. In each boy's hand was a tiny paper boat.

Son Son folded his arms on the window sill and prepared to watch the boat race. As each boat was launched a chorus of jockeying cries went up. Not all the boats managed to stay afloat. One or two turned over and sank at the push-off, some foundered in the mud-banks soon afterwards while the others followed a swift, uneven course over the swirling streams and eddies.

"Foul!"

"Wha' gone wrong?"

"I see Baba pushin' away the obstruction wit' his toe."

"Liar!"

"You mustn't do that. Keep yo' foot out o' the channel."

"I only just. . . ."

"I disqualify you."

A tall, thin, black boy with feet set wide apart and knees knocking together entered the compound trailing a live, leaf-green iguana on a string. When the newcomer saw what was going on he lifted the iguana off the ground and ran forward with it.

"Rosetta!" cried Son Son, gazing into the darkness of the corridor, "Come quick!"

No answer. Where was she? Didn't she hear him calling?

At the sight of the iguana the boys engaged in the boat race had turned and fled. Now they were hurrying up the steps of the verandah as fast as their legs could carry them.

The knock-kneed boy proceeded to parade the iguana before the barrack. He strode to and fro slowly, menacingly. He walked up and down, backwards and forwards. He raised his arms above his head. He began to swing the iguana round and round. Nearer and nearer to the boys cowering in panic on the verandah went the rasping buzz of the animal's tail.

"Rosetta! Rosetta!" cried Son Son. He wanted to slip down off the chair and fly along the corridor to see what had happened to her, but he could not tear himself away from the window.

Sated with one form of terror, the knock-kneed boy decided to try another. He stopped whirling the iguana above his head. He moved away from the verandah. And the boys began crowding out of the shadows as though the danger had passed. Of a sudden the knock-kneed boy wheeled round and flicked the iguana into their faces again and again.

"Rosetta!"

One by one the terrified group on the verandah crept out of sight, but the knock-kneed boy continued to amuse himself with the iguana . . . trailing it back and forth tirelessly . . . stopping now and again to splash the iguana about in the ochre-red mud and water until it was no longer green.

"Bring me that 'guana here!" cried a short, fat, black woman bustling through the door of the end-room in the barrack.

"Yes, ma."

She leaned over the verandah, cuffed him on the head and took the limp, mud-coated carcass of the iguana away from him.

"You good for nothin' scamp!"

She went back inside and the knock-kneed boy strolled round to the rain-water cask beside the barrack. He unhooked the dipper and scooped up a drink. Something was wiggling in the water.

"'Ma, a congery!"

The eel slipped back into the cask. Wiping his mouth on his shirt sleeve, the knock-kneed boy turned and faced in Son Son's direction. Son Son got ready to duck. ("You little big-eyed, poor great,* hot-house brat . . . wha' all-yo' lookin' down here for? Bet yo' ah tek up a rock stone an' lick all-yo' down?") But as the knock-kneed boy crossed the yard he did not look up at the window.

A moment later Son Son saw him again. The knock-kneed boy was staggering under the weight of a bench of the kind Son Son and Cora sat upon in the meeting room of the Plymouth Brethren.* He set the bench down in the mud, close up to the verandah and opposite the door of his mother's room. Then he stepped over and sat down upon it. Leaning forward on the verandah, he began drumming on it with his fingertips. His voice rose on a long-drawn note of sadness:—

Ah Chichi* lay
Ah Chichi lay

and then fell to a deep, quick rumble:-

Chichi's the washer
The July washer

Son Son wondered what the song meant. Who was Chichi? And what was a "July washer"? Maybe Rosetta could tell him. He would have to ask her.

Naked feet splashed in the mud. A woman emerged into view from the building under Son Son's window. To Son Son the troop of five others that followed her seemed in one or two essentials to be almost identical with her. They were tall, young and black. They sashayed across the yard in a wavy line, gathered up their calico skirts, stepped over the bench one after the other and sat down on one side of the knock-kneed boy.

"Wha'm is she got, nuh?"

"'guana."

"Smells mo' like pepper-pot* to me...."

"Hey, I wonder wha' I was hearin' all afternoon. Just like somebody poundin' plantain."

"Dreaming o' foo-foo* music again?"

John Belly
Quakin' belly
Big like a t-a-y-c-h-e!
Tee hey
Tee hey

The fat black woman appeared at the door. "All-yo' is all wrong," she said, "'Um is salt fish an' green bananas stewed. *De 'Guana fo' tomorrow!*"

Son Son slid down off the chair.

"Rosetta! Rosetta!"

Rounding the end of the corridor Son Son braked. He slowed to a hesitant walk. There she was, sitting in the kitchen door combing her hair.

He eyed the miracle which comb and fingers had deftly wrought, transforming Rosetta's tight, low-grown curls into a minute set of squares and furrows. As he crept up behind her Rosetta turned round and swept him into her arms.

Son Son found that lying in the warmth and the perfume of Rosetta's embrace was strangely like being sung to sleep on his mother's swaying knees on a Sunday evening. Only Rosetta was not singing. Nor was he dozing off. He was wide awake. And instead of seeing the moving reflections of long white dresses on the floor Son Son glimpsed a metal object. He struggled out of Rosetta's arms and picked it up.

It was a piece of lead piping about a foot long and an inch in diameter. He hefted* it. Nice and heavy. Then he grasped it with both hands and brought it down hard on Rosetta's head.

The sight of blood spurting out of a furrow and dyeing a plaited tuft of hair mingled in Son Son's consciousness with the sound of Rosetta's outcry as she put her hands to her head. A chilling sensation flowed through him. He heard as from a distance the rustle of a skirt, the swish of black sage twigs and Cora muttering: ".... boy must be going out of his head ... thinking he can crack a body coconut." Then, as he trembled in anticipation of a whipping, Rosetta jumped up.

"Do,* Miss Humphreys," she begged, thrusting herself between him and the twigs, "You mustn't lick him. He ain't went* to do it. He didn't know what he was doin'. He don't know no better. He didn't mean any harm."

"The Coolie's Wedding"

February 1953

"Run down to the dispenser's like a good little boy and get me a gill of tincture of rhubarb."

"Yessum."

The sound of Ruth's voice interrupted William's pacing. He looked round and saw that she had come out upon the gallery. She stooped down beside him.

"Here's your sailor hat."

"Yessum."

After he had put on the hat Ruth placed a silver coin in his hand and closed his trembling little ebony fingers over it. Then she drew him gently towards her. "What is it I send you for?" she asked.

Here was something William had not thought of. He swiftly perceived that before he would be permitted to set out on the errand he would have to satisfy Ruth that he was competent to run it.

"A tinko," he stuttered, "A tinko o'—"

"A gill of tincture of rhubarb!"

"Yessum."

He turned to go, glad at having got off so lightly but Ruth pulled him back.

"What is it," she asked again, "I send you for?"

"A gill," cried William, "A gill o'—"

He paused, eyelids aflutter.

".... tincture of rhubarb, boy!"

"Yessum."

"Say it let me hear."

"A gill of tincture of rhubarb."

"That's right," said Ruth, rising and placing an arm about his shoulder, "Now run along and don't loiter in the road. And if you should see the carriage with the coolie bride and groom stand one side and let it pass. You musn't get run over, you hear?"

"No'm."

As he sped over the polished mahogany of the hallway, William felt as dizzy as he had been on the occasion of a visit which he once paid to his maternal grandfather who lived deep in the Guiana woods in a white, round-roofed house in which all the rooms opened so confusingly on to a circular porch that once the doors were closed there had been no way on God's green earth for him to distinguish one from another. His head was in a whirl.

. . .

"You tell he he could go out?" asked Mirrie, the Negro servant girl, poking her head through the kitchen door. William did not hear Ruth's murmured reply, but the shrillness of Mirrie's voice pursued him out upon the landing:—

"Take care all-yo' don't get knock down!"*

Too small to take more than one step at a time, William held on to the banister and began the steep descent. He could not get down the stairs fast enough. He was in flight from the monotony and boredom of going from window to window on the gallery and flicking the shutters up and down. He'd escaped from the prison—4 ft. wide, enclosed with lattice work of a light shade of green and extending along the front of the house—in which he had been condemned to spend the long mornings and the hot, drowsy afternoons. An occasional descent upon the Lamaha . . . tadpole fishing in the Canal?* That was for boys in rags and tatters or with no clothes at all and often with the midwife's cord hanging from their navels. Not for a boy in a blue and white outfit, his knees well coconut-oiled and with shoes on his feet.

When he reached the bottom of the stairs William almost broke into a run. All around him the soil was like a sea of black mist with here and there the white-hooded speck of a toadstool floating on it. The piles on which the house stood seemed to be swaying like the legs of dancers on stilts.*

Emerging from the darkness under the house William yielded to the so-
bering touch of sunlight. A hummingbird in the garden zizzed by before
him, going from flower to flower, charting an elusive, emerald-lit course in
the sun. The movement of the butterflies was languid, languid. Lizards scur-
ried up and down the trunk of the coconut palm. A blue duck's egg peeped
from beneath a rose bush, not one but two. Ground doves breakfasting on
mustard seed strode to and fro. There was honey in the green coffee pods—

"Almonds!"

He picked up one from under the tree: a ripe, bat-pecked one with a
bloom on it. He ate the scarlet meat beneath the skin, tapped open the seed
with a stone and popped the almond into his mouth.

Opening the gate, William stepped out upon the plank lying across the
Lamaha Canal. He placed one foot before the other and slowly walked on
to a high, round-surfaced road paved with dark bluish stone from the bed of
the Mazaruni River. As he turned down the 'road to freedom'—the canal,
flowing on both sides, was dark and untroubled, islanded with water lilies
and still with the shadows of palm trees, rows of planks, the overhanging
boughs of fustic* and star apple trees* and the silvery fronds of fern upon
it—William saw that the stretch ahead of him was empty. A quick backward
glance was reassuring: the upper part of the road was empty too. Nothing
marred the purity of line of the little white-steepled church at the top. Nothing remotely threatened to encroach upon the morning's silence save the
swelling notes of the church's pipe-organ.

The solemn beauty of the music—what was it. . . . a wedding march?—
arrested William's wayward emotions. The music stirred something deep
within him; brought back to him, strangely, the picture of a house in another
part of Georgetown and the sound of two different kinds of music that used
to float up from beneath it.

It was the house in which William had first seen the light of day. It stood
in meadowland and a water-course filled with cus-cus grass* lay beside it.
And from the stairs at the back William had often seen, squatting in the light
of a cow dung fire, a Hindu coolie who slept under the house at night.

"Foot-loose vagabond! Stinkin' up the place—"

If Mirrie, the servant girl, could have had her own way she would have
turned the Hindu off the premises. To her the facts about him had been
simple enough. 'Too lazy' to work out the terms of his contract in the cane

fields the Hindu had given the planters the slip.* Between "this, that and the other body" he was doubtless on the run. Then, seeing that no palings* surrounded the house, the Hindu without so much as a 'by your leave,' had moved in underneath it.

But from the beginning the Hindu, a tall man with a bearded face and a white speck on the ball of one eye, had had 'the good sense' to keep severely to himself. He would break camp in the morning before William's father went to work and he never showed up again until after dusk had fallen. And had it not been for the songs which he sang and the smoke from, and the smell of the cow dung which he gathered up off the streets and burnt under his pot of curried greens and mutton nobody in the house would have known that he was there at all.

Often during the long dry season that followed the Hindu seemed to imagine himself back upon a sugar estate on the evening of a pay day and, red-eyed with rum and twirling a cutlass above his head, was drunkenly dancing under the open sky in a torch-lit circle of his countrymen sitting on the ground and swaying, clapping their hands and filling the black, star-gemmed night with Hindu chants. Only instead of reeling to the throb of goat-skinned drums the Hindu would squat in solitude and beat a tattoo on the back of his frying pan. . . .

"Less noise, Babu! And let a body sleep in peace. You and your 'Coolie bam bam ku bam, Coolie bam bam ku bam.'"

Then, as the gay frenzy wore off, all would be quiet. Long nights of silence would follow. But when the October rains began the Hindu would find his tongue again. He would give way to lamentations now. Had the fear of a Mahaica River overflow already become part of his existence in Guiana?

Akbar-la-la
Akbar-la-la
Mahaica is comin' down!

After an interval of eighteen months William could still see the Hindu eyeing the cus-cus grass, watching the long blades topple and fall as the watercourse brimmed over. He could still hear the Hindu's cry going on and on in the night. Its echo filled his ears, muffling the sound of horses' hooves on the road.

He looked back and saw a landau approaching: a small, enclosed one drawn by two big, jet-black horses.

"It's the coolie wedding."

He stepped aside and stood with his back to the Canal, almost getting his heels wet. He could hear and see a commotion developing on both sides of the road: at garden gates and jalousie windows and behind the lattice-work of galleries.

As the landau passed with wheels and gleaming sides mirrored in the Canal, William caught a glimpse of the bride. Small and dark, full of the delicate loveliness of the East. Then he saw the groom. A Hindu in a silk hat and with a white chrysanthemum in his buttonhole. *What was that flickering in his eye? A white cast?*

William stood gazing after the landau. He watched the horses with sparks flying from their hooves burning up the Mazaruni road. As they mounted the culvert at the corner, William held his breath. The horses' heads suddenly appeared above the landau's flat square roof. Then, without dropping on all fours again, the horses leaped aside, scattered the flimsy wooden rail and tipped the landau out of sight.

Next thing William knew he was running behind a crowd of Negro women whose white calico skirts were billowing out in front of them. When he sped around the corner a crowd had already begun to assemble on the cross-road. The horses, under the driver's care stood lathered in foam and with quivering flanks on high ground.

Worming his way through the silent and impassive throng, William reached the water's edge. The landau with the two wheels on one side still spinning, lay half-buried in the Canal. The Hindu and his bride, trapped inside, were making frantic efforts to ease themselves up through the paneless half of the door.

"Hey," breathed a female onlooker as though recovering from a shock, "Fancy Babus goin' to the Church of England and gettin' married! Whuh they think they is, nuh?"

And as the landau rocked and rolled, sinking deeper in the mud, no one offered the bride and groom a helping hand; but a newcomer in the crowd reached out and grasped William by the ear. He looked round in agony and saw Mirrie, the servant girl.

"You wait till you get home," she said, dragging him off, "Yo' mudder gwine wash yo' skin fo' you, too."

"Woy, woy!" cried William, flying along on the tips of his shoes.

"Two Sisters"

(A Story in Three Parts) March–May 1953

I

At the top of Barbary Hill, where four roads met, the carter pulled up. An electric tram had begun turning directly in front of him around the corner from Baxter's Road, turning with the driver pressing hard on the foot-bell.

Ping-a-ling-a-ling. . . .

A small Negro boy and a young Negro woman sat beside the carter. He had picked them up on the edge of Trafalgar Square (his had been one of a number of donkey carts standing wheel to wheel round the base of Nelson's statue),* as they stepped ashore from a sailing vessel that had put into the Careenage* an hour previously.

"Where you want to go, soul?"*

"Jackman's Gap* in Black Rock village."

"Above the rum refinery?"

"Yes."

"Over St. Stephen's Hill?"

"Yes."

"Below the Cave Hill stone quarry?"

"Yes."

A pause.

"Then get in, soul."

Women from the neighbourhood's backyards, pushing and elbowing one another, and almost drowning out with the impact of bucket on bucket and kerosene tin on kerosene tin the tram's ping-a-ling-ing, surrounded the stand-pipe on the corner. Water was exploding in a vessel which one of the women, her bare feet planted wide in a pool of mud, held under the tap; but neither the 'battle of the stand-pipe' nor the glimpse of Spooner's Hill stretching white and dusty between fields of Indian corn, sweet potato and sugar cane out into the country was sufficiently novel or restful to engage the attention of the young woman perched on the sea beside the carter. Phinee's head was turned in another direction. She was looking beyond the aerial of the turning tram at the jalousies of a house across the road. It was the house in which her sister lived, and as she looked she was possessed by the certainty that from behind the shutters on the gallery someone was quietly watching her.

Ping-a-ling-a-ling. . . .

The carter pursed his lips, pulled on the reins, sucked in his breath and the donkey moved off again.

There was absolutely no doubt in Phinee's mind about the identity of the person whom she could still feel looking down at her. Her sister Dinks, no one else. How surprised Dinks must have been to see her! *Hey, what happened, soul? Is your marriage broken up? Has the man left you? Why, I thought you were going to settle down in Demerara* for good. I didn't know you would come back to Barbados. And with a boy child besides?*

As the cart turned down Baxter's Road, Phinee's gaze flickered from the corn field on one side to the row of houses on the opposite side. One of the immediate tasks ahead of her was to get in touch with the Plymouth Brethren—to let them know she wanted to take the sacrament. Her husband was not converted and he was not with her—he'd gone to Colon; so there would be much eyebrow raising with the silent exchange of glances. Yet she could not foresee anything in the nature of an ordeal. Had she not been breaking bread and sipping wine with the Brethren in Demerara?

Ah, there's the Meeting Hall . . . standing without a daub of paint less than a hundred yards from the cross-roads, so that Mr. Seafort could easily afford to give his pony and trap a rest on a Sunday morning. He and Dinks could walk to 'meeting' in no time at all. Whereas she and Henry would have to come on foot all the way from Jackman's Gap.

"Look, mama!" cried Henry, "the trams don't go any further."

The marl dust through which the donkey was labouring and the cart creaking and wobbling sparkled like powdered sugar in the sun. It was so thick it obliterated, outside the gates of Jenkin's Insane Asylum,* the end of the tram-line from Bridgetown.

"No, son."

Staring unseeingly at the spiked railings which enclosed the Asylum's grounds, she had begun to think (and the thought persisted while the cart moved on into the shade of the big evergreen oak at the foot of St. Stephen's Hill and even as it emerged again into the sunlight on the slope of the hill and continued over the hill down into the valley) how nice it would be to worship with a fragmentation of the Brethren that she knew of. The group was within easier reach and she would thus be able not only to save shoe leather but, from a spiritual point of view, the idea of worshipping with them had much to commend it.

There was nothing at Walmer Lodge to spoil the beauty of the Sunday morning service. No trams racketed past the door. The meeting house, reached by steps cut in the rock, stood by itself on an eminence high above a white, tramless stretch of the island's coral girdle. Here . . . except for the sighing of the wind in a nearby 'shack-shack' tree* and the lazy murmur of the sea in Black Rock Bay . . . there was no noise. Even the occasional passing of a horse-cab was muffled in the marl.

Yes, that's what she would do. She would worship with the Brethren at Walmer Lodge and thus avoid an encounter with Dinks.

"Here's Jackman's Gap, soul," said the carter, stopping in the white marl road. He threw the reins on the donkey's back and got down. Then he went round to the back of the cart and lifted out the canister, the folding chair and the hat box.

Nothing had changed. In the sun-parched field opposite the Gap the cane cutter's knife, topping and felling, flashing with one up and down stroke, would soon be at work on the thin, reedy crop.

"Ratoons,"* observed Phinee drily, "More like little lady canes."

Aloes, cochineal and nettles formed a hedge around the garden and the fruit trees in front of a cottage at the Cave Hill side of the Gap. A blacksage fence, tall and thick and well-trimmed, surrounded the two-storey stone house on the other side.

As she entered the Gap, preceded by Henry carrying the hat box and followed by the carter with the canister and the folding chair on his head, Phinee immediately saw the refuge she'd left Demerara to fly to: a two-roomed cottage standing in half an acre of ground. As she approached it, Phinee's heart almost stood still. The roof of the cottage was intact, but a number of the shingles on the lower half of the side facing her were missing. Spreading over the yard on to the roof, the breadfruit tree at the top of a water-course that divided the half acre in half, was still flourishing . . . with ripening fruit on it; but on the front, the back and the shady side of the cottage there were no shingles at all.

"Only bare boards," cried Phinee, "for the wind to come through the cracks. If only Old Jojo* had put a fence round the place—"

What was she saying? To let herself go like that, to speak so ungratefully of the dead was not only wrong but contrary to her make-up. As if Old Jojo the father of her mother's mother, had not been the idol of the golden days of her childhood at Flat Rock!* She could see him now . . . an early riser, clad in spotless white drill and so tall that he had to stoop to come through the front door of 'Mess House'* . . . with a silvery goatee and a lean, ochre-brown face beneath a cork helmet; his boots caked with mud and shining with dew from the morning's turn around the estate grounds; his big coat pockets filled with okras plucked from the vegetable patch behind the crumbling walls of the old sugar-mill; unloading the okras on to the big dining table and slowly ascending the stairs to occupy himself in the seclusion of the room above with the affairs of the Vestry Board of which he'd been a member for forty years and the Burial Society which he'd founded and the large family (no longer concentrated on Flat Rock) of which he was the head.

The carter, short, stocky and middle-aged, set the luggage down before the door. Then he stood up, wiping the sweat out of his eyes.

"How much do I owe you?" asked Phinee, opening her purse.

The carter hesitated. He eyed the cracks in the ground under the bread-fruit tree, noted the condition of the half acre ("a wilderness") and the absence of the shingles. ("Ripped off in the night by prowlers from down in the Gap, burnt as firewood or tacked on to a lean-to.")

"Would a shilling be too much for you?"

She inserted a key into the lock, opened the door and entered. A small, empty room with bare walls revealed itself to her. Insects' eggs ("ground pearls") and the skeletons of dead centipedes lay on the floor. Opening a window to let out the smell of long untenancy, Phinee then went to the door of the adjoining room. She paused, peering into the darkness.

"Come, son," she turned to Henry, "Let's get to work. We have plenty to do."

II

All day Phinee toiled in the sun. She had come back to Barbados secure in the knowledge that she was setting foot on native soil. Her dreams of a new life in Demerara had not endured long. They had ceased to occupy her when Robert decided to join the exodus to Colon which had begun to spread around husband, wife and small son like a cane field fire; but the promise of an early family reunion sustained her and generated the intensity and oneness of purpose with which she now set to work clearing the half acre of long grass, shrubs and weeds. Until the tickets arrived and everything was in readiness for her and Henry to embark on the steamer to Colon, she had resolved (the piece of property Old Jojo had bequeathed to her enabled her to do this) to bury herself in an out of the way corner of her old island home, remote in her pride and disenchantment from relations and friends.

"Oy! A 'pimpler'* jook* my finger!"

She dropped the hoe and fled across the field. She found Henry crawling out from beneath a tangle of briar and mustard vines.

"What are you doing under there, boy? Didn't I tell you to pick up the rocks in the water-course?"

He stood up and faced her with downcast eyes, sucking the blood from his thumb.

"I thought it was a turkey egg."

"A what?" she asked, eagerly parting the bush. A turkey's egg—a fertile one—would be as good as a gold piece. She would hatch the egg under a fowl hen. Then she would lavish on the chick the utmost care. Nothing would be too good to feed the young turkey . . . to make it fat and heavy. And on Christmas Eve she would take it down to Westbury Road and with the money which she would get for it she would buy enough shingles to cover the wind-ravaged 'hip' of the cottage.

She rustled the fallen leaves and prodded the bramble. All she could see was a round white stone.

A wry smile gathered about Phinee's thin lips. What had she been think-ing of when she airily planned to hatch the turkey's egg under a fowl hen? As if she had any poultry of her own! What she really had in mind was that she would have asked one of the Brethren at Walmer Lodge to accommodate her. Not the black, long-limbed brother who, on the Sunday morning after everyone was seated, had come up the long flight of stone steps dragging a bicycle along with him. No, not him even though in discharging the duties of 'Responsible Brother' he had seen to it that she had secured her rightful place among the converted minority in the congregation . . . Standing the bike outside the door of the meeting room, the brother had walked in with bloodshot eyes and approached a table in the centre on which stood two loaves of bread and a silver and china service. He had then taken out of his hip pocket the bottle of wine which he had procured for the sacrament and, holding it between his knees, had uncorked it with a noise more suited to a rum-shop.

"Oh, look! A forty-leg!"

"Where?" she asked, standing up.

"Here."

She pulled Henry aside, gathered up her skirts and stamped on the centipede.

"Now go along and pick up the rocks in the water-course."

He got an empty sack and went down to the dry, rock-strewn bed of the water-course. He filled the sack with stones and went and dumped them in a heap under the breadfruit tree. Then he went back and got another sackful. After he had combed the water-course dry, Henry turned his energies on to the field; first one half and then the other—popping into the sack every stone that he could find and adding them to the rising pyramid in the yard. Then, perspiring but still tireless, Henry tackled the reef of limestone at the top of the water-course. Using an iron stake he dug out the lumps of rock from between the veins of red earth as though gold prospecting was in his blood. He employed so much vigour prying loose the 'nuggets' from beneath the overhanging roots of the breadfruit tree that Phinee stopped him.

"That will do," she said, taking the stake away from him, "Do you want to bring the breadfruit tree down upon your head?"

He crawled over to a gnarled root on the other side of the tree and sat down facing the rock-pile. The silence all around him was only broken by the song of a bird overhead ("Kiss-kiss-ka-dee!")* and the clink of steel on stone from afar: the quarrymen's drills on Cave Hill.

He picked up the sledge hammer and began wielding it. Gently, not with all his strength. He must not reduce the limestone, the marl rock and the coralline chunks to powder. He had only to break them down to size.

"Mama!"

He brought the hammer down slowly. An old Negro, his body almost bent in half, was passing by. He walked without a stick and with his chest hovering low above his wide-spreading knees.

"What's wrong with you, boy?" cried Phinee. She had interrupted her dawn to dusk labours to prepare and sit down at 11 o'clock to their big meal of the day.

"Come see the—"

The old Negro, his eyes glinting, walked out of the sun into the shade of the breadfruit tree.

"Who you is, nuh?" he asked, eyeing Phinee with a toothless smile, "One of Old Jojo's grands? You too favour one of Old Jojo's grands."

Here was someone before whom, Phinee felt, she was not required to make any concessions to adversity. Occasionally folk from the bottom of the Gap passed by and observing her at work in the field, had stopped and gaped. Others, seen on their cabin doorsteps or in their sunflower gardens, had attempted to engage her in conversation:—"You going down to the Bay? To Walmer Lodge? To Miss Goodridge's shop? Well, take that turning down yonder. You looking for Miss B—? Soul, she is in the Asylum." But sometimes, much to her bewilderment, it had not been all curiosity. What was she to make of the action of the person who, ducking out of sight, had thrown a pail of soapy water over a fence directly in front of her? Or the behaviour of the woman who had jumped up out of the chair in which she had been rocking and fanning herself and, turning round, had thrown up her skirt and stomped off the porch into the house:—"And if you don't like 'um, you can phlegm!"

"Breaking stones to sell to the road menders?" cried the old Negro, turning to Henry.

"H'm?"

"Trouble is, they does only pay a cent a donkey cart load."

"Tell me," cried Phinee, "Do you know anybody who can help me fork up the ground?"

The old Negro reeled as though someone had struck him a blow. When he finally managed to steady himself he placed his hands on his knees and glared sidewise at Phinee.

"See I here?" he cried with a quiver in his voice, "I usta wear a silkerchief* around my neck, and rings 'pon every finger!"

"Of course," said Phinee, "I haven't got any money to pay you. You will have to wait until the corn is ripe."

"Why," Emptage Hart went on, not paying any attention to Phinee's remark, "I can remember when cane holes was half a cent a hundred I usta could out-dig any field hand in Black Rock. 'Pon a Saturday night you could always find me at the Constitutional Club on Westbury Road."

Seeing him forking up the half acre, raking over and furrowing it, shaking out the vines, roots and stones from the soil Phinee groaned in despair. The ground seemed so hard and dry.

To help 'diversify the crop' Emptage came up the Gap one morning with a pocketful of dry okra pods. ("Corn meal and okra does go well together.") In the barrow which he was pushing lay a tub of water with a maze of sweet potato slips floating about in it.

Next day Emptage gave Phinee a mango plant to graft into the breadfruit tree. The barrow was constantly yielding surprises: a white, pink-eyed rabbit, a pair of pigeons to mate with the wood doves nesting under the eaves. Emptage even took the barrow out into the road to gather horse manure to spread over the field.

Up in the breadfruit tree Henry lay outstretched on a limb . . . dangling the loop on the end of a long blade of grass above the head of a lizard on a browny green leaf. A donkey cart, creaking and swaying, coming up the Gap half full of cassavas and yams earned the lizard a reprieve. On the driver's seat sat a fat, black man in a black serge suit. A town buyer. He sat with the donkey's rein clasped in one hand. In the other hand was a stout piece of sugar cane, a couple of joints in length. Around the man's bleeding lips—cut by cane peeling*—cane juice had dried and whitened. He tapped on one of the cart's wheels with the cane as though to expel a maggot from it. Then he bit into the cane, sucking the juice and spitting a trail of blood-stained trash behind the cart.

Presently another cart emerged from the same direction. The driver sat with his hat tilted forward, dozing. The donkey, moving surefootedly on a slack rein, appeared to be successfully avoiding the pitfalls in the Gap when one of the cart's wheels sank into a depression; some of the sweet potatoes from the cone-like heap with which the cart was filled rolled off the tailboard. The driver was unaffected by the cart's sudden tipping to one side and the donkey, carrying on as though aware of this, swerved out of the rut only to be jarred by the wheel on the other side jolting against a rock that jutted up sharply. An avalanche broke from the summit of the sweet potato pile.

Henry watched the cart disappear out of sight. Then he dropped to the ground and, rushing out into the Gap, gathered up the potatoes in a sack.

"Mama!" he cried, "look what I've got!"

"Instead of you studying your lessons," she grumbled, not at all pleased with him.

Going to school in Barbados was to Henry like a form of torture. On his very first day at school his class-mates gave him a thorough going over.

"Where you does live, bo?"

"Jackman's Gap."

"That God-forsaken old hole?"

"You mean Jack-me-Nannie Gap, don't you?"

"No, I don't!"

"Where you come from, bo?"

"Demerara."

"What, from that place so muddy the houses have to be built on stilts?"

"It's better than here!" cried Henry with heat.

"Hey, hear the 'Mud-Head' spouting!"

One boy tugged at the collar of Henry's sailor jacket. Another crept up behind him, made a circle of thumb and forefinger and released it against his ear. A third boy spotted a tiny blue square on Henry's white short trousers.

> Patch in the crutch
> Is nothing much
> But patch in the knee
> Is poverty.

"What school in Demerara did you go to?" asked one boy, continuing the Inquisition.

"Rob Street School," answered Henry.

"What they teach you there, bo?"

"Latin and Greek."

"Oh!"

The bell rang for the end of recess and the boys, full of ugly suspicions, walked with him in silence into the crush on the schoolhouse steps. Running up the steps, Henry stumbled and fell. The boys burst out laughing.

"That ought to knock the Latin and Greek out of your head!"

III

Next day at recess Henry turned his back on 'bat and ball'* and the scrimmages on The Green. Though in Jackman's Gap he shared with Phinee the condition of a new sort of exile in Barbados, she had her roots in the island; but at school he was like something cast up from the Sargasso Sea,* a newcomer from Demerara, and the fact that his class-mates drew a line between him and themselves added to his feeling of isolation.

Passing a group of small Negro girls holding hands in a ring and swaying in unison—

> There's a young girl in the ring*
> Tra-la-la-la
> There's a young girl in the ring
> Tra-la-la-la
> O! show me your motion
> Tra-la-la-la

Show me your motion
Tra-la-la-la
For she likes sugar and I like plum

Henry wandered between the Headmaster's house and the Girls' School to the top of the long playground. He stood under a tree-shaded part of the wall of St. Stephen's churchyard looking down upon a marl road (the drop over the edge of the soft green turf was steep) lying blindingly white in the sun. The marl was restive, moving in billowing clouds to and fro, spiralling up and up and powdering as it lazily descended the blue sand, the sweet potato vines and the gaping mouths of myriads of soldier crabholes* in the dune on the opposite side of the road. Further down the slope, blotting out the beach, the log cabins of Negro fisher folk appeared amidst the dark foliage of manchineel trees;* but in a clearing below the rum refinery the sea rolled in upon white and golden sand. Nets lay outspread in the sun between overturned fishing boats undergoing repairs. The tall, smokeless chimneys of the refinery loomed across the flickering green dome of the sea as though to dispute the passage of a flying fish fleet serenely tacking in the Bay.

Lay, lay
Bessie Down
For the sake of the pumpkin
Bessie down.

Of a sudden Henry began to hear the sound of timber creaking and groaning as in pain. Nothing that was not nailed down on the floor of the poky* little cabin could be relied on to stay put. Everything was sliding forward and back and sideways. Up on deck a never to be forgotten view met his gaze: cartwheels of foam spinning out from under the schooner, the sea at once a clear and a dark blue stretching away to a horizon that was forever expanding, shoals of silver-winged flying fish and the green swirl of Tobago's palms fading away in the dusk.

When Henry turned to go back to the schoolhouse the playground was empty. The Headmaster was pacing the verandah. A small, lean, black man in sombre attire.

Still full of the day and the sleepless night—or was it longer?—which he and Phinee had spent on the voyage in the schooner from Demerara to Barbados, Henry mounted the steps.

The Headmaster paused, put his hands under his coat-tails and stiffened.

"Didn't you hear the bell?"

"No, sir."

"Where were you that you didn't hear it?"

"Over yonder," answered Henry, glancing in the direction of St. Stephen's Church, "Looking at the fishing boats going up to Bridgetown."

"Oh, I see," said the Headmaster, "You are the new boy."

Hurrying home from school late one afternoon with a slate held over his head to ward off the rain slashing across the playground from the sea, Henry attempted to steal past the Headmaster's house; but behind a pink mass of bougainvillea on the lattice-work the Headmaster, his tall son and six comely daughters were sitting in a row on the verandah.

"Heard from your mother yet?" called out the Headmaster.

"No, sir."

"Poor boy."

As he stood at an open window deafened by the raindrops falling like bullets on the broad, coarse-grained leaves of the breadfruit tree and eyeing the water swirling out of the Gap and weaving a channel through the grass and over the stones into the water-course, Henry resigned himself to the fact that there was nothing he could do to end the deception. He had tried again and again to explain that it was *only* his father who had gone to Colon, but the Headmaster had dreamily persisted in regarding him as a "Panama orphan." After a while he had even waived the payment of Henry's school fees. Thereafter Henry went to school feeling like a party to a fraud, but Phinee had welcomed the Headmaster's gesture with delight.

"Let him go on thinking I'm in Panama," she had said, "It won't do him any harm, and the Lord won't hold it against you."

She was weeding the bed of thyme and keeping an eye on Henry. She did not want him to get over-heated romping with the rabbit in the cus-cus grass on the boundary line.

Crunch . . . crunch . . . crunch . . .

"Is that you, Emptage?"

Ever since he had helped her with the sowing the old Negro had stopped coming round in the mornings. She had not seen him since he had brought her a scarecrow to combat the plague of blackbirds in the corn field.

She glanced round at the gravel path on the shady side of the cottage. Over the border of seashells she glimpsed the pink haziness of a parasol, a suede shoe buttoned up at the side and the trimmings on the hem of a white muslin skirt.

She stood up. "Oh, it's you," she said. To what did she owe the unexpected 'pleasure' of a visit from her sister? Had Dinks come to pour salt into an open wound or had she come to show off her town finery?

Dinks pushed up the veil over her hat. She paused about ten feet from Phinee . . . on a spot still showing evidence of having been occupied lately by a rock-pile.

"You mean to say," she began in a tone of honeyed reproof, "You've been down here all this time and you haven't been to see me? Fie upon you, Phinee!"

Phinee leaned the hoe against the closet over the latrine-pit. "Cho'!"* she said, stepping over the bed of thyme, "I've got too much to do to think about you, girl."

Dinks pulled off her long cotton gloves. "Hey," she drawled, wide-eyed and open-mouthed, "But what have you done to the place, no?"

Beyond the dark, cool shade of the breadfruit tree the water-course was like a mirror in the sun. The pigeon pea trees along its banks were heavy with a golden shower of blossoms. The two halves of the half acre fairly bulged with the promise of a mixed crop in which maize predominated. Silver tassels flowed from the budding ears of corn. Here and there in the green density of a wide range of side-lines (yams, sweet potatoes, eddoes, pumpkins and cucumbers whose vines, spreading over the furrows entwined themselves round the stalks of the young corn) appeared the big, velvety leaves of the okra and the pale green of the cassava.

Dinks moistened her lips. Up at Eagle Hall Corner she had one foot in town and the other in the country. She was almost equally distant from the mercantile bustle of Bay Street and the rural calm of Jackman's Gap. When there was a glut of flying fish at Cheapside (the never-failing tumult on Barbary Hill would inform her of this) she could always send the servant girl with a penny to buy a basketful. But money was scarce; and though she was raising a kiddy goat* and had one or two fowls in the yard and Mr. Seafort arrogated to himself the luxury of a Shetland pony and a 'tra-la-la' buggy,* the day to day business of finding money to buy not only cod fish and fat pork but maize and ground provisions was a perpetual nightmare.

She turned to Phinee with a smile in her eyes. "You must let me take away some of the green ones when they are ripe."

Phinee eyed her in silence.

"But we will count them in," Dinks assured her, "We don't want to rob one another. And when the balance of the corn is dry I will come and we will reap them and husk them together."

"Yes?"

"Then," Dinks went on, "I will get Mr. Seafort to come down in the tra-la-la and carry away my share."

"Your share?"

"Yes."

"Your share of what?"

"Don't play the fool, Phinee!" cried Dinks, "You know full well that half the corn is mine."

Phinee's dry, mirthless laughter brought Henry running out of the cuscus grass. He put the rabbit back in the hutch and joined the two women.

"When Old Jojo died," Phinee was saying, "Who did he leave the place at 'Arise'* to? Three quarters of an acre of ground, two big alligator pear* trees, a house with only a little needed doing to it . . . who did he give them to?"

"As his favourite grandchild," answered Dinks, "He gave them to me. But I don't see what that has to do with the case. Some people without stopping to weigh the consequences can go off to a 'Mud-Head' country and marry a mulatto man. If I choose to live in town, that's my look-out."

"And this," said Phinee, waving an arm around the half acre, "Who he gave this to?"

"To you, of course," said Dinks, "But you seem to forget—"

"Forget what?"

"That all the years you were in Demerara somebody had to keep the place from going to pieces. You say the air in the house was musty? You found dead forty-legs and 'ground pearls' on the floor? Soul, you were lucky to find a house at all! After I sold the place at 'Arise' and moved to Eagle Hall Corner I used to come every so often to have a look round. If I didn't carry away the ripe breadfruits somebody else would have! Sometimes I had to hold back coppers Mr. Seafort gave me to put in the meeting room box so as to pay the taxes."

"Taxes?" cried Phinee with a frown, "What taxes, soul?"

"Oh, you didn't think of the taxes, no? Dada! You think the taxes could pay themselves? No, soul. Somebody had to pay them. And to pay the two and six* a year unbeknowingst to Mr. Seafort I had to go without tea* many a morning."

"So you paid the taxes all the time I was away?"

"Yes, and it was a struggle too."

"Nine years at two and six a year is twenty two shillings and sixpence."

"Yes," said Dinks, "but you can't count it like that. You've got to consider the interest too. And besides if I didn't pay the taxes the Collector would have auctioned off the place long ago."

"That's right," nodded Phinee.

Dinks' eyes brightened. "I know," she said, "You wouldn't be so bad-minded as to deprive me of my share!"

"And so you want half of the corn?" asked Phinee.

"After all, that is only fair," smiled Dinks.

"Don't worry, soul. I will give you your share." Only Phinee reserved the right to determine when she should do so. Not when the corn was ripe but now, while it was still young and tender and green. "If it's half you want," she cried, turning from Dinks and striding across the bed of thyme, "Here—take it!" She uprooted a corn stalk and pelted Dinks with it. She tripped over a potato vine, turned and pulled it up and with both hands grasped at the surrounding corn. "If it's half you want—"

"Hey, soul!" cried Dinks, dodging a shower of stalks, "You haven't got to cut off your nose just to spite me."

"But, Mama!" cried Henry, pulling at her skirts, "What are you doing?"

"Let me go, boy!" she cried, shaking him off, "If it's half you want—"

Losing all self-control she plunged into the field, pulling up the corn, kicking loose the entangling vines, felling everything that came within her grasp. She snapped the brittle limbs of the cassava, ground the pumpkins and cucumber underfoot. She destroyed the pigeon pea trees limb by limb, one after the other. Nothing that she passed was left standing. Not until the two halves of the field looked as though a hurricane had swept over them, not until they were strewn with everything she had so hopefully planted—not until she was satisfied that she now had nothing to share with Dinks—did she call a halt.

When she got back to the yard Dinks was gone. Henry alone was under the breadfruit tree. He was sitting on an age-encrusted root of the tree with his head on his arm, sobbing.

"Bliss"

July 1953

"Okay, report for work at 7:30 Monday morning." Not a word about the janitor, nothing to prepare Boysie for the encounter with Old Brown.

"You the new office boy?" asked the janitor, looking up from mowing the lawn.

Boysie hesitated on the plank that stretched across the lawn.

"Yes."

"A Jamaican?"

"No."

"Where you come from then?"

"British Guiana,"

"Demerara, eh?"

Boysie wondered what else the janitor wanted to know. He was not the boss. He was not Mr. O'Malley.

"You been in Colon long?"

"Five years."

"You go to school here?"

"I used to go to Teacher Bailey's—"

It was strange not to be with the 'overflow' of Teacher Bailey's pupils in the Vestry of the Wesleyan Chapel on Cash Street; not to be sitting on a porch with a roof slanting down to a sunlessly cool, tree-shaded yard—the beginning of an overgrown strip of garden; not to be aware of the stench of the "G" Street sewage canal flowing across the bottom of the garden or to see the hands of prisoners clasping the iron bars of windows in the egg yellow wall of the Colon jail beside it.

"Him is a Jamaican, no?"

"Who?"

"Mr. Bailey."

"Now that you mention it—"

Yes, Teacher Bailey was a Jamaican, an old Wolmer's College* boy . . . but what difference did that make? What was the janitor driving at? What was he trying to say?

"All right, come inside. Mr. O'Malley told me to expect you."

Boysie followed the janitor into the office. The janitor give him a feather duster, told him to make himself useful and went outside again.

Boysie set to dusting and tidying the desks. Here and there daylight, flowing in under the gallery outside both the front and the side doors and through the shutters on one side of the room only, penetrated the darkness. Above him the oak-beamed ceiling seemed about as low as that of the Vestry porch at Teacher Bailey's . . . Who would be sitting on that porch half an hour hence, watching the hands clasping the iron bars and listening to the noises coming out of the prison cells? Edna, black-eyed Chinese Monica, Ramon Perez—

Not Ramon surely! No, Ramon had no time for anything like that.

A queer aggravating sort of boy, Ramon. Small for his age and with high cheek bones in a broad, sallow, pock-marked face. Son of a Colon police lieutenant, an energetic, quick-stepping giant of a man of Spanish and Indian admixture who walked with his big shoulders hunched up, wore a gold-braided cap and a gold badge on his white tunic; a man who, looking ahead, had set his heart upon Ramon acquiring, speedily and even from a Jamaican immigrant source, the rudiments of a 'Gringo' education. So much so that even before Ramon had passed through all the grades in the big Spanish school at the top of Bolivar Street he had whisked him off to Teacher Bailey's.

Recess. . . .

Balls flew back and forth across the fenced in handkerchief of the yard. Ramon alone sat on the porch, his head buried in a book. (Monica, still as a flower, eyed him in silence.) The noise and the gaiety, the eruption from the Vestry swirled about him in vain.

"Come on, Ramon!" cried Boysie. "Don't you want to play?"

No answer.

"Don't you want to join us?"

The thin, curving jut of Ramon's lower lip paled, grew bloodless.

"No, no, no! My father . . . he does not like!"

Boysie mounted the steps. He spoke softly to Ramon, almost in a whisper:—"I saw you in the crowd coming out of church last Sunday morning. You were with your father. I smiled and waved at you from across the street. Didn't you see me?"

"Yes, yes, I see you but you have no right to speak-o-ty* me outside school! I am a Panamanian . . . white! You . . . a 'Chombo' from the Antilles . . . black!"

The whirr of the lawn mower stopped. The figure of Old Brown darkened the doorway.

"You empty the waste paper baskets yet?"

"No."

"Well, empty them, no?"

After he had finished passing the duster up and down the legs and over the black, leather-upholstered tops of a row of tall stools under the leaf of a long counter, Boysie started on the baskets. Returning from tipping the contents of the first one into the dustbin the janitor, rummaging in the locker under the stairs, growled at him:—"You don't have all day for that, you know."

As he passed back and forth, keeping an eye on the janitor, Boysie observed how, commencing with the panel under the bills of lading* clerk's window, the woodwork below the metal railings on the outside of the walls of the inner office had begun to shine and glow with a new application of the janitor's elbow grease. Then, suddenly, Boysie saw the janitor sweeping up.

"That the last one?"

"Yes."

Old Brown put down the broom. He grasped Boysie by the arm and led him through the backdoor into a courtyard. Under a stonewall stood a bench with a row of dirty spittoons, a tin of brass polish and a rag upon it.

"All right," said the janitor, "You can clean them."

Boysie's chin slowly went up. He steeled his jaw.

"What are you playing, eh?" cried the janitor. He had served the firm long and variously—on the wharf at his home in Port Antonio, Jamaica, on a banana plantation in Changuinola and in the Colon agency for the past six years—and he had never met anyone on its pay-roll quite like Boysie.

"I wasn't employed to clean any spittoons," said Boysie.

"So you don't want to clean them?" asked the janitor. The sweat was pouring in rivulets down his cheeks and lying in pools under his bloodshot eyes.

"No, I don't," answered Boysie.

"All right," said the janitor as if that was all he wanted to know, "You wait till Mr. O'Malley come in. Me gwine repo't you!"

He stomped out of the yard.

Sauntering back into the office, Boysie saw the janitor sprinkling water from a bucket on to the floor.

"Boy ah form fool," grumbled Old Brown, seizing the broom and continuing with the sweeping up, "Don't want for to clean the spittoons."

Boysie watched him closely. In the midst of the spectacle of the janitor working himself up into a steaming fury the gate in the low railing began swinging to and fro. The clerks had started coming in one by one. First to make his appearance was a tall, slim, light-haired youth (flushed a coral pink and faintly perspiring) in a straw hat and a blue suit. After him came a short, stocky older man with dark shining hair. Hatless. Palm Beach coat folded over one arm. . . .

"Boy ah form fool," grumbled the janitor, struggling out with bucket and broom through the backdoor.

Presently Boysie saw the cashier approaching. Mr. Jasmine was a Creole from Mexico who had fled abroad after the fall of Porfirio Diaz* three years previously. Firmly gripped between Mr. Jasmine's teeth was a pipe with a long curving stem and an enormous bowl. He was crossing the plank stretching over the lawn with a quick sagging step. Under the brim of a Mexican sombrero (a headgear less common in Colon than a Hindu coolie's turban) his glaring eyes were flying from side to side. . . . Later, keeping his ears cocked Boysie discovered as the room began to buzz with the summery accents of Louisiana, Florida, Georgia and Texas that Mr. Jasmine's English was fluent and that his voice was deep and husky.

"Boy ah form fool," grumbled the janitor, shuffling in with the spittoons. None of them was now stained with tobacco juice. Each one was shining with a bright glow.

"H'm," said Boysie to himself, "I've got your number, Mr. Brown."

But when Mr. O'Malley, a native of Bowling Green, Kentucky, breezed down the stairs from his apartments on the floor above Boysie's new accession of confidence threatened to desert him. Mr. O'Malley shed his coat and hat and seated himself at his desk. The janitor flew over with a dust cloth and, still grumbling away, wiped the arms and the legs, the back and the springs of Mr. O'Malley's swivel-chair; while Boysie, expecting the worst, waited for Mr. O'Malley to say something to him. But Mr. O'Malley didn't say anything to him. Rolling up his shirt sleeves over his milk-white, slightly freckled arms Mr. O'Malley lit a cigar and spoke to the janitor instead.

"Yes, sir!"

The janitor wagged a finger at Boysie. "You form fool and see if me don't—"

He slipped on his coat and went out through the front door. Big, angular, six foot tall. . . .

Boysie moved about the office wondering whether he was going to like it there. He'd had the temerity to invade the oldest part of the town where the houses served a dual purpose: shipping agencies and foreign consulates on the ground floor and residences on the floors above. Some of them even had wire screens, like the bungalows on the Canal Zone—

"The coach is here, Mr. O'Malley!" announced the janitor from the pavement outside the door.

Mr. O'Malley gathered up a pile of shipping documents on his desk, swivelled himself out of his chair and reached for his straw hat.

"Come on, Boysie. Get your cap."

"Yes, sir."

Mr. O'Malley, coatless, emerged into the light of the doorway. When Boysie trotted out behind him the janitor turned and gazed at them in silence.

At the end of the plank Mr. O'Malley turned his back on the line of white, one-storey buildings running down to the shore of Limon Bay. He faced the newer part of town, a mushrooming world of tenements. Ahead of him a horsecab with top thrown back and with a Negro on the driver's seat was turning round against a background of palm trees in the old native half of Slifer's Park.

"To the Port Captain's office first," said Mr. O'Malley, stepping into the cab almost before it had stopped at the curb.

"Yes, sir."

"And then on to the Cristobal docks."

"Yes, sir."

Mr. O'Malley moved over to the farther side of the cab. As he sat down he put his hand over the side and began tapping the ash off the end of his cigar. Then he saw Boysie climbing on to the seat beside the coachman.

"Not up there!" frowned Mr. O'Malley.

"Sir?" cried Boysie, bewildered.

"In here."

"Yes, sir."

Boysie sat down beside Mr. O'Malley in a daze. Was he dreaming? Would Ramon Perez see him when the cab drove down Bolivar Street? Not if he was at school. Nor was Boysie particularly anxious for Ramon, poor boy, to see him. He did not wish to destroy Ramon's sense of the fitness of things.

"The Iceman"

August 1953

After the amputation of his leg and a spell in the Rehabilitation Ward of the hospital on the beach, Natty Boy found that he could get about quite as easily as before. Yet however much he prided himself on his resiliency Natty was obliged to admit that going about the streets of Colon hawking ice from a wheelbarrow was not exactly an occupation for a man with only one sound leg.

"Why the rass* you don't look where you goin' eh?" shouted Natty, taking refuge in the gutter, "You t'ink you own the road, eh?"

In a narrow street on both sides of which the wide verandahs of two, three and four storey tenements extended all the way across the pavement the darkness combined with deep ruts, quagmires, broken glass and refuse was bad enough; but to have to contend as well with a crazy, slack-turbanned Babu jogging around the corner in a donkey cart as if he was on a West Indian country road was the limit.

Natty stepped out into the middle of the street. He turned his head from side to side as he gazed upward at the verandahs. Then, trying in one melodious flow to reach his Spanish-speaking hosts, immigrants from the West Indies and anyone else whose idiom might not have been too 'pure,' Natty cried:—

"Hielo! Hielo!" (It sounded like "Yellow, Yellow!") "Ice!"

Doesn't anyone want any ice today? You mustn't imagine that it is not going to be hot. It's going to be a scorcher! Do not be deceived by the slow way the sun is mounting the rooftops or by that whiff of a breeze from Limon Bay. Or is everyone still asleep?

Where is the buxom, velvet-voiced occupant of Room 17-B on the balcony yonder? The girl from Barbados with a complexion like a ripe pomegranate?

"Jamaica turkey* does fly high, nuh?"

No, she's too pretty and well-nourished to say anything like that, not to know a John Crow from a turkey or to harbour designs upon a bird that lives on carrion. A John Crow sitting in a coconut treetop or prowling along the sea-shore would not be in any danger from her.

She, whose 'six-months' marriage' seems to be going on and on as if 'Old Ivory'—for that's what his skin looks like: a dapper little Italian tailor with a moustache curled up at the ends and a shop on Front Street—was really in love . . . hasn't she got up yet? She has always been a good steady customer.

He pulled the barrow out of the gutter and started to push it forward again.

> *Tee day, tee day*
> *Bajan!**
> *Bajan, Bajan*
> *Tee day!*

He was moving in one direction while the darkness on either side of him was flowing the other way. The shadows contained by the pillars which supported the verandahs of Bottle Alley* streamed off behind him. It was now possible to see beyond the open doors of the ironmonger's, the ship chandler's, the aerated bottle works. The pavements even began to shine. Then, suddenly, the white roof of a little bandstand set amidst the dark green of trees, the splashing of fountains and the scarlet blooms of hibiscus appeared directly ahead of him in a golden burst of sunlight.

Natty paused, still gripping the barrow's shafts; and as he stood gazing at the beauty enclosed by iron railings within the lower half of the public park named after Joe Slifer, one of the engineers who had pioneered the railway on which he had lost his leg, Natty's eyes misted over . . .

Back in 1850–1855, more than half a century before Natty Boy set out from Kingston to help Uncle Sam dig the Panama Canal, William Aspinwall and his partners in a New York syndicate had built, mainly with Chinese coolie labour, a railway that was so vital to the construction of the new waterway that one of the first actions of the French under Ferdinand de Lesseps in their abortive attempt from 1880 to 1889 to 'pierce the Isthmus of Panama' was to acquire control of it. The railway, which the line of the canal closely followed, ran through forty-eight miles of swamp and jungle and reduced to approximately two hours the time it had formerly taken to cross from the Caribbean Sea to the Pacific Ocean. On the Caribbean side of the Isthmus the line, diverting traffic from and ringing down the curtain on the ancient seaport towns of Porto Bello and Chagres, stretched from the mainland over a causeway on to the old Indian island of Manzanillo in the Bay of Limon. In 1850 the Provincial Assembly had honoured the town that sprang up round the railhead with the Spanish name of the Italian discoverer of the New World, Cristobal Colon; but for a long time the town was known under one or the other of two names, Aspinwall and Colon. . . .

The cattle trucks of a labour train, terminating beside the palm trees in the open half of Slifer's Park stood at the top of the railhead. Long grey whiskers of steam shot out from under the engine. On one side of the tracks the vapours fell across cinders, tufts of grass and the pavement—right up to the lower half of the park's iron railings. On the other side the hot bursts moistened an area of the Freight House, an old stone fortress of a building which, from the rising of the Liberals under Pedro Prestan in 1885 down to the secession of Panama from Colombia in 1903, had now and then found itself in the line of fire during political disturbances in the town.

"All aboard!" cried Natty Boy, wiggling a gloved hand above his head.

The engine driver shut off the exhaust. He leaned out of the window and with a smile in his eyes watched Natty in a polka-dotted bow tie, a white silk shirt, blue serge trousers and patent leather shoes striding along the pavement beside the railings. Then he opened the throttle.

Natty continued walking. He was getting quite used to the driver's smile. At 6:45 a.m. when the train began its first journey of the day to Mount Hope in the Canal Zone the driver, eyeing Natty after he had given him the signal to pull out, had smiled. At noon when Natty coupled the engine on to the train for the return journey to Slifer's Park the driver had smiled again. And now, at 12:45 p.m., on the way back up to Mount Hope, the driver had smiled once more.

The pavement ended on the curve of Fifth and the beginning of Front Streets. Here the guardian of the crossing, a big, six-foot tall, grey-haired Negro who'd lost a leg in a premature explosion during the blasting at Culebra, stood outside a dog kennel of a hut with a blood-red flag unfurled in the sun, checking the onrush of a multitude of donkey carts bound for the Colon wharves.

"Hello, Natty, m'boy."

"Okay, Mr. Riley."

Passing between the engine and the row of bobbing asses' heads Natty mounted the end of a snaky strip of concrete. As the engine swerved in towards him and then bounded along the play in the couplings conveyed to Natty the substance of a challenge. It was as if the driver, instead of taking men to work not directly connected with the cutting of the Canal was engaged upon a more urgent task: hurrying (through the green smear of jungle on the opposite shore of Limon Bay) to the ever-lengthening tip of the Toro Point break-water with dirt waggons filled with the black gold of Culebra Cut.

The low, flat roofs of the trucks in which the Italian, Gallegan and West Indian workmen were travelling doubtless made the journey in the midday heat almost intolerable. But the desire to escape from the suffocating conditions in the centre of the trucks had not been the only reason for the eagerness with which most of the men—streaming through the emerald gloom of royal palms at the top of Slifer's Park from the Chinese cook-shops and the tenements of Colon—had begun from about 12:30 p.m. onwards to occupy all the places at the windows on one side of the train only. The driving force behind the pushing and shoving had been more than the need for a breath of fresh air; behind it lay the desire to see on the ribbon of concrete the lone, perspiring figure of Natty Boy in a fever of rhythmic motion.

He was delaying the moment when he would board the train longer than he had ever done before. He was doing this not in the spirit of an actor performing in an open air theatre before a tense audience. No, he was not putting off the moment in order to impress anyone with his fearless courage. Nor was he doing it to 'spite' the engine driver who, still with the flicker of a smile, was keeping an eye upon him. Something else of which Natty was but vaguely aware, something connected with the mastery of a new craft, was involved.

Running down the line ahead of a locomotive moving at a pace too rapid for the eye to gauge, throwing a switch and then turning with arms outspread to step coolly back on to the cow-catcher;* climbing to the top of a long freight train and passing from the roof of one box car to the next in the opposite direction from which the engine was chuffing; alighting from the iron ladder on the side of a box car turning a curve at top speed—all these had been in the nature of exercises in preparation for the supreme test of a brakesman's skill which Natty Boy had been gradually working himself up to.

He pulled off one of his arm-length gloves, reached in his hip pocket and taking out a clean white handkerchief mopped his face, chin and neck. He pressed down firmly on his clean-shaven head the grey cloth hat that he wore with the brim turned up not only in front but behind as well. His shirt sleeves, shortened at the elbows, rippled in the wind. His brass check, hanging from a strap on the Ingersoll dollar-watch in his fob, swung from side to side.

Two, three, four of the ten cattle trucks flew past him. Turning his head slightly to the rear Natty commenced a kind of jog trot. Then he broke into a sprint, moving in closer to the train. When the end of truck No. 8 drew up alongside him Natty leaned over the edge of the pavement and with one hand grasped the iron bar extending round the side of the couplings, while with the other hand he strove to reach the bar on No. 9 with the object of levering himself up into a position astride the two trucks. With an ominous jangling of the couplings the train leapt forward under a sudden burst of speed and shook him off. He stumbled and fell on to the rail and the wheels of Trucks Nos. 9 and 10 passed over his right leg, shattering it just below the knee....

> O! poor me one
> Too much o' them 'pon poor me one
> Too many Babajans in the room
> An none o' them can buy a broom

Natty turned west. He hugged the sweeping curve of pavement under the verandah of a two-storey building stretching from Bottle Alley to Front Street and facing Slifer's Park across the mellow flagstones of Fifth Street. He followed the clean, gently sloping pavement which was wider than the Bottle Alley ones, past the open doors of and the glitter of elegant furnishings in a bar frequented by the more successful of Colon's politicians.

"*Lora!*"* screamed a parrot from the top of a wide stairway in the centre of the building, "*Lorita real!*"

Natty stopped. He lowered the barrow's shafts to the ground and stood up. Wiping the sweat off his face and neck Natty was struck by the eerie calm, the emptiness all around him. Nothing now flowed into or out of the curve of Fifth and Front Streets. So few trains now passed by that the crossing was not even guarded; and only the ghost of old, stiff-legged Mr. Riley inhabited the flagman's hut. The Freight House was like a tomb. The waterfront was still, drowsy, sun-drenched. As though the tide in Limon Bay was swiftly running one old wharf, curving up narrowly under a zinc roof, swayed and rocked, creaking and groaning, breaking up. New and safer and less windy anchorages deeper in the arm of the Bay across the boundary into the Canal Zone had drawn all the big steamer traffic away from the sovereign old port. Now only the cayukas* of Mache aborigines from the coast of San Blas and the sloops of coconut growers on the Colombian island of San Andres found their way to the decaying wharves and jetties.

Natty removed the sacking from the ice and brushed the thin layer of sawdust off the top. Then he unhooked the pincers from beneath the shafts and began to work a chink between the two big 75-lb blocks.

"*Hielo, hielo!*" cried Natty, "Ice!"

He started chipping the ice with a hatchet.

"The Loan"

November 1953

"Anisette?" asked Sam Ty, the Chinese proprietor of the canteen, after pouring white rum into the three small glasses on the counter.

"I am not a Spaniard!"

Curly Mendez's response was not for himself alone. It was for Buster and Rufus the Silent One as well.

"Some of this?" continued the Oriental, fingering the siphon on a flask of Angostura bitters.

"No!"

"Water?"

"When I light a fire," exploded Curly, "I like for to see it burn!"

Buster stepped back from the bar and gazed into the hazy depths of the canteen. He wrinkled his brows. "Stop, tell me something ... is no' that the Spaniard wha' borrowed the three dollars from Curly the other day?" Like Curly and Rufus, Buster was a Jamaican immigrant of ten years' standing in Colon. And though he could not possibly have had any interest in breathing new life into the old connection between the people of the Isthmus and Imperial Spain and though he knew in a vague way that the only tie now existing between them and Old Castile was pretty tenuous, even in the matter of language, he still could not bring himself to think of a Panamanian save as a 'Spaniard.'

"Where is he?" asked Curly, wiping his lips. After a long morning in the sun, driving a new electric truck on the Cristobal docks, the white rum seemed in an instant to have put a scarlet film over his eyes.

"See him over yonder," cried Buster, "Ah treat him friends them."*

Among the group of men standing midway between the wet and the dry goods ends of the counter was one with a palm leaf hat with a shredded brim. The face beneath the hat was a dark yellow and lean. The man at whom Curly was looking was small and compactly built. His white cotton shirt fell outside a pair of dirty pantaloons. He had just bought a round of drinks and as he raised his glass in a toast to his companions, he cried:—"*Salud!*"

It was he all right; the little mestizo who, a fortnight before, under the palm trees on the road from Cristobal to Colon, had approached Curly for a loan of three Panama silver dollars.

Although he had never seen Pablo Pequeno before Curly had given him the money almost with a conscience, as though there was something a little immoral about him, Curly Mendez, a West Indian, earning good money on the Panama Canal while a native of the country through which the canal passed had for whatever reason been reduced to the condition of a panhandler.

"Go tell him say* yo' want yuh money, man!"

Curly strode over to Pablo Pequeno and gave him a couple of taps on the shoulder. Light, if somewhat urgent taps; but the effect of having administered them worked a kind of transformation within Curly. He realized with a shock of delight that by the service which he had rendered Pablo Pequeno he had lifted himself on to a dazzling new plane. He was now on terms of social equality with a 'Spaniard'; so much so that he could even tap him on the shoulder.

Ten minutes' walk from the canteen was the Fox River jetty, opposite the reed-choked swamp on the edge of Silver City in the Canal Zone, where Pablo Pequeno's canoe (hewn out of a tree trunk) lay. He had brought it down the river early that morning filled with sacks of charcoal which he burnt in the blue Santa Rita foothills.

"You wish to speak to me, Chombo?" cried Pablo Pequeno.

Curly's Adam's apple travelled up and then down. Chombo? Did that mean that, in spite of everything, his status—the dusky counterpart of a Gringo—had remained unchanged? "Don't you know me?" he asked softly. He searched Pablo Pequeno's eyes in vain for a gleam of recognition. "I'm the fellow who gave you the three dollars on the Cristobal road, after I came away from the pay car. Don't you remember?"

Pablo Pequeno flicked the ash from a yellow paper cigarette. "You?" he asked, without even an embarrassing flush, "I never saw you before."

One of Pablo Pequeno's friends, Jose Diaz, a Santa Rita herdsman, stepped forward to try and smooth out the difficulty. A few years before, when the construction of the Panama Canal was nearing completion, Jose Diaz had lived for a short time in a Colon tenement with a swarm of immigrants newly arrived from Jamaica, Barbados, Trinidad and British Guiana and he had always maintained that they were really no different from other folk.

"Tell me, boy, what do you want? What do you wish to say to Mister Pequeno? He no comprend you."

"No comprend me?" cried Curly.

"Mister Pequeno—he don't know you."

"Don't know me?" shrieked Curly, "Hafta* him stand up before me and Buster and Rufus and cry big cry-water and tell me say him don't got no job, no money, nowhere for to sleep. . . ."

"Oh, don't pay any attention to the monkey," muttered Pablo Pequeno in Spanish.

Silently, and without a suspicion of premeditation, Pablo Pequeno and his friends drifted away from the bar and began to encompass Curly in two encircling lines. The tread of their cloth-topped, hemp-soled shoes was soundless. Half of the group went one way while the other half moved in the opposite direction. Both halves continued to pass round and round him ominously. Then one of Pablo Pequeno's friends stopped in front of Curly. He fell upon one knee, flicked out his arms and then leapt back safely out of range. Knotting his fists and turning from side to side Curly watched the net which the peons were weaving about him. What on earth were the devils up to?

Again the little mestizo dropped upon one knee before Curly; slowly, inch by inch, he began to work his way forward, his dark eyes burning into Curly's. He flung out his arms and kept them suspended in mid-air. He started to move them up and down, up and down. Then, taking a swift backward step, he shot up his right leg and the rope-matted tip of his shoe caught Curly flush under the chin, jerking his head backwards.

The sea of palm leaf hats trembled in a blur before Curly, but when it closed in upon him a change seemed to have taken place. It was no longer a churning onrush; it was legs—millions of pantalooned legs. He felt as if he was standing on the foot-board of the truck which he drove on the Cristobal docks with his hand lightly touching the lever and with his shirt, behind and then in front, billowing out in the sun and wind—turning and twisting the truck from side to side, backwards and forwards ("Hey, what do you think you're doing?" "Testin' the brakes, boss!")—jerking the knife edge of the flat, low-trailing top of the vehicle to a sudden stop within an inch of some bystander's shins; spurting clean out of the sunlight into the dim darkness of a pier (as though the endless passage of cement, the muck of Chilean hides and nitrates and the perspiration from bags of West Indian sugar had not left a black slippery skin on the concrete to add to the dangers of a collision) with the big steel shutters pulled down so low that only a thread of light showed and with the freight piled in squares that grew taller and taller and with gangs of dockers, Buster and Rufus among them, moving about shadowily . . . but he was not at work now—he had, only half an hour before, come off the 4 a.m. shift—antagonizing everyone by the manner in which he went about seeing to it that the brakes on his beautiful new truck were in perfect working order. ("There's no sense in forever testin' them," had come repeatedly from Buster.) He was somewhere else . . . in a Chinese canteen in Colon. A dark place. Like the inside of a pier with the shutters down. Only the floor wasn't mucky. There was gravel in the dust on it though. Dust and gravel made a fine breeding place for chiggers. Did they harbour ants, too? Big red stinging ones?

Then, as Curly slowly rose, shadows like the white sails of the coconut boats in Limon Bay flew around him. *Where are you off to? Don't run out through the side door on the alley!* Ah, here was something. He opened his fist and found a scrap of clothing in it.

"You button up your shirt in the back?" cried Curly steadying himself, "You like for to wear your shirt-tail loose? Well, me gwine show you the Jamaica style! . . . Button up your shirt in the front! Tuck in your shirt-tail! . . . Come playin' you don't know me. 'Mistah Pequeno, he no comprend you.'"

Pablo Pequeno, his hands fluttering up, started to back away.

"You look out, ah?"

At the other end of the canteen. Buster and Rufus stood in the light that entered over the top and under the bottom of the two halves of the swing door on Cash Street.

"Use your head 'pon him, Curly!" cried Buster.

Slowly, step by step, Pablo Pequeno retreated to the door and over the still and down into the alley. He was as good as in the clear now. A flow of soapy water, a banana peel or two, the okra-green slime on the pavement which sloped upwards gently from either side of the gutter, under the shadow of overhanging tenement balconies, presented a slippery set of hazards for anyone with ideas about embarking on a chase through the alley, especially if like Curly he had studs on his boots. That was where Pablo Pequeno with his rope-soled "pusses"* had a decided advantage over him.

Pablo Pequeno muttered something under his breath. "Say that again!" cried Curly, leaping through the door after him, "And see if me don't. . . ."

He slipped and fell on the pavement. When he scrambled to his feet

Pablo Pequeno, his shirt-tail flying, had almost reached the "G" Street end of the alley.

Back in the canteen Curly called out to Sam Ty: "John, three white rums."

There was the slip-slop of Sam Ty's stockingless feet in backless straw slippers. Then, with a light swish and a jingle, the curtain of beads over a door in the solid wall of shelves behind the bar parted and the presence of Sam Ty with his ivory dome and his pigtail again grew remote, begrudging.

Buster took a trial sip of the rum, his lips moving with a sound like running water. Satisfied that the rum was barely tolerable, Buster swallowed the remainder in his glass at one gulp. Then he whirled on Curly: "Of course, Curly, me blame you for having anything at all to do with a Spaniard!"

Rufus nodded assent.

"It seems," Buster went on, "that being second cousin to a brown man in Ocho Rios in Jamaica you don't like for to 'sociate with your own—a English black people but ah try to palm yourself off as a Spaniard."

"Cho', Lawd!" cried Curly. He paused, eyeing with sudden interest the peaked top of the empty cement sack in which Rufus was hooded. Then, heaving a sigh of utter weariness, he brought his gaze down on a level with Rufus' eyes: "Why don't you take that thing off your head? You aren't out in the sun now."

"A Piece of Hard Tack"*

October 1953

Had she been at her old home at Flat Rock in Barbados, Glen would have had no occasion to feel nervous about the tinkling of a bell on a gate. True, at the back of "Mess House," on the edge of the five acres of cane-growing land which surrounded the dwelling on three sides, there was a pen (with a carpet of grapevines on the roof) in which an old sow rooted; but elsewhere on the windy little plateau—across the mouth of the drive, around the armless cone of the windmill and the big, empty shell of a tenement on whose floors some of Glen's relations used to hear chains clanking at night, a sure sign that *duppies** were about—there was not even a fence. Moreover, "Mess House," facing a sandy strip of road that led through cane fields and woods to the neighbouring sugar estates, facing the dawn as it broke over the tops of shaddock* and golden apple trees* in the gully beyond the road, sat plunk on the ground. It was a stone and timber construction one storey high and square as a cube, with no shutters on the windows (only storm blinds), no verandahs, galleries, front or back porch—the lifelong residence of Glen's grandfather, a mulatto born in St. George's parish in 1829.

Often during the two months since she (no longer exposed to her Great-Aunt Muriah's* outbursts over the emptiness of the kitchen larder) had exchanged the marl dust and the chiggers on the ground floor of "Mess House" for a husband and a big, six-roomed house of her own in Georgetown, British Guiana, Glen had been seized by fears of a kind previously unknown to her. These fears were rooted in the fact that the house in which she now lived scorned to touch the ground. It was mounted on piles approximately fifteen feet tall.

"Is that the bell, Vangie?" Glen asked the servant girl.

"Ma'am?"

"On the gate."

"The gate, Ma'am?"

"Yes, is that the bell on the gate tinkling?"

"Tinklin', Ma'am?"

"Never mind."

"Yes, Ma'am."

Glen moved along the corridor in the centre of the house. When she reached the gallery she tiptoed over to a window. She bent her head and listened. No sound came from the gravel path in the untidy little rose and coffee garden in front of the house. Glen then gazed down through the jalousies. Whoever had opened the gate had taken the precaution to latch it again.

Glen looked out on the road beyond the gate. One solitary person was in sight: a short, thick-set Negro in a preacher's cast-off frockcoat, limping along with his hat in his outstretched hand. His bearded face was dripping with sweat, his lips drooped, the expression in his eyes was mournful. The old Negro was a mendicant whom the urchins in the neighbourhood called 'Br'r Goat.' ("Who stole the goat?" "The man in the long coat!" "What smells so high?" "You mean like a billy goat?")

As she watched him passing by, Glen's brows came together in a frown. Her eyes glinted with suspicion . . .

One of the mendicant's legs was wooden. The other was so big (there was 'water' on it, Glen had once heard Vangie say) that even with the aid of a stick he could scarcely drag it along.* She saw him weaving slowly in the sun, stepping painfully (his barefoot was scaly and puffed up across the instep) on to plank after plank lying across the Canal which flowed on both sides of the road; devouring here and devouring there the scraps of food handed to him over zinc paling, black sage fence or garden gate.

Suddenly, there flashed into Glen's mind the moving image of a village which she had seen from a window in the train which had taken her and Ramsey on their honeymoon to Plaisaunce:* huts thatched with dry plantain leaves, swamps and rice fields glistening in the sun and with here and there a Negro field hand, Chinese or Hindu coolie bent over in toil. It was a village which the early Dutch settlers in the Colony had founded; a village with an unpronounceable name—the village whence both Vangie and the mendicant had come. Was there a family connection between the two of them? Had 'Br'r Goat' been trying to attract Vangie's attention? Was it he who had rung the bell on the gate?

Glen turned back into the house. When Ramsey came home to breakfast at 11 o'clock from the Portuguese dry goods store where he worked she would tell him about the bell. She would try to get him to take it off and put on a bigger one. One that she would be able to hear, not only on the gallery but in the depths of the house—in the kitchen and beyond; so that if anyone should open the gate she would know instantly.

Beyond....

Outside the kitchen door Glen turned into the hallway. Crossing the landing at the top of a flight of stairs, she was conscious of her shadow dimming the shaft of light. Involuntarily she turned her head and glanced down the stairs.

"Good Lord!" she gasped, "'Bucks!'"*

Ten of them . . . squat, mat-haired and bronze of all ages and both sexes . . . standing at the foot of the stairs with outstretched hands and up-turned faces silently gazing at her. She had seen Amerindians enough aimlessly wandering about the streets of Georgetown (at first she had thought that they belonged to the 'coolie brethren' and that like herself they were newcomers, but she had soon come to realize that however poor the East Indian immigrants in the Colony might have been they all wore clothes, whereas the Amerindians, an aboriginal folk, scorned raiment) but this was the first time any of them had ever sought her out. How long had they been standing there? Ten minutes . . . a quarter of an hour . . . half an hour? Ever since she had heard the bell on the gate?

"Poor things!" murmured Glen.

Confronted at meal-time with a swarm of children in "Mess House," Glen's Great-Aunt Muriah in Barbados had been noted for the miracle of pacification which she could work with a sugar cake. She would crush the cake between the palms of her hands, reducing it almost to crumbs, so that each child would be certain to receive a portion—if not a flake of the co-conut or a piece of the brown sugar, then surely a taste of the spice, ginger or orange peel. Keeping Muriah's example in mind, Glen strode into the kitchen. When she came out again she had half a ship's biscuit in her hand.

"Hey, where you goin', soul?" drawled Vangie, wiping her hands in her skirt and following Glen out on to the landing.

Glen's lips tightened. So it was *soul* now, was it? And the servant girl, a fresh upcountry product, had only been with her about a month or so. Next thing Glen knew Vangie, using a term of friendship which the Negroes had appropriated from the Amerindians, would be calling her *matti*.*

"Oh, my Gawd!" cried Vangie flying down the stairs as she spotted the Amerindians. Glen turned halfway from the bottom and faced her.

"Do you want to get a 'swell foot,' soul?" cried the servant girl.

"What's wrong with you, girl?" frowned Glen. She was looking at the nutmeg on a string which Vangie wore around her neck . . . looking at it without seeing it . . . seeing only as if she was again on the gallery the perspiring figure of 'Br'r Goat' and now suddenly wondering how he had come by his afflictions.

"You want to waste away with a disease no doctor can cure?" asked Vangie looking Glen anxiously in the eye.

"What nonsense are you talking, girl?"

"A disease," Vangie went on imperturbably, "that you would have to cross the ocean three times before you could shake it off?"

Three times. . . .

"No, I don't!"

"Well, then, send them away, soul. Let them go to the almshouse."

She turned from Glen and surveyed the gathering at the foot of the stairs. Into her vision flowed a forest of outstretched hands, ten pairs of eyes (black as the polished seeds in a sapodilla plum), the glitter of coloured bead aprons which a wizened old woman and a big 'teen-age girl wore, the lean, patriarchal figure of an old man in a loin cloth and the broad chests of two young men, the pot bellies of four or five small children, more yellow than bronze, bunched together in front.

Vangie lifted up the tips of her skirt. "Shoo!" she cried, shooting out a leg. "Go away! ... go along about all-yo' business. *Matti* ain't got nothin' today."

The upturned gazes fell. The hands dropped. For a moment the Amerindians remained motionless. Then, slowly and in silence, a churning movement among them began.

Vangie, dwarfed in Glen's shadow, squatted on the stairs. She watched the Amerindians winding in single file through the empty space under the house. She saw them move out of the darkness into sunlight. As one of the children reached up and unlatched the gate, she heard the bell on it tinkle. She saw the Amerindians clear the garden. As the old man turned at the tail-end of the procession to latch the gate, she heard the bell tinkle again. Then, with a sigh of relief, Vangie rose.

The two women stood face to face on the landing. Then Vangie lowered her gaze. She stared at the moiety of a ship's biscuit in Glen's hand. At last she spoke:—"If you ain't got enough to go around," she said, "you must harden your heart against them, soul. You must never give one be-out you give all, udderwise the naked vagabonds will think you does play favourites. Then, after taking all you got to give them, they will go out through the gate without a word, but when they get back upcountry you can be sure they will start working *obeah** for you."

Obeah? Witchcraft?

Glen permitted herself a wan smile. She had indeed come to a strange country.

"Wind in the Palms"

September 1954

A north wind, driving down on Colon from the Caribbean Sea, agitated the curtain of bamboo reeds at the door of the one-room flat. On the premises next door, a Chinese shop on the 3rd and Cash Street corner of the tenement, a lively racket was also going on. The tall doors of the shop, each one of which was divided in the centre from top to bottom, were swinging to and fro in the wind ... with the heavy, loosely hanging cross bars of iron which fastened the two halves of each door together at night sliding up and down like half-a-dozen see-saws. But in spite of the banging and the swaying of the reeds Coolie's old Jamaican mother slumbered on.

If she was lying in a soft feather bed under a canopy of pink silk, Coolie mused, it was because she had him to look after her. Indeed she was fortunate to have a son broad-minded enough to shut his eyes to the continual embarrassment of her ebony skin. No, he was not one to take the easy way out. He was too good a boy for that. "Disown 'er? Tu'n 'er out in the street? Not me, me, son." It even gave him a feeling of pride and satisfaction to know that he could provide for her now that she was no longer young, although he always kept her out of sight whenever any of his friends visited him in the evenings.

From his East Indian father whom he'd never known Coolie had derived certain physical attributes of which he was rather proud. Beneath the velvet darkness of his skin was a faint trace of yellow; but if Coolie's bronze skin and soft wavy hair set him apart from his mother's people he still was not quite on a par with a "brown man"* with his mixture of European blood. And so, to secure admission to the society of "brown men" and their women-folk among Colon's immigrants Coolie had perforce to fall back upon the line of his nose bridge. It was so fine and delicate a line, despite the horsey width of the nostrils, and the degree of respect which it could command was potentially so great that Coolie had come to look upon it as his chief asset when the time came for him to marry. Already on the occasion of a West Indian ball in a private dwelling on Bolivar Street when all the girls wore pink frocks and the men turned up in dinner jackets he'd even gone so far as to confide to a friend on the latticed, jasmine-scented balcony during a break between dances that no girl whose nose was all fat, gristle or "sprawl"* would stand a chance with him. "No, me son, all me picknee* dem must 'ave me own-a nose, an' de gal me tek to de altar—she no must bring me dat nose?"

All day she had sat, still as a flower, with hands clasped on the sheet of glass that lay thick and cool upon the vast surface of her new mahogany desk. Her head was turned as by the magnetic pull of the view outside the wire-screened window: white pillars on the balcony, the softly caressing motion of the wind in Cristobal's palm trees. The room in which she was sitting—it smelt like a doctor's surgery* and she shared it with Coolie who sat facing the wall opposite to her, checking and filing the day's stack of sanitary reports—was sandwiched between the two others in the Health Office, the connecting doors of which were both open.

No sound came from the Major's room behind her, not even the scratching of a pen; but in the front room the Chief Clerk's voice could be clearly heard. He was talking to one of the sanitary inspectors. "Sure, sure—by all means," cried the Chief Clerk. "Be zealous!" His voice, a wheezy whine in which there was a total absence of anything to connect him with Minnesota or a Scandinavian ancestry, was heavy with the controlled passion of a dabbler in Colon real estate and the authority of an "old timer" familiar from the beginning with the campaign to rid the Isthmus of malaria and yellow fever. "Fumigate every outdoor sink, W.C.* and garbage can in the alleys of Colon; flood the 'G' Street sewage canal with all the oil and tar the budget can stand; tear down and set fire to anything that looks like an invitation to pestilence—but for Pete's sake limit the action to the haunts and the breeding places of the mosquito and let perfectly good racing stables, cattle pens and tenements not yet condemned alone!"

"Don't you ever get bored?" ventured Coolie. He was regarding her, suddenly and without a trace of self-consciousness, from over his shoulder. Crepe de chine blouse of a dusty shade of pink, milky stem of a neck, small nose with the tiniest of freckles on it, wavy auburn hair, eyes of a sea-weed green—

"Not at all," she said. "I like it here."

A Pennsylvanian, new to the tropics, she had come into the office on a Civil Service appointment, preceding Coolie by a couple of months. Her capacity for stillness was something quite new to him. He had never known anyone who could sit so still for hours on end. The fact that she was in the middle of a long slack period did not trouble her in the least.

"Who wouldn't?" he blurted out. "With nothing to do all day long."

She laughed. "Why, it's worth a hundred and fifty dollars a month just to come down here."

She pulled open a drawer on the far side of her desk, in front of the small table on which stood a typewriter with a note book and pencils lying beside it. She took out her handbag and closed the drawer again. Then she rose and passing close behind him turned and stepped out of the room. Coolie listened to her tripping on the tiles in the corridor. Then with a sigh he turned back to the reports on his desk.

"Will you go downstairs—"

The aroma of a cigar teased the air, the large shadowy form of the Major loomed above Coolie.

"—and tell Charleroy not to wait, to go home? I shan't need him any more to-day."

"Yes, Major!"

It was funny how deceptive the topsoil in a field could be. All the brisk striding to and fro, the agate eyes, the austere bearing, the fragrantly trailing veils of smoke—all these now seemed to Coolie to have no more than an external significance. Not once had the Major, after walking in one morning to find that the Chief Clerk had given Coolie the job, alluded to the encounter outside the Washington Hotel.

The Major had been swinging along in the dusk of the tropical evening with a kind of ponderous nonchalance: stout, with iron-grey hair and a chubby, rose-pink countenance wearing a khaki uniform (rather tight fitting) and with his legs (slightly bandy) encased in highly polished leather leggings. It was as though he had for the moment thrown off the cares and responsibilities of Medical Officer of Health for the twin cities on the shores of Limon Bay and was now looking forward to an evening's quiet relaxation in his rooms in the big hotel on Colon beach.

"Beg pardon, Sir!" cried Coolie catching up with him on the pavement outside the walled gardens of the hotel, "I would like to speak to you."

The Major's arms dropped. He brought himself rigidly to a stop. He took the cigar out of his mouth, pursed his lips and waited for Coolie to go on.

"Now that you've moved from the old Panama Railroad building on 3rd Street to new quarters in Cristobal, I understand you have been getting in a lot of new equipment. Metal cabinets from the States, furniture from Hayti—"

He did not say mahogany desks and chairs beautifully made by the prisoners in the Caco-filled jails of Occupied Hayti.

"—and so on."

Coolie paused for breath.

"I also understand," he went on, "that you're looking for someone to help out with the work in the office. Do you think, Sir, that you could give me the job?"

The Major tapped the ash of the end of his cigar. He unpursed his lips. "Is this," he answered icily, his blue eyes hardening, "the right time and place to apply?" And before Coolie could recover from a feeling of shock the Major had swept past him into the driveway of the hotel.

Nor had the Major shown in any way that he held the encounter against him. He had opened up a new vein, telling Coolie how as a poor student of medicine, obliged to keep a "stiff upper lip," he had worked his way through Valparaiso University in Indiana—waiting on table, washing dishes and stoking fires, just as though between him and Coolie there had been at no time any difference at all and as if to suggest that Coolie might even be persuaded at some future time to emulate him.

The car was parked by the side of the palm-fringed road. Charleroy, the Major's chauffeur, was sitting in it fast asleep. He sat slouched over the wheel with his head cushioned on his arms.

"Hey," cried Coolie, jumping on to the running board and tugging at Charleroy's coat sleeve, "Wake up!"

The side of Charleroy's face glistened with a greasy ooze in the heat. It was blotchy, a yellow brown. He opened his eyes slowly.

"Wha' up now?"

Despite a peevish disposition and a languid disagreeable manner Charleroy was no enemy of gaiety. No ten-cent. dance on the dim, moonlight, balconied edges of the *barrio* at the lower end of Cash Street was complete without him; waxing and winding to the rhythm of a Jamaican mento* was with him a nightly diversion.

"Tell me something," said Coolie, "is bleach you been bleachin' again?"*

Charleroy turned his head over on the other side. "Cho,' go 'way, boy."

"You're lucky, me son," said Coolie mysteriously.

"Lucky?"

"Yes—what time is it?"

Charleroy pulled a watch out of his fob pocket. "Three o'clock. Why?"

"The Major say you can go home now. Him don't need you any more today."

"Cho," cried Charleroy, sucking his teeth* as though it did not matter to him in the least whether he finished work early or late. He sat up, wiped his face on his sleeve and adjusted his cap. "Tu'n 'er over for me, nuh?"

Coolie stepped off the running board. "Lahd, but you lazy, me son." He turned the crank and the old Ford spat and sputtered into convulsive life. Under Charleroy's touch the engine soared no less than three times into high gear and then settled down to a gentle throbbing.

"Kiss me neck back—!" drawled Charleroy, leaning out of the car and gazing towards the entrance to the Cristobal docks. "Is no dat the crew off the German boat?"

They were coming off the pier under a naval escort. They all seemed as they marched out into the sunlight to conform to a single pattern: short and blond with closely cropped hair. They all wore the small round caps and the blue jackets of the German merchant marine. When they got to the gate there was a pause. Some sort of pow-wow seemed to be going on. The men slung their kit-bags down on the ground and relaxed. One man nonchalantly rolled a cigarette. Another turned to the parrot perched on his shoulder and began talking to it—Far out on the slumberous green rim of Limon Bay, beyond the path of vessels in transit through the Canal, a prize crew had boarded their ship. Off the coast of Colon early that morning the German captain had received from a Yankee cruiser in the vicinity a wireless order to heave to; but instead of complying he had hurriedly got up steam in a wild endeavor to reach a neutral haven in the Gulf of Mexico. Shortly afterwards a shot had come whistling across the steamer's bows.

"Where are they taking them to?" whispered Coolie. Charleroy didn't say anything. "I suppose," Coolie went on, "they will be interned until the end of the war."

"To Gambo to rass!" exploded Charleroy, slowly driving off. "That's where dem gwine tek dem. De stockade fo' dem blood-hole!"*

Coolie watched the car chugging along under the tall column of palms. His agitated countenance, yielding to a slow smile, began in spite of himself to brighten. The smile flowered into a grin. Then the grin broadened with the flash of dazzling white teeth into a hearty laugh. As he turned to re-enter the white concrete building, Coolie shook his head. Amusing fellow, Charleroy—

◇
◇
◇
◇

ROUNDWAY REVIEW

FICTION, UNITED STATES

"Success Story"

February–July 1954

I

The street car stopped. Alighting, Jim followed the curve of the elevated railway around the corner. An area, overshadowed by a blank wall—the end of an elm-shaded block of brownstone houses on Grand Avenue—yawned where No. 1 Lexington Avenue should have been. In a window on the first floor of No. 3, a tall, brick-red loft, stood an Italian glass manufacturer's sign. Hanging over the sills of second and third storey windows on the other side of the building was an assortment of rugs, mattresses and bed linen.

Jim mounted the steps. He strode across the stoop out of the Saturday noon day sun into the hallway. Groping around in the dark with his feet making the only sound that was audible to him, Jim climbed one and then another flight of stairs. He set down the suit case that he was carrying and for a moment fanned himself with his straw hat. Then he knocked on the door in front of him.

The door slid ajar and a small kinky-haired girl put out her head. She looked Jim up and down slowly before she spoke:—"Yes?"

It was so long since Jim had had any sort of communication with the Seaforts that he hardly knew how to begin. And his knowledge of them was so scanty, too. "I'm looking for some people from Barbados," he said, "They used to worship with the Plymouth Brethren and before they came to America they lived for a time in a house across the road from the stand-pipe on Eagle Hall Corner in St. Michael's parish. The people I'm looking for had two children, a boy and a girl. You would easily know the boy because every time he got a little peckish* he used to suck his fingers. Nothing that Aunt Joe could do to break him of the habit was any use."

"Who?"

"Aunt Josephine," cried Jim, "She tried everything she knew. She would get hold of the fingers and pickle them in green aloes—"

"What did you say was the name of the people?"

"Seafort," answered Jim. "Mr. and Mrs. William Seafort."

A voice from behind the door called out:—"Who is it, Hyacinth?"

The little girl reached out and picked up Jim's suit case. "Come inside, bo," she said, "And mind the door. It only got one hinge."

Squeezing his way into the room Jim closed the door behind him and leaned against it. Nothing in the room was clear to him, everything was deep in shadow and it was sometime before he perceived, beneath the flare of a gas jet, the ebony nudity of a playfully smiling, ten-months'-old baby seated on the darkly shining top of a big round table. Another child, somewhat older, lay in a crib beside the door. On the opposite side of the room, upon a day-bed beneath a window, Hyacinth had joined two other girls and a boy in a silent exchange of blows—their erect heads and flailing arms warring in the light that fell through a crack between the room and the back of a house on Grand Avenue.

The washing on a clothes line stretching across one side of the room parted and a woman, tall and thin and with a lemon-peel complexion stepped down from the kitchen alcove.

"Hey," she drawled, "Well, if it isn't my sister's boy child!" She paused and with repeated nods of the head stood drying her hands in her skirt. "I can remember now," she said, more to herself than to Jim, "It was night before the last. I was mending one of Mr. Seafort's collars and every time I had to thread the needle I would go close to the kerosene lamp on the dresser.

And every time I went I could see, clear as day, the hull of a steamship in the chimney. I ought to have known then that I was going to see somebody from overseas. Hey, what a big man you've grown, boy!"

She held Jim at arm's length and looked at him long and closely. "I would have known you anywhere," she said, thrusting out her long underlip and wagging her head, "Anywhere . . . why, you're the spitting image of your father!"

Jim shot her a sidelong glance. That Aunt Josephine should have seen a close likeness between him and his father was touching; but had she forgotten that Bodie Prout had been short and stocky, with sea-green eyes and a brown skin? And could she not see that he, Jim, was more like her sister. . . . tall, spare of build, more deeply pigmented?

"And to think," she went on, "that the last time I saw you—come kiss me, boy!—you were only so high."

An eager light crept into her dark, deeply-set eyes.

"Remember," she said. "Down in Jack-me-Nannie Gap?"

"Yes," answered Jim.

"Under the Cave Hill stone quarry?"

"Yes."

"Above the rum refinery?"

"Yes."

"You were only eight to nine years old then."

And with an empty quaking belly most of the time, too; spending more days that Jim now liked to recall on a rockpile breaking stones to sell to the roadmenders at a penny a donkey cartload; lying with legs crossed and with hands clasped under his head on a limb of the breadfruit tree in the yard, dreaming—with mute reminders of the songlessness of the yellow breast, the twitter of pee-wits and the exuberant outburst of the kiskadee ("Kiss-kiss-ka-dee!") all around him—of a house on stilts with long cool galleries beside the Lamaha Canal in Georgetown, British Guiana.

"Jack-me-Nannie Gap!" snorted Nimta, initiating a truce in the set-to on the day-bed, "Pooh!" She was glaring across the room at Aunt Josephine, but Aunt Josephine was so full of the blue skies and the cane fields and the white marl roads and the flying fish and the sea eggs* and the other things, even the idiom of the country folk, which Jim's presence had brought back to her that she seemed to be sensuously revelling in the joys of an imaginary return to her old island home.

"And how is Beatrice, no? How is yo' mahmie when you left she? I ain't see she for so long."

"Hear that, Nimta?" Hyacinth whispered aloud.

Nimta stamped her foot. "Can't you say 'mother,' mother?" she demanded.

Aunt Josephine paled. Her lips trembled. She searched Jim's eyes, in panic and in vain, for a gleam of something more than a frigid non-commitment. Then:-

"Why all-you don't let me alone, no?["] she cried, stomping round on the children, "Why unna* don't stop persecuting me, no?"

Hyacinth started to giggle.

"Aren't you ever going to speak properly, mother?" cried Nimta, "You are in America now, not in Barbados, don't say 'unna.'"

"Go along, unna pack o' good-for-nothings," retorted Aunt Josephine, "Mock unna murrah!"

"Oh, dear," sighed Nimta wearily. "If it isn't 'mahmie' it is 'murrah.'"

Aunt Josephine snatched up something off the ice box and approached the day-bed. It was a heavy, wire-bristled brush scented with pomade.

"Make fun of me," she cried, "Mock me and see if I don't clout all-you round wunna* head."

Beneath the menace of the hair brush Hyacinth's eyelids quivered, Vashti's hands flew to her skull, Nimta sat with hers lying still in her lap while Lonnie remained curled up at the head of the bed with a smile of amusement in his eyes and the two middle fingers of his left hand in his mouth.

A child's cry wedded to the sound of a crib violently set in motion, suddenly arose out of the darkness near where Jim was standing. He turned and saw the child gripping the sides of the crib and furiously rocking it. Then through the loosened slats in the bottom the child fell to the floor. Aunt Josephine picked him up, tucked him under one arm and fitted back in the slats. Opening the door of a cupboard, she pressed back a threatened avalanche of rags, pulled out some clean bedding and closed the door again. She spread the bedding in the crib and lay the child back in it. Clad only in a skin-tight woolen vest the child, still yelling its lungs out, again strove to reach the sides of the crib. Aunt Josephine bent over the crib and with one hand gently rocked it, while with the other hand she held down the child. Then, seeing that this was having no effect, she lifted the child out of the crib, clasped him to her bosom and swaying from side to side began to sing a lullaby to him:-

*Love was once a little boy**
High ho!
High ho!
Now he is a little man
High ho!
High ho!

But the child, resentful of the warm embrace and the gentle cooing, remained unpacified. Aunt Josephine turned him over, slapped him on his buttocks and thrust him back in the crib.

"I know," grumbled Aunt Josephine, "unna wasn't gwine rest till all-you disgrace me before my sister boy child."

Jim crossed the room. He leaned over the day-bed and recklessly thrusting his head through the window, almost grazed his forehead against the stuccoed brick wall of the house on Grand Avenue.

"You Mister Lonnie," cried Aunt Josephine, "Get up and speak to your cousin."

Untangling his legs from the folds of the patchwork quilt on the day-bed Lonnie rose. He had a large dome of a head, a thick mop of kinky hair and a long stringy neck. His lips, closing upon a mouth that was forever on the verge of opening, masked purple gums and overlapping teeth. As he crawled off the bed the stone which served as a substitute for one of its legs rolled away and the head of the bed slumped. Scowling with reluctance Lonnie stooped to prop the stone back under the bed. He slipped and fell in the thin stream of water oozing from underneath the leaky ice box.

"Serve you right!" cried Nimta, flouncing off.

Aunt Josephine caught her by the shoulders. "Take your mouth down off your head, miss, and speak to your cousin."

"Lonnie," cried Nimta, eyes brimming, "Didn't you hear me say howdy do a long time ago, when he first came in?"

Aunt Josephine turned her eyes toward the ceiling. She threw up her hands in despair. "Lord," she said, "What I gwine do with these children, no? Why, I can't even speak to them now," she added, turning to Jim, "And if I was to touch one of them they're all ready to jump down my throat."

"All," she ended wearily, "except Miss Block."

"Here comes Miss Block now," twittered Vashti, as the bedroom door opened and a girl in a pretty summer frock stood fastening a rose in her bosom, "And with my ribbon in her hair, too!"

"I smell perfume—"

"Freddie gave me that flower, girl!" cried Nimta, "What are you doing with it?" She snatched the flower out of Miss Block's hands and stamped on it. The bloom on Miss Block's cheeks, a smooth dark brown, blossomed into flame.

"Never mind, soul," said Aunt Josephine, "She is so . . . so . . ." She bit her lip. "So begrudgeful* and bad-minded," she blurted out, "the only body she could possibly favour is she father!"

"Jim," she said, "this is my god-child."

"Hey," cried Nimta, "Look how she is blushing!"

"See how she is vamping* him already," whispered Vashti.

"You go on razzing me," flared up Miss Block with an engaging lisp. "And see if I don't throw something at you."

"Dress round, Vashti," said Aunt Josephine, "and let a body sit down." She reached across to the table and tickled the baby under the chin. His two little teeth, white as rice grains, shone in a dazzling smile. She gathered him up and coiling his little arms around her neck, again settled herself on the day-bed. "Go inside, then," she said to Vashti, "and stop your whimpering. You look just like Jonah when he come out the whale belly." She turned and smiled over her shoulder at Jim. "Sit down, no?" she said, making room for him, "And tell me is Beatrice still with the Brethren or did she go and join the Off-Side?"*

Her tones were elaborately casual but if it had been her intention to stun the children into silence she could not have employed more effect[ive] ones. Vashti glanced at Nimta; Hyacinth gazed at Jim; there was a long thread of saliva as Lonnie pulled his fingers out of his mouth. A sudden stillness even descended on the crib beside the door. Polishing the table with a dust cloth Miss Block alone took refuge in brisk, active unconcern.

II

"Well, after Papa was shot—"

"Shot?"

"Yes."

"Why, I didn't know he was shot," drawled Aunt Josephine uncoiling the little arms from around her neck and laying the baby face downwards across her knees.

"Yes, he was shot on the Isthmus."

"Hey, what for, bo?"

"It's hard to say exactly," answered Jim looking quickly into Aunt Josephine's eyes. "At the inquest the man who shot him was the only witness, and he swore that it had been a case of mistaken identity."

"What happened, bo?"

"Well, one night they sent him and another officer out together on a special assignment—"

"You mean to say," cried Aunt Josephine, "that Bodie went and joined the police force after all the trouble he had in Saba?* You would have thought that he would have had more sense than to do that. Hey, what a man for you!"

"It was the only kind of job that he was happy in, I suppose."

"Why, I can remember the toime* he sent Mon Tout, Edgar and St. Helise to the gallows for killing that little girl."

"Yes, that was one of the reasons why he decided to leave Saba. Mon Tout's, Edgar's and St. Helise's friends swore they would get him." *Men who dominated the African witchcraft cult on the island, spoke a French creole patois and who, during Carnival season at the end of Lent when everybody went about masked and in gay costumes, paraded up and down the streets menacingly twirling stout walking sticks and singing Calypsos which they made up as they went along.* "He didn't pay much attention to their threats at first, but wherever he went he could feel a black wall of hatred rising up against him. Then one morning when he got out of bed in the cottage where he lived alone he found a lot of eggs on the floor."

"Eggs? What kind of eggs, bo?"

"Ordinary fowls' eggs."

"Did he step on them?" asked Aunt Josephine breathlessly.

"They were almost under his feet, and he barely managed to avoid stepping on them."

"Hey," cried Aunt Josephine, "They were trying to work obeah for him. Wo-lay! Wo-law!"*

"Yes, Mon Tout, Edgar and St. Helise had killed the girl in the woods on a dark night in some sort of obeah blood sacrifice, but their accomplices got away. The island was in a ferment. For his work on the case Papa was commended by the Administrator, but he wasn't popular with everybody. The feeling against him was particularly strong because he was an outsider. Then after the eggs appeared in the room he didn't know who to trust. 'No patois man* is going to poison me,' he said, 'or make me think I'm bewitched.' So when a labour agent who'd been active in the island signing on men to work on the construction of the Panama Canal, approached him with the offer of a job on the force that was being organized to police the ten-mile wide strip of territory through which the Canal was to pass, he accepted the offer and the next thing we knew he'd left Saba for Colon."

"A dirty old hole," frowned Aunt Josephine, moving her knees from side to side and now and then giving the limp, outstretched body of the baby a gentle pat, "The way the women in Colon does carry on. . . ."

"Then, instead of going to join Papa in Saba as she had planned, Mama and I went from British Guiana to Barbados to live on the little place in Jackman's Gap in Black Rock which she'd inherited. . . ."

"From our grandfather," said Aunt Josephine, slowly nodding her head.

"And when we arrived in Colon about a year and a half later he was stationed at Tabernilla. The place is now under water."

"Under water?"

"It's at the bottom of Gatun Lake."

Orchids now bloomed, flamingoes and cranes nested on the little islands that floated round the top of Tabernilla's tomb like emeralds on a mirror. There had been no ceremony to mark the occasion when from two sides the water rushed in. No tears had been shed. Tabernilla, lying in the path of history, had merely failed to survive the marriage of the Caribbean Sea and the Pacific Ocean.

"He didn't say much about it, but from the first we gathered that he was having trouble with someone on the force. He would come home and say, 'I had a tiff with Corporal Rowde again today.' 'What about?' 'Oh, nothing important. Just something trivial.' And so it went on until one evening. . . ."

Holes gaped in the pier's rotten pinewood flooring where the planks had been torn up and ferried in flat-bottomed boats across the old French canal (not a dangerous undertaking, unless a new Yankee tug coming down the Chagres River into the narrow incision in the jungle was passing by, billowing the water) to stoke Tabernilla's fires; barnacled, mossy-green piles jutted up here and there through the openings, swaying like dancers on stilts. Down in the water under the pier there persisted the lazy swirl and the golden shimmer of bobo fish. And further along the cut, beyond the pier, the bush was thick with guava trees with fruit ripening on them only for the birds.

"And Rowde—"

"Yes, sergeant!"

"Take one of the new men with you."

"Sir?"

"One that knows a bit about the ropes. Let me see—"

The glow of the green-shaded light over the sergeant's desk only partly dissipated the shadows in the station house.

"Yes, take Bodie Prout with you. He used to be a police constable in the West Indies. Once did a smart piece of work in a voodoo murder case."

Involuntarily Rowde's fingers closed in a white-knuckled grip over the railing in front of the sergeant's desk.

"A good man, Prout," said the sergeant with a shake of the head and a frown, "Handy with a pistol too."

A pink flush crept upward from the neck of Rowde's khaki tunic. His gaze fell. With his eyebrows raised as in agony he stared at those curious relics of the French in their attempt to trap and destroy the malaria-carrying mosquito: tin cans of water in which the legs of the sergeant's desk stood.

"You two ought to get on well together," said the sergeant, turning to gaze through the thin wire screen* in the door at the glimmer of raindrops rippling down off the station house roof into the Camino Real.

In spite of himself Rowde relaxed. He frankly did not think much of the choice. It was as if the sergeant had never seen Bodie Prout stroll into the station house in white flannel trousers, open-necked shirt and green sports jacket with a cricket bat in his hand. ("Where are you off to?" "For a work-out on Tabernilla Green.") Or had never heard the sounds that arose from the Green at dusk of an evening in the dry season. ("Stroke! Well played, sir!") Or had never been tempted, just for the fun of the thing to egg Bodie Prout into unburdening himself about his origins. (No—this in explanation of his thin lips, high-bridged nose, brown skin and faintly green eyes—there was no East Indian coolie or "Buck" Indian in him. The light-skinned side of him was pure Anglo-Saxon!) Or had never seen the light that would steal into Bodie Prout's eyes or heard the words that would fall from Bodie Prout's lips whenever he spoke about his home in British Guiana: how his father enjoyed the distinction of having had a village named after him; how the old mulatto once owned a couple of windmills and still paid taxes on odd holdings scattered about the Colony. How one sunny afternoon in the midst of the grinding season at the old man's place ashes and fine grains of sand had begun floating down out of the sky. ("It happened on a Friday . . . Christ was crucified on a Friday.") Then the sky turned black. A wind rose. The lime trees in the garden, the breadfruit trees down by the pond, the sugar canes still uncut in the field all began trembling, swaying and moaning. The sails in the windmill flew round and round with a harsh, a grating noise. The roof of the boiling house shot into a field and the rain deluged down into the vats in which the cane juice had been fermenting, coming to the boil, crackling. The fires under the vats went out; the water poured as through a sieve from the loopholes in the red brick cone of the mill. The staves round the puncheons of molasses out in the yard fell apart and for days after the storm the water, sweet, then merely brackish, flowed over the edge of the sand-hill until it almost covered the tops of the star apple trees in the gully.

"And Rowde—"

"Yes, sergeant!"

"If our spick-o-ty* friend should turn up to-night in the vicinity of those freight cars on the siding down by the old French wharf for the sake of all that's dear to you don't let him see you first and don't forget there's a price of five hundred dollars on his head. The moment you think you've spotted him let him have it."

The sergeant paused. Spread out before him was a document which he appeared to be studying.

"*Soy hombre libre! No soy enganchado!*" ["I am a free man, not a contract labourer."]*

"Sir?"

"When our French predecessors on the Isthmus decided to call it a day, Manuel Fonseca, known as the "One with the Twist in His Neck," was a man with a grievance. The compensation which he'd received from the Company for his property in Tabernilla had seemed to him inadequate, and he could get no redress anywhere. After we moved in[,] the Division of Civil Affairs promised to see what could be done, but something went wrong and Fonseca by the ease with which he can walk on and off the Canal Zone has since been committing various acts of sabotage: cutting the telegraph wires, tearing up sections of the Panama Railroad and dynamiting our goods trains."

"Yes, sergeant!"

" . . . always wears a blue alpaca suit . . . never moves a step without a .44 Colt revolver on his hip and knows how to use it too."

The sergeant looked up from the dossier. "As a matter of fact," he cried, eyeing Rowde sharply, "he is uncannily swift on the draw."

Rowde spread his bow legs and tilted back his head. There was a twinkle in his luminous black eyes.

"Did you say he's got a twist in his neck?"

"Yes!"

"We'll soon straighten that out," chuckled Rowde.

"This sabotage is holding up work on the canal. It's got to stop or else some big-mouthed Congressman in Washington will want to know why."

"Yes, sergeant!"

"Twisted Neck" won't attempt on a dark, wet night to distinguish between leather leggings and puttees.* In the event of a showdown he won't draw the Colour Line. To him a Gringo was a Gringo whether he was dark or fair, spoke with a Texas drawl or a British Guiana accent.

"Good night, Rowde."

"Good night, sergeant."

"Good night, Prout."

"Good night, sir."

Buttoning on black waterproof capes over their khaki uniforms, the two officers passed in front of the sergeant's desk, opened the wire-screened door and went out into the night.

"Exactly what happened after that," Jim said, "no one knows. All we've got is Rowde's word at the inquest that after looking the ground over he and Papa decided to separate. Who said, 'I will go this way, you go that,' was never revealed. Then just before dawn, after the gas lamps in the section went out, Rowde said he saw a shadow moving between two lines of freight cars on the pier. He pulled out his gun and fired and when he ran up and turned the body over with his foot, he saw that it was Papa. 'I reckon,' he said, 'I mistook him for the spick.'"

"Poor Bodie," murmured Aunt Josephine.

"When the body came down from Tabernilla," Jim went on, "a delegation of men from the fraternal society to which Papa belonged went to the railway station and took charge of it. It was then that the trouble started."

"You mean to say," asked Aunt Josephine, "that Bodie was so dazzled with the world that he turned his back upon the Lord and went and joined a lodge. Hey, look 'pon my trial!"

"Mama was so broken up," Jim continued, "that she was only too glad to have someone take the funeral arrangements off her hands."

"Knowing Beatrice as I does," said Aunt Josephine, "I ain't at all surprised. I can remember when she first met your father . . . she was so in love!" She checked a wry smile at the memory of Beatrice flitting like a humming bird between Barbados and British Guiana, ignoring all the warnings about the folly of a girl marrying only for love and allowing nothing or no one to stand in her way.

"Then on the night before the funeral," said Jim, "the Brethren turned up in a body and forbade Mama to attend it. Told her that as a Sister in the Lord it would be wrong for her to appear in a procession on Bolivar Street with a lot of lodge men wearing gilt aprons, purple sashes and white gloves and that if she persisted in going to the funeral she would have to give up taking the sacrament. As if she could desert Papa now," cried Jim bitterly, "after all that he had suffered."

Aunt Josephine's eyes narrowed to slits. She slowly chewed over the dilemma in which Beatrice had found herself. "Of course," she said, her eyelids aflutter, "the flesh is so weak that if I was to foine* myself in Beatrice's place and the worst should come to the worst I suppose I would have the courage to put aside the Lord and follow Mr. Seafort to the graveyard."

She paused.

"Not," she hastened to add with a deep frown, "that Mr. Seafort is so worldly as ever to go and join a lodge."

She sat back, a nice warm feeling of contentment flowing over her. "Um is too bad though," she said, "because if Beatrice was to come here she would be worse off than she is in Colon now. We ain't got no Off-side Brethren in Brooklyn yet, bo, thank the Lord, and there would be nowhere for she to go to meeting."

She rose with the sleeping child in her arms and moved towards the bedroom door. "Nobody," she said, "can say that Beatrice is not a woman of character, but sometimes it doesn't pay to be too ownwayish* in life. She has made up she bed, now she must lay down 'pon it."

III

The clothes line was no longer burdened with washing and Jim, seated on the edge of the day-bed, could dimly see Aunt Josephine going all out to place before him on his first day in America a hot, steamy ball of *cou-cou*.* Into the pot of corn meal simmering on the gas ring she emptied a tin of green peas. Didn't she have any okras to whip into the maize to give it a soft and mellow lightness? Or hadn't okras yet begun to follow the wave of Negro migration across the Caribbean Sea to Brooklyn?

Slowly and laboriously Aunt Josephine turned the thick, adhering mixture round and round with a long wooden spoon.

"Lonnie," she said, "put on your cap and slip down to Bohack's* and get me a can of tuna fish."

Lying on the day-bed with his legs outstretched behind Jim and with his arms folded under his head, Lonnie was eyeing Miss Block who, profiled in the light sweeping through the room at the front end of the apartment, stood slapping faint dabs of a cyclamen-hued powder* on her face before the mirror in Aunt Josephine's bedroom. *(An unheard of proceeding . . . why wasn't she using the room which she shared with Nimta, Hyacinth and Vashti?)* He drew up his knees, planted one leg firmly over the other and growled:— "What's the matter with Miss Block that she can't go? She better than any of we?"

Aunt Josephine's face loomed out of the kitchen alcove. She shook the ladle at Lonnie:—"You lazy disobedient boy, get up and go I say!"

"But mother!" protested Lonnie, almost in tears.

Miss Block's lisp, falling on Jim's ears like a sound from another world, penetrated the awkwardness of the ensuing silence: "I'll go. I've got an errand to do anyway. Down at the shoemaker's."

"The money is on the dresser, soul."

"Yes, mum."

After Miss Block had gone Aunt Josephine went back to the task before her. In the matter of preparing the favourite dish of all Barbadians she had no doubt at all that she could easily hold her own with her sister in Colon. Yet she knew that it won't be a *cou-cou* to make anyone's mouth water, even if it was swimming in butter. Nor did she have anything to serve up with the *cou-cou* which would compare favourably with the fresh, blue-water choice before the poorest of the poor in Barbados. No dolphin,* mullet, flying fish or the pink flesh of the sea urchin.

"Oh, Nimta, you are clumsy."

"Why don't you look out the way then? Suppose you make me fall down?"

"Children!" cried Aunt Josephine.

"Well, tell her to draw in her feet and not sprawl them out so. She is always tripping up a body."

"You stepped on my toe on purpose," cried Vashti.

Aunt Josephine flicked a hunk of the *cou-cou* on to a plate and tasted it. "You know, Jim," she said, "in America we does eat three square meals a day, not like in the West Indies. No bread and tea 'pon a morning, but a big breakfast."

A spasm of pain, surprise and bewilderment twisted little Vashti's face almost out of recognition. Nimta smothered a titter. Hyacinth's eyes shone on her mother with a smile of fascination. Lonnie guffawed:—"I wonder when that is!"

"Oh, by the way, Aunt Josephine," said Jim, "I forgot to tell you that I asked the expressman at the dock in New York to bring my trunk here."

"Of course, boy," she said, "Let he bring 'um here for the toime being anyhow, till you get settled."

"I don't want a very big room," said Jim, "Just somewhere to stay till I know where I'm going to live. I don't know yet. But if you can put me up for a while I'd like that."

It was not only that to remain in close and intimate contact with God-fearing folk was with Jim a necessity. Jim was thinking of his mother back in Colon. It would be such a relief to her and such a comfort in her loneliness to know that he had followed her advice not to go up to Harlem (" . . . that sink of iniquity? Avoid it like you would the plague, boy") and had chosen instead to stay with the Seaforts beneath the tall spires of the City of Churches.

Aunt Josephine gazed down into the dining room. "You can sleep in the front room to-night," she said, "and use the looking glass on the dresser in the girls' room and in the morning I'll speak to Mr. Seafort." She went on turning the *cou-cou*. After a while she paused. "Is Cora Island's top room still empty, Nimta?" she asked.

"No'm."

"It is so!" cried Lonnie, "Didn't Freddie tell me he father come home one evening and ketch the boy what he rent the top room to coming down the front steps with a woman—"

"Lonnie!"

"What I do now?"

"Mind your tongue, boy!"

"Hey, a body can't even talk in this house now," cried Lonnie in a sulky peevish tone, coiling himself up closer to the wall under the window.

The door opened and Miss Block entered.

"Tell me, soul," said Aunt Josephine, "Cora Island got anybody for she top room yet?"

"No'm."

"Put 'um down there for me, soul, and make the vermicelli pudding for the baby for me like a good girl."

Miss Block placed the parcel with the tunny fish on the table and disappeared through the bedroom door. When she came out again she was tying an apron's strings around her waist. She emptied a small packet of vermicelli into a bowl of water and stood the bowl on the ice box. ("Yes, let 'um soak there, soul.") Then, going over to Jim, she said: "Wouldn't you like to go up front till dinner is ready?"

"I'd like to," agreed Jim with alacrity.

He followed Miss Block through Aunt Josephine's bedroom into the living room. It was a hot, dusty Saturday afternoon in July and all the furniture in the room was shrouded in cheese cloth. To satisfy his curiosity about the reason for this, Jim turned to Miss Block but Miss Block, clairvoyant, mindful of the force of his tropical background, had already divined what was going on in his mind.

"It's to keep off the dust," she explained.

"All the time?"

"No, only in the summer. The windows are always open then."

"I see."

She went over to one of the room's two curtainless windows and removed the rugs from the sill. Whether they were sufficiently aired or sunned was now of no moment. She rolled up the rugs and stood them in the hall outside the door of the girls' room. When she came back in she gathered up the pillows lying on the sill and the bed sheets and blankets hanging out of the other window, and strode with them into Aunt Josephine's bedroom.

Jim sought the comfort of an armchair by one of the windows. After the noise and the ceaseless bickering that went on in the dining room Jim was inclined to put a new evaluation on the virtues of peace and quiet.

How restful it was to be sitting there by himself! How free of spiritual and emotional torture!

A curving sweep of the tracks of the Lexington Avenue elevated railway lay outside the window. Beyond the tracks the Brooklyn skyline was dominated by the chimney pots in a sea of roofs. Under the shadow of the "El" the entrance to a garage opposite looked as if a garden hose had been playing on it. A black limousine descended the wet sloping driveway and, flanked by a row of the steel girders supporting the "El," proceeded along the avenue with the slowness of a hearse in a funeral procession, taking an eternity to pass the crates of eggs, fruit and vegetables on display outside the door of a grocer's shop on the corner.

As the car disappeared out of sight the slow grinding of wheels and the screeching of a train pulling out of the "El" station around the corner disturbed the silence. Jim glanced up and beheld the wheels of a long wooden coach almost on his eyelids! He expected the coach to jump the rails and crash into the wall of the girls' room behind him, but in some miraculous way it managed to stay on the line. And the train, plunging the room in darkness, flew past.

The swift return of the light found Jim gazing into space. The roar of the train died away in the distance and he was beginning to get used to silence again when the rails began to hum and vibrate anew. The music grew less remote, gathering volume on the way. Then, in a dark and sudden flash, a train from the opposite direction thundered by.

"Come, Jim, dinner is ready."

As in a daze he rose. Aunt Josephine was in the room. Jim looked into the black, softly smiling eyes. Aunt Josephine's thin, lemon-pale face was newly scrubbed. Her flat, narrow bosom was imprisoned in a pleated calico bodice Jim had not seen before. The whale bones in the collar were bent and rusty.

"Come, Bo," she said, "before 'um get cold."

Nine o'clock.

And still the evening sky was filled with light. How different from the early fall of darkness over the palm-fringed shores of Colon!

Down in the street there was the crack of bat on ball, the whizzing of cow hide through the air and the scurrying of feet round the steel girders of the "El."

Lonnie's voice floated up from the stoop in the dusk:-

Tee tee san
Tee tee san
Ah hole 'e!

Ending Lonnie's game of tag the girls raced up the stairs. Forbidden to turn Aunt Josephine's room into a "public thoroughfare" they gaily resolved to take the hurdles in the hall. Jim could hear them laughing and joking, stumbling and falling in the dark over the chaos of household litter. For a brief instant one of them stuck her head round the side of the living room door.

"Warm enough for you, Mr. Prout?" she whispered softly. It sounded like Hyacinth but Jim wasn't sure.

Miss Block came in, lit the gas and went out again.

"Lift it up, sir!"

"Oy, it cutting my fingers, mother!"

"Lift it up, boy!"

Straining under the weight of one end of a cot, Lonnie backed into the living room through the door from the hall. When Aunt Josephine got inside the room with her end of the cot, Lonnie dropped his on the floor.

"My fingers is sore," he growled.

Jim got up from the chair by the window.

"Go inside," said Aunt Josephine to Lonnie, "and tell Miss Block to give you the sheets and the pillow." She sat down on the edge of the cot and proceeded to regale Jim with its history. It was a very handy thing to have about the house, even though it sagged rather badly in the middle and had obviously seen better days. She had got it for little or nothing from a second-hand furniture dealer's on Myrtle Avenue and six lodgers had already slept on it—green country girls newly arrived from Barbados whose stay with her had varied from two weeks to a month after which they had invariably left to take up housework jobs where they could sleep in.

"Here they is," said Lonnie.

Aunt Josephine took the sheets and the pillow from Lonnie. "And now," she said to Jim, "let me show you how you must sleep in America. I does always have to show the new girls. . . ."

"Sleep?" asked Jim

"Yes, bo. You mustn't think you does sleep in America the same as in the West Indies. No, bo."

She proceeded to show him. "You must not lay down 'pon the sheets, but betwixt them. That is the secret. And you must never forget to do that wherever you da-go. You must not let anybody think you just come. You must remember that in America everything is different, even sleeping."

She got up from between the sheets, bade him goodnight and closing the sliding panel of her bedroom door after her left him there looking at the cot.

IV

As Jim and Miss Block tripped down the stairs from the apartment on the second floor of the tenement on Lexington Avenue and turned the corner into Grand Avenue nothing was clearer and more reassuring to Jim than that the spirit of Sunday worship was abroad in the Promised Land. At one end of the block the Lexington Avenue "El" curved and lengthened off behind them. Across the other end the Fulton Street "El," partly obscured by the foliage of elm trees, loomed up. But instead of the thunderous roar of "El" trains on either line the pealing of church bells filled the morning sky.

White folk devoutly clad in black, and Negroes too, singly and in twos and threes, descended the brownstone steps. Each house in the block seemed to be adding its quota to the stream of churchgoers spontaneously forming on either side and moving along the sunli[t] pavements in the direction of the dark pools of shadow under the elms.

The chimes rose and fell over an ever-widening area. They accompanied Jim and Miss Block across a broad avenue (devoid of both surface car and elevated railway lines but with the sound of trains on the Long Island Railroad rumbling beneath it) out to the fringe of a Polish immigrant quarter.

Up a flight of new, unpainted stairs to what had once been a furrier's show room the pair softly crept.

"I'd better go in first," whispered Miss Block, "We are late."

"Okay."

It was a few minutes after 11 o'clock and the meeting room, unutterably still and warm, was deep in the silence in which the service had begun and was solemnly continuing.

"Of course," Aunt Josephine had said, "You mustn't think that this is Golden Lodge or the Eagle Hall"—at opposite ends of a white marl road in Barbados where only the presence of Negroes darkened the meeting rooms of the Plymouth Brethren. We're all mixed up in Brooklyn, bo, the coloured and the white together but with nothing that you could safely call 'poor buckra.'* All our white folks is quality."

Jim had wanted to ask the mother of Mr. Seafort's children if she realized what she was saying. She had sounded not as one who since early girlhood had embraced the Lord, but rather as if ten years in America had given her a sense of values that was vaguely disturbing. Even though he was not converted Jim had been appalled to perceive the change. It was something which he had been disposed to place on a par with the spectacle of Aunt Josephine showing him on the previous evening how to sleep between two sheets.

"There's Mr. X," she had gone on before Jim could tell her about the solitary West of England man who worshipped with the Negro Brethren in Colon, "who owns a factory. A tall man with a commanding appearance as though he was cut out for the Army."

A pause.

Aunt Josephine's thin, yellow face had then contracted in a frown.

"Mr. X has not been with us long. Before he joined the Brethren he was with the Quakers, but he fell out with the Quakers over a dispute in the coal mines. You weren't here at the toime but the way the Pennsylvania miners was carrying on you would have thought that they wanted the Kaiser to win the war! So when the Quakers joined with a so called All-Denominational body to find out what was behind the trouble Mr. X broke away."

Another pause.

"Then there's Old Miss Y, who is so rich she could easily afford to drive up to the meeting room in a motor car with a chauffeur in livery. And I for one would be the last person to deny she the privilege! There would be nothing sinful if at her age she should put aside the Lord long enough to give she poor legs a rest. And there's Mr. Z, who has shining black hair but who looks as if he could do with a blood transfusion and whose eyesight is so poor he has to wear glasses—comes from poring over the books of the gas company where he does work, I guess. And the young lady he's courting. . . ."

"Mr. Seafort!" ejaculated Miss Block in a whisper.

"H'm?"

"Mr. Seafort."

From the edge of the square in the centre of the long, crowded room where the Brethren sat facing a table with a decanter of wine, two loaves of bread and a silver and china service came a ripple on the sea of silence. A small black man had opened a hymn book and was calmly turning its pages. His face was not only aglow. It looked as though there was beginning to stir within him a secret impulse to deviate from the concept—mirrored with Arctic bleakness in the faces of both the converted minority, white and dark-skinned, sitting together side by side on three rows of benches around the square and the unconverted Negro majority who, like their *congeners** on the other side of the invisible line which divided the two groups, consisted entirely of Barbadian immigrants—of a religion that was dry and austere. Then, as he gave out the hymn and the congregation rose to sing it, Mr. Seafort's ebony countenance expanded gently in a smile.

Jim remembered as a small boy in Barbados how Mr. Seafort had always seemed to him to be a man with an all-consuming passion. This passion expressed itself in the care which he found the time to lavish on the Shet-land pony and the buggy—curry combing the pony to death and constantly polishing the sides and the spokes in the wheels of the buggy—in which he occasionally drove to town. Possession of a pony and trap had automatically given Mr. Seafort a certain status at the cross-roads on Eagle Hall Corner. Yet Mr. Seafort had not been happy there. The noise used to get him down. Not everyone on the Corner was privileged to have a rain-water cask in the yard and in consequence the clatter of buckets and kerosene tins and the commotion that now and then arose from the eternal jostling for position at the stand-pipe across the road from the house in which he and Aunt Josephine lived sometimes bordered on the unlawful. And after the sugar canes in the fields had ripened and had been harvested and milled the fury of the cavalcade of mule drays, five and seven mules to a dray, coming down Spooner's Hill from the estates in the country with hogsheads of molasses foaming in the sun and spilling over in the dusty road outside the door, the crack of the drivers' whips and the shouts of the muleboys running alongside of their charges and urging them on by name ("Dandy! Hector! Bright!") would become almost unbearable. Then there was the clangour of the tram cars coming up Barbary Hill from Bridgetown and wheeling around the Corner at top speed, turning up Bank Hall Road and turning down Baxter's Road. . . .

"Sit down!" whispered Miss Block, tugging at Jim's coat sleeve. *Where was he that he did not know the room had ceased to vibrate with the glory of the Lord?*

Scarcely a breath of air stirred. The minutes slowly crept by. Some of the young folk in Jim's vicinity seemed on the verge of falling into a doze, but within the area of the converted the Brethren continued to sit and sit solemnly contemplating the parquet floor. At last one of them, a big, six-foot tall mulatto with a sandy complexion, raised his eyes and glanced rather pointedly at the window along the top of the front, glass-walled end of the room. The window was shut tight, muffling the sound of traffic in the street below.

"Mr. Island."

"Who?"

"The responsible brother."

Mr. Island rose and with the eyes of the congregation upon him strode up to the sacrament table. He removed the stopper from the decanter and poured out a cupful of the red sparkling wine. Then he returned to his seat, sat back and took a leisurely sip. Wiping his mouth with a handkerchief, Mr. Island then turned and gave the cup to a little white-haired old lady in a black silk dress beside him. Miss Y sipped the wine, flushed a deep pink and passed the cup to a buxom Negro woman whose face beneath a hat trimmed with red roses was lightly freckled. The Negro woman, who bore a close family resemblance to Miss Block, placed the cup to her lips and then handed it to Mr. X. Still faintly smiling as though moving in a realm remote from the narrower limits of ecstasy, Mr. Seafort awaited the arrival of the cup.

As the cup passed from lip to lip Mr. Island rose and approached the sacrament table a second time. He placed a loaf of bread on each of two silver trays and proceeded to send them on their rounds. He gave one tray to Aunt Josephine and then turned and gave the other tray to Miss Y but not before he had broken off a piece of the loaf reposing upon it. Then, gathering up his coat-tails, Mr. Island sat down again.

Looking at Mr. Island munching the crust of bread Jim's eyes filled with the sun. Shadows, too. Dim and cool in the meeting room on the ground floor of a wide-balconied tenement building in Colon, Panama.

"So you're going to America?"

"Yes, I sail tomorrow."

The brother fixed Jim with a mirthless gaze. "You believe in the Lord, boy? Believe that Christ came down from Heaven to save the world? That he died on the Cross of Calvary like a common man . . . between a thief and a murderer . . . so that you and me and your mother here shall be saved?"

"Yes."

"Then you is converted! You is a child of the Lord, a servant of Christ Jesus!"

Something in Jim's manner must have told the brother, who was Mr. Island's counterpart among the Off-side Brethren in Colon, that Jim had been exposed to enough missionary zeal at home already.

"Hey, Sister Prout, what is to become of this boy, no? The Lord says, 'This is my beloved son in whom I am well pleased.' Embrace him, boy! Don't wait till 'tis too late. Don't stand off there like you 'fraid. The Lord ain't gwine bite you. He died for you! Conversion won't take away any of your pleasures. You will still be able to carry on as before. 'In my Father's house there are many mansions and if it were not so I would not have told you.' The Lord is not a story-teller, boy! 'I go to prepare a place for you.' The Lord is inviting you, boy! He is making a way for you. All you've got to do, all the Lord is asking you to do, is to believe and thou shalt be saved."

"Let us pray."

Long after Mr. X sat down the silence endured. Languidly fans were plied. A brother gave out a hymn and the congregation rose and sang it. Then the longest period of silence of the morning—a silence that steadily deepened into an expectant hush—ensued. Suddenly there was a general relaxing of the tension. On both sides of the line of demarcation the Brethren, converted and unconverted, still seated or rising and dispersing, turned to greet each other amid a swelling tide of conversation.

Mr. Seafort's approach—old funeral serge suit newly pressed and whisk-broomed in places to a fine transparency, white cloth tie frayed at the edges and celluloid collar* bright with a blue duck's egg shine—was sidling and unobtrusive. His tread was soft, almost feline. His face shone with a happy, coal-like glitter.

"Well, well," he cried, seizing Jim's hand in an iron grip and pumping it, "I'm glad to see you, boy! When I came home last night and Josephine told me you were in the front room I could hardly believe by ears."

"Yes, I arrived yesterday at mid-day," said Jim, freeing his hand.

"And you had no trouble finding the place?"

"None at all."

"And how was Beatrice when you left her, no?" asked Mr. Seafort tenderly.

"As well as can be expected in the circumstances."

The smile faded out of Mr. Seafort's eyes. "You will find America is a great country, boy. A great country." His manner, crisp as potato chips, underwent a sudden change. His voice, no longer shrill and high-pitched, grew low— filled with scorn and sarcasm. His gaze as he now looked at Jim was hostile with a kind of impersonal hostility. "When I think of the way the big men at home used to waste the taxpayers' time and money debating the size of a cane hole—whether it should be two-and-a-half, two, two-and-three quarters or two-and-one third feet square—how my blood does boil!"

"Sir?"

What was Mr. Seafort getting at? *A cane hole?* What on earth did a cane hole have to do with the price of eggs? Here was a veil between him and Mr. Seafort which Jim would have to tear aside sometime. Mr. Seafort, before coming to America, only knew the soil of his native island and his vision of life, unlike Jim's, had not been coloured by long sojourn in a Latin-American country.

"A great country, boy. But wait—you'll see," ended Mr. Seafort cryptically, relaxing and beaming again.

Mr. Seafort's work in the pantry of a well-to-do family [in] Brooklyn Heights began early in the morning and often did not finish until after midnight. Mr. Seafort, who was happy in his job, had only one regret. He had so little time to spend with his own family. In the morning when he went out the children were not yet awake, and when he came home at night they had already gone to bed. Indeed, he hardly ever saw them except on Sunday afternoons—his one half-day off in the week; which to Mr. Seafort was lamentable because he did not wish his children to get out of hand. He wanted to exercise more control over them and to bring them up not "properly" in a worldly sense, but with a true understanding of the religion of the Plymouth Brethren.

"Didn't I tell you not to read newspapers?"

Jim, sitting alone in the living room, was startled out of a doze by the sound of Mr. Seafort's voice in the dining room. He sat still and listened.

"I'll make you remember fast enough. Take down your trousers and get across the day-bed."

"Don't lick he, Seafort, he ain't do nothin'," pleaded Aunt Josephine.

"Turn over, I say and get your spitty hand out of the way. Hand me the strap, Vashti."

"Hush, child, don't cry—"

"You must obey your pappy, you hear? When he tells you not to read newspapers you must listen to him, you hear? H'm! Even if your mother should tell you you can go ahead and read them you mustn't listen to her, you hear?"

"Yes, pappy."

"Seafort, for God's sake!"

"Move your hand, boy, and don't aggravate me! You mother is a stupid, weak-kneed woman but that is no reason why you should disobey your father, you hear? Now get up and don't let me catch you with any funny sheets again."

"You Miss Nimta, come here! Who gave you that brooch you got on?"

"I found it, pappy."

"You found it—where?"

"On the ground."

"Give it to me. Hey, look how these children gwine get me in trouble, yes. She found a brooch—where did you find it, girl?"

"On Greene Avenue."

"What were you doing on Greene Avenue?"

"Vashti and I went down to Fort Greene Park."

"Josephine! You mean to say you sit here and let these children go all the way down to Fort Greene Park, naked as they are?"

"Think I ain't got nothing else to do but wet-nurse big able girls—"

"Come here, soul. You mustn't do it again, you hear? You mustn't drag your little sister farther than the stoop, you hear? A motor car might knock she down and run over she, you hear? And when your pappy speaks to you you mustn't wall your eyes and suck your teeth, you hear? Turn round! Turn round, girl! You musn't walk about the streets like you haven't got a home, you hear? And you mustn't find rich ladies' brooches, you hear? They might see you with them on and come and take your pappy away to the lock-up, you hear? Now go to your room and stop bawling before I really give you something to cry for!"

"Faith to God, Seafort, it's a sin the way you does maltreat these children—"

"Swear! Go along, swear! Take the Lord's name in vain this fine Sunday afternoon."

Jim put on his hat and climbing noiselessly over the obstructions in the hall crept out of the house.

V

After tramping the streets all day in search of work Jim had found the arm-chair by the window in Aunt Josephine's living room easily the most restful spot in the flat. He sat there now, listening yet not listening to the noises coming from a baseball game down under the "El" in the dusk-filled street below and marvelling—he never ceased to do this—at the white, luminous glow in the evening sky.

An "El" train, pulling out of the Grand Avenue Station, swung up high on to the horizon. Swiftly the view of the heavens was obliterated. As the screeching and grinding of the long curving line of coaches mounted to a crescendo Jim felt someone clap him on the shoulder.

He turned just as the soft grey haze of the Northern twilight had begun to flow back into the room and saw Timothy Cumberbatch standing beside him.

"What do you say there, fellah? I ain't seen you in a monkey's age. Where you been keeping yourself?"

"Hello, Timothy. I didn't hear you come in."

Timothy was tall, slim and black. He wore horn-rimmed glasses and a blue serge suit. He had been born in Barbados but the outward manifestations of his powers of adaptation were so impressive Jim had found it difficult to believe Timothy had spent only ten of his twenty-one years in Brooklyn.

"For crying out loud, fellah!" grinned Timothy, shaking Jim by the shoulder, "Don't let it throw you! Buck up, boy, you ain't down in the jungles now. You can't git nowheres going all moony like-a so."

He strutted about the room crunching a grape, his ostentatious air of well-being masking the best of intentions. He paused with puckered brows and with the passing interest of an amateur in antiques to examine the cheese cloth in which the harmonium*—a disused and purely ornamental concession to worldliness on Mr. Seafort's part—was embalmed. He moved on, jaws still working. "Come to think of it," he threw out as a kind of afterthought. "You're to call me second cousin."

Not only he, silently acknowledged Jim with less than relish, but his two sisters and small brother as well. His father, Amos Cumberbatch, was an up and coming go-getter. ("Amos Cumberbatch from Carrington Village in Barbados? Man, he is rugged, rugged!") He was caretaker and janitor for a string of apartment houses in Flatbush. Amos was Mr. Seafort's half-brother and he broke bread with the Plymouth Brethren on Sunday mornings but unlike Mr. Seafort, who was only just beginning to accommodate himself to the idea that perhaps the time had come for him to start thinking about placing his eldest daughter Nimta in domestic service, Amos partly because he was personally in a position to do so, had put every member of his family to work.

The family lived in rent-free quarters (access to which was now and then restricted by scores of ash cans) in a remote corner of the vast, low-ceilinged basement of one of the monster blocks of flats which Amos looked after. It was so dark down there the electric lights had to be kept burning all day long. The air, never free of coal gas, was almost unbreathable.

Upstairs in the white-tiled hallway Timothy tended the switchboard; his mother, armed with mop and pail, kept the tiles all the way up to the top floor nice and clean while his father, a wheezy little dynamo of a man, strode from house to house tending the boilers, shaking down and building up the fires, filling and wheeling out the ash cans. Timothy's little brother, who was in the fourth grade, ran errands after school for the local trades people. One sister was just big enough to push a pram* along Ocean Parkway in the afternoons: the other one, too big for anything so light as nurse-maiding, was at nineteen a full-blown general houseworker. She cooked, washed and ironed for a family of eight persons.

"The folks been saying," said Timothy, rocking himself on heels and toes, "that you ain't got nothing to do yet."

"That's right."

"How long is it since you've been here?"

"Just three weeks," answered Jim, looking out the window, "Three weeks today."

"And you ain't got nothing to do yet, huh?"

"No, not yet."

How many times during those three weeks Jim had not had, from the window of an "El" train, a close-up of the white and gilt dome of the Borough Hall? Or skirted, still on the "El," the West Indian slums of Third Avenue on the long ride out to South Brooklyn? Or paused beside one of the houses going up on the flat marshes of Ridgewood on the crest of a real estate boom? Or tramped—dusty, foot-sore and weary—the sidewalks along the endlessly "El" shaded length of Brooklyn's Broadway? Yet no matter how early Jim had got up in the morning to answer the "Help Wanted" advertisements in the *New York World* he never seemed to have got up early enough. Someone was always there ahead of him. Or maybe he did not have the required kind of experience. Or maybe they wanted a woman. Once or twice—at the foreman's shed of a building contractor, in the dimly-lit office and the back of a hardware store—he had been definitely looked at (there was no mistaking it) with askance.

Through the dark cavernous mouth of the "El" and trolley car terminus at Park Row on the Manhattan side of Brooklyn Bridge, Jim, assaulted by the hot breath of the subway and with the ground quaking beneath him, squeezed and jostled, had even joined the disgorged multitudes out into the sunlight. As he entered the canyon of Nassau Street he always seemed to be less conscious of moving under his own power than of being propelled forward by a force within the anonymous mass of which he had now become a part. He had ventured into all the side streets and worked the skyscrapers floor by floor. Very seldom had he managed to get past the office boy. Sinking ankle deep in the carpet, he had on one occasion come up against a perplexing kind of brick wall. This was on the umpteenth floor of a skyscraper overlooking Trinity Church at the top of Wall Street. Ebony flunkeys resplendent in blue uniforms trimmed with gold braid moved with stately pomp in the distance. Silently, without a word and before Jim had had an opportunity to state the nature of his business one of them had conducted him to the stairs. Yet all had not been bitter aloe. Sometimes he had met a person in authority face to face. He had become accustomed to being bowed out with a promise that he would be sent for should an opening occur.

Timothy's lips parted in a dazzling smile. "Well, I've got another job for you," he said, tearing back his coat and jamming his hands down in his trousers pockets, his long legs spread wide.

"What is it this time," asked Jim without turning his head, "Operating a switchboard?"

"No, it's a better berth than that. And with plenty of pickings. Know anything about indoor chauffeuring?"

"You mean operating an elevator?"

"Yeah."

"No, I'm sorry, Timothy, I don't know anything about running an elevator."

"But there's nothing to it," cried Timothy, "It's a copper-bottom cinch!"

"No, Timothy, I shouldn't like to risk it. I might get stuck between floors or something."

"But there's nothing to it!" repeated Timothy in dismay, "Why, anybody can learn to operate an elevator. Dumber guys than you learn."

Jim shook his head. "It's no use, Timothy, I'm not ready to throw in the sponge yet."

"Yeah?"

"No, I think I'd rather wait a while."

Timothy's lower lip drooped. He fingered the elk's head on his gold watch chain. "Wait for what?"

"For the kind of job I want," said Jim.

It would take more than the persuasion of Timothy to deflect him from his goal. After all that he had come up through, to capitulate now, before he had given the thing a fair trial?

"No, Timothy," said Jim dreamily but firmly, "I'm not ready to kick in yet."

"But listen, fellah!" cried Timothy with a frown of exasperation, "You don't seem to realise that you is in America. Don't nobody wait for jobs in America. You goes out [after] 'em and grabs 'em—"

"You don't understand, Timothy."

"Yeah?"

"There are lots of places I haven't tackled yet."

"Okay, brother, suit yourself."

Slowly, with a shrug of the shoulders, Timothy turned and went out of the room. Passing through Aunt Josephine's bedroom to the dining room he neglected to close the door behind him. Then, clear as a bell, Jim heard Aunt Josephine's voice "What did he say, Timothy?"

There was a deep audible sigh. "No use. Still too proud to break down."

"How long he been here now, ma?" asked Vashti.

"Three weeks today."

"That guy takes the cake," declared Timothy. "Why, he must be nuts to think he can get the kind of job he had in Panama in this country. Running an elevator ain't good enough for him, huh? Well, you wait till the cold weather sets in. He will come crawling, you wait and see."

"He'd better hurry up," said Aunt Josephine, "and get something to do because when Saturday night come he does have to pay me, job or no job. Mr. Seafort is a funny man when it comes to money . . . Show Timothy the tam Miss Falladin gave you, Hyacinth."

"Did I tell you, Lonnie, about the new bathing suit I got?" cried Timothy, "Boy, it's a honey! Wait till you see it. It's got a big yellow oval on the chest—some lodge sign or other, I guess. And, boy, is it thick? Ordinary wool is lisle* to that! Guy up in Six "D" gave it to me, the sporty guy what got the meat ball stand at Far Rockaway. *You* know. All it's got is a hole in the leg, down here. Why, I can fix that myself."

"Last night," said Aunt Josephine, "Mr. Seafort brought home the leavings of a big 15 lb. turkey, didn't he, Nimta? Miss Falladin was having a banquet night before the last. . . ."

"Don't talk to me about eats, please!" cried Timothy. "Why, we never buy any food. We haven't bought a thing to eat all summer. Our ice box is chock full of stuff. All we've got to do is lift it off the dumb waiter. Spiced Virginia ham, cold chicken, pork chops, liverwurst, tomato and rice—"

Jim got up, crept noiselessly across the room and softly closed the door.

VI

On the way into the skyscraper Jim found himself in a crowd that moved with the briskness, almost the grim resolve of folk committed to a return to the treadmill after a week-end at the seaside or in the country. "Going up?" Nobody nodded assent. Nobody paused to consult the directory on the wall. Everybody without even a glance in the direction of the starter made directly for the long row of elevators.

Jim sauntered over to the young man in the dark blue uniform. "Which elevator do I take for the Gold Dust Twins* Soap Company? It's on the nineteenth floor, I believe." The starter waved an arm past the locals. "Take No. 6 and get off at the first stop. Going up?" *Click!*

Jim followed a part of the crowd into an express. ("Going up?") The starter *clicked a signal to the operator, the two halves of the automatic door came together and the dizzy ascent began. Jim held on to his straw hat. His breath seemed to him to be escaping fast. It was being coaxed up and up out of him. The conviction that he was "soaring on ether" grew within him. Then, as the operator pulled a lever and suddenly arrested the motion of the flying cage, Jim's heart almost flew into his mouth.

"Nineteenth floor!"

Light from the windows on two sides of the building met and mingled across the width of the floor. An early arrival—a young man with a deep sun tan, clad in a black smock and with a pen stuck over one ear—sat on a high stool before a counter with an open ledger on it. The office boy, pushing open the wicker gate, came out.

"I'd like to see Mr. Runck," said Jim, feeling in his pocket for a letter. "Is he in? I have an appointment."

"He hasn't come in yet," said the boy, "but if you'd care to wait . . ." He motioned Jim to a settee and disappeared. The private offices at opposite ends of the landing were in darkness. The one with which Jim was *not* familiar was marked "Domestic Manager." He now noticed it for the first time. It must be a million-dollar outfit! Just the sort of firm ("a manufacturing plant in Chicago"—"the home market carved up in regional blocs"—"a big new demand overseas for the company's products owing to the war in Europe")

Jim had always wanted to be connected with. If he should get the job he would give up sleeping on the bug-stained cot in Aunt Josephine's living room and move into proper lodgings. ("Now that you're going up in the world you won't forget us, will you?") Possibly with the Islands. Then after a while he would send for his mother in Colon to come and join him and when she arrived he'd see about getting a flat.

He looked at the clock on the wall above the line of steel and glass doors before the elevator shafts: a line that was blurred by the shadows of elevators noiselessly ascending and descending. Five minutes to nine. Now and then an elevator would pull up before him and someone would get out and, occasionally with the whirl of a skirt and the flash of high-heeled shoes, hurry past him. Then two, three persons at a time. Everyone seemed to go straight to a metal cabinet, open the door and then bang it shut. A swing door sounding as though its edge was padded with rubber bumped to and fro. The switchboard buzzed. Half a dozen typewriters clicked. Stops at the floor grew less frequent. Then, through a panel of frosted glass in the upper half of the door, Jim saw the light go on in the Export Manager's office.

The office boy appeared again. "Mr. Runck will see you now," he said. "Step this way." Jim rose and followed him along the landing. Opening the door at the end, the boy stood aside and Jim walked through.

Mr. Runck, an oldish man with a bullet head, sagging jowls and a paunch, was seated at a roll-top desk. A Havana cigar hung, unlit, out of the corner of his mouth. He turned slightly in his swivel chair and with a twinkle in his blue eyes regarded Jim over his pince-nez. When he spoke, his accent was that of the Middle West. "Close enough for you?" he said with a grin, showing a set of horsey teeth. If New York was sweltering in a heat wave Jim did not know anything about it. He felt quite cool in his Cordovan shoes, pongee* silk shirt and brown serge suit with its faint weavings of green. "Sit down," said Mr. Runck. He indicated a chair beside his desk. "Did you get my letter?"

"Yes, sir."

Mr. Runck bit off the end of his cigar. He gazed at Jim with lowered head. His face broadened in a smile. "How about the elevators," he asked softly, "have you got used to them yet?"

"Not quite," answered Jim not at all resentful of Mr. Runck's crack but, on the contrary, pleasantly feeling that Mr. Runck was trying to put him at his ease. "They still give me a funny turn."

"You'll get used to them," said Mr. Runck, obviously dealing with a phenomenon he had encountered before. Twirling the cigar around in his mouth, Mr. Runck went on: "Now, we've gone into the matter of your application and we find there's a position open. . . ." He paused and bit at the cigar again. "We can take you on at eighteen dollars a week."

"Thank you, Mr. Runck!"

"You will be taking over from a young man who is going into the Army."

"I see."

"Can you start right away?"

"Yes, sir."

"That's fine."

Mr. Runck pressed a button on his desk. Then he flipped off his eyeglasses and swivelled his enormous bulk around just as a plump and rather attractive brunette in a pink crepe de chine blouse and a white corduroy skirt entered the room in response to his ring. "Miss Guzman," he said, "this is Mr. Prout, Mr. Alejandro's new assistant." For a brief moment Miss Guzman stood squirming in confusion. She pursed her lips, furrowed her brows, bravely managed a faint attempt at a smile and proceeded to shift her weight from one silken leg to the other.

Jim rose.

"And, oh! . . . the reference from that manufacturers' representative that you worked for in Colon," said Mr. Runck, picking up a long envelope off his desk. "Here! You don't want to lose that."

"No, Sir."

Into the glare and hubbub of the general office Jim followed Miss Guzman. Uncertainly she tripped ahead. Not far away a young man sat facing a line of desks against the windows along one side of the room. Miss Guzman went round beside him and paused in the aisle. "This is Mr. Prout," she said, "the new assistant." Then she turned and went back to the big roll-top desk in the corner outside Mr. Runck's door.

Mr. Alejandro rose, shook hands and drew up a chair. He was not much older than Jim: about twenty-one. But the fact of Mr. Alejandro's youth ("offset" or "compensated for" by nothing that was associated in Jim's mind with dignity) was not the only thing that gave Jim a shock. It had not occurred to him that Mr. Alejandro might not be white.

Mr. Alejandro reminded him of those *paysanos** often to be seen on the market jetty at Fox River on the borders of the Canal Zone in grass-woven hats and hemp-soled shoes with cloth tops and with their shirts (buttoned up in the back) falling over the tops of their white cotton trousers: burners and vendors of charcoal who, out of the blue mists of the Santa Rita hills and in the path of the morning sun, had descended the river in *cayukas* laden with the commodity on which they depended for a livelihood. Only Mr. Alejandro, fairer skinned, did not possess the ebony tint of the *zambo* or the febrile yellow colouring of the *mestizo*. His complexion was an unusual blend: a fresh, sandy olive (and there was even a pink, almost crimson, glow under the high cheek bones). His nose was beaked and his black shining eyes, spaced wide apart, slanted beneath heavy lids. His hair, stiff and bushy and jet black, bristled on top of his head like a pineapple. He was the Andes and the Orient, with a touch of Old Castile, rolled into one.

"Mr. Runck tells me you are from Panama."

"Yes," said Jim quickly, "but I am not a Panamanian. I was born in British Guiana."

"Demerara?"

"Yes."

"Why, we're next door neighbours!" exclaimed Mr. Alejandro with a smile, "I'm from Venezuela." His white even teeth shone like pearls. His whole manner was bewildering. He was the first Latin-American Jim had met who did not seem to have to make a psychological adjustment in order to breathe the same air as a person of colour from one of Britain's colonies in the Caribbean region.

Mr. Alejandro cleared his throat and leaned back in his chair. "Now," he said, "the work here isn't hard, but it is often very rushed. In the time that I have been here not a shipment has been late for a steamer yet, and the record must be kept up." He paused, and looked Jim in the eye. "Can you make out consular invoices?"

"Yes."

"Ships' manifests?"

"Yes."

"Bills of lading?"

"Yes."

"Operate an Ely-Bunson machine?"

"No," replied Jim, "I'm afraid not. I don't even know what one looks like."

"You must learn to operate the Ely-Bunson," said Mr. Alejandro, "because you will be required to use it quite often. All right," he said, nodding in front of him, "there's your desk."

Jim cast furtive glances at his neighbour. With the index finger of each hand John Gonzaga was striking the keys on the overslung body of a machine set high upon a wide metal gauge. Obediently the machine chugged across the dim lines of a bill of lading. John pressed a lever and the machine slid forward along the bright shining rails. He banged on the keys some more, then he squeezed the lever again and the machine sprang lightly to the top of the gauge.

Without any warning at all John suddenly stuttered into song. "Ki-ki-ki-kaytie! Beautiful Kaytie. . . ."

Mr. Alejandro nipped the outburst in the bud. "How about it, Caruso, still on the Jose Rivas shipment?"

"Yep."

"How much is there left?"

John hesitated. "Let's see . . . two thousand cases of blue cloud, fifteen hundred cases of brown soap. . . ."

"All to Cienfuegos?"

"Yep."

"No gold dust at all?"

"No twins."

On Saturday morning the Italian organ grinder's tune would float up from the street to John Gonzaga for the last time. On Saturday John would be leaving the office for good. He won't be bringing his bathing suit to work with him because on Saturday at midday he won't be going straight from the office to the Battery to take the ferry across the Hudson River to the warm sun and the green cliffs and the white golden sands of a resort on the Jersey shore. Not any more. Miss Guzman, after she came back from lunch on Friday, won't be able to purse her lips and elevate her eyebrows in mild reproof as she listened to his tale about finding an old sock in his coffee down at Max's Busy Bee,* a place where he never ate. No, not anymore. At that he had been clever. No one could say now or in the future that he had evaded the draft or had even waited until he was called up. Son of a pushcart peddler in "Little Italy," an immigrant from the Old Country, John Gonzaga had grown so tired of the slowness with which the local Draft Board seemed to be getting around to him that he had joined up.

*When the moon shines over the cow shed**
I'll be waiting at your kitchen door.

"Carlos!" cried Mr. Alejandro.

"What do you want?"

A round baby face, yellow as assafoetida, looked up from a typewriter. The eyes staring with a kind of dull melancholy out of the face of Carlos Jimenez were large, sleep-haunted pools of jet. The hair on top of his little peanut of a head was black but thin and wispy.

"The invoices back from the C.S.A. de V. yet?"

"I haven't seen them."

"Where is Bill?"

"He should have left the Lackawanna ferry over an hour ago."

Mr. Alejandro got on the telephone. "Chilean Line please." Jim gazed beyond the stand in the aisle on which he had hung his hat. He could see the girl in a taffeta dress, a blonde with a chalk-white face and wet, mice-like curls on her brow, who operated the switchboard over in the Domestic Department. Mr. Alejandro jiggled the hook. "Step on it, Sally. I'm in a hurry." Then Carlos, tall and thin with stooping shoulders, a pigeon chest and the lower part of his stomach, curving outwards, passed in front of Jim and placed a batch of newly-typed letters before Mr. Alejandro.

"Compania Sud Americano de Vapores? Freight Department, please. Hello, Pablo. This is Alejo … trying to get me? Why I've been here all morning. Hasn't Bill showed up yet? Oh, don't worry. They'll be down in time. I'll let you know as soon as he rings up."

An elevator bounced up to the floor and a big, silver-haired man stepped out. He pushed open the wicker gate and strode in puffing and blowing. His weather beaten face was flushed.

"Had to go down to the Hoboken warehouse. Awful mess down there."

"What about the Mazatlan shipment, Bill?" asked Mr. Alejandro looking up at him.

"All set."

"Don't forget, the *Acapulco* sails at three."

"I won't."

He fished in his pocket and drew out a thick roll of bills of lading. Mr. Alejandro waved them aside. "Oh, John!" he sang out, gazing down the line of desks at which Jim, John Gonzaga and Carlos Jimenez sat profiled opposite him.

"Spill it."

"When you get through with what you're doing show Mr. Prout how to use that machine, will you?"

"Oke."

At noon that day Mr. Runck, twirling a cigar around in his mouth, met Mr. Palmer, the manager of the Domestic Department on the landing waiting for the elevator. Mr. Palmer, who wore spats and was carrying a cane, was pulling on a pair of yellow kid gloves.

"I see," said Mr. Palmer, "that you've got a nigger in your department."

Mr. Runck took the cigar out of his mouth. "He is not a nigger," he growled with a glint in his blue eyes. "He is a foreigner."

"The Lieutenant's Dilemma"

May 1955

"Don't see many of the darkies about now, do us?"

"Ah, they da put 'em on a round the clock grind now, see. Unloading convoys at Avonmouth Docks."

"Is that what 'tis?"

"Aye."

Up on the landing I glanced at the clock. I was early. Five minutes to seven. A moment later the G.I. stamped into the hallway. He strode through the door as if the disposition to step warily and take nothing for granted had, less than a month after the "black Yank" invasion, given way in him to something sharp and vaguely hostile.

"Where do you want to sit?" I said.

The G.I., short and chubby, a jockey at a Long Island race track in the days before the Japanese attack on Pearl Harbour, turned his head from side to side obviously not caring whether we joined the crowd down in the saloon bar, sought a refuge in the private bar or wandered out on the lawn where carp had been blown up during the Sunday evening raid on Bath when a huge, black, low-circling monster of a German bomber with a Spitfire on its tail had jettisoned one of its bombs in the canal flowing between the rear of the tavern and the wooded slopes of a hill.

"Oh, anywhere."

"Hang on a moment. . . ."

I turned and went down to the bar. I got two foaming pints of beer, came back up the short flight of steps and rejoined the G.I. Across the hall from the landing the door of the private bar was half open. We walked in and sat down at a vacant table at the back of the small poky room. Two old women in black, a silver-haired old man and a middle-aged couple occupied three of the four tables standing at right angles from us.

"Cheers."

"Looking at you," said the G.I., raising his glass to his lips.

"Have a cigarette."

"No, you have one of mine."

"Okay."

The G.I. unbuttoned the flap on the left breast pocket of his tunic, produced a packet of cigarettes and shuffled out a couple on to the black gleaming tiles with which the table was inlaid.

"Haven't seen any of you boys lately," I said, lighting up. "I thought maybe you'd been confined to camp or something."

"We've been on strike."

"On what?" I cried.

"On strike. We boycotted the town."

Gently inclining himself towards me the G.I. lowered his voice. "You know how it is with the people in this town," he said, rolling his eyes *away* from me and over in the direction of the five other people in the room. "'Hello, darkey.' 'Good morning darkey.' 'Oh, mummy, look at the darkey soldier!' 'Have you got any chewing gum, darkey?'" He paused, sat upright and stared ahead of him. "Well, we'd had enough of that 'darkey' stuff. We went to the company commander and told him we weren't going to have any more of it. We wanted to be sent back to the States."

The captain in command of the G.I.'s unit was a Regular Army officer from Georgia. One evening while firewatching I'd met him beside the waterless fountain in the Market Place. This, he'd told me with his eyes shining behind gold-rimmed spectacles in the black-out, was his first experience of Negro troops and he was thoroughly enjoying it. He'd even got so that he preferred Negro to white troops. Yes, sir, when it came to commanding troops give him Negroes every time.

"What did he say?"

"Oh," replied the G.I. "He hemmed and hawed and tried to soft soap us a while till some of the boys sagged and now the whole thing is beginning to fizzle out."

"When did the strike begin?"

"About a week after we got here."

I reached for my glass. . . .

"Another thing," said the G.I., "one of the boys in the outfit and I were standing on the river bridge one afternoon when a blonde passed by. A hayseed with a pitchfork on his shoulder strolling along on the other side of the bridge winked at us, jerked his head in our direction and sang out, 'All right, snow!'"

The G.I. paused, turned sideways and regarded me with a glitter in his black, low-slanted eyes. "What on earth did he mean? Was he trying to be funny? 'All right, snow!' We were so mad . . ."

I stubbed out my cigarette. "Drink up," I said. "The evening is young yet. You don't want to pay any attention to a remark like that. 'Snow' has nothing to do with colour. It's Wiltshire dialect. It means 'dost thee know!'"

"Dost thee what?"

"Know."

"Yes, yes, but what was he trying to say?"

"Something nice about the blonde. Something like 'righteous,' or . . ."

"Oh, I get it," cried the G.I., nodding his head.

I picked up the empty glasses.

"What will it be?"

"Same as before."

Outside the door the light was dim but not so dim that I could not see two of the officers from the G.I.'s unit standing in the hallway. I went down to the saloon bar and got two more pints of beer. When I came back up the steps the officers had not moved. They were still there.

Re-entering the room I saw that the G.I. was sitting with his legs stretched out under the table. He appeared to be taking things easily.

"Here's how," I said

"How," murmured the G.I., taking a long drink of the beer.

Outside in the hall the two officers from the G.I.'s unit were slowly pacing back and forth. It was probably only a coincidence but every time they passed the door one of them—a big, husky, bespectacled six-footer—would turn and look in our direction.

The G.I. suddenly drew up his legs. He sat perfectly still, almost rigid. "The lieutenant," he growled, "he keeps on walking up and down, up and down..."

"Was he the officer you were waiting to drive back to camp when I saw you in the jeep this morning outside the jeweller's shop?"

"No, that was another one."

"Oh."

The two officers passed by again.

"Any idea where our friend comes from?"

"Iowa," cried the G.I. "He played football at college. And owns some sort of a manufacturing business. He never had much to do with Negroes before he joined the outfit and he seems to be feeling his way along. He once told me that all the employees in his business have got to be educated, but since there were no educated Negroes in the small town in Iowa where he's located he has no Negroes on his pay-roll. I didn't know how to take that."

"Here he comes now."

Leaving his brother officer outside the lieutenant, pale as ivory, slowly entered the room and without a flickering glance at anyone else came straight towards us. He rested his hands on the edge of the table and leaned forward with his eyes fixed unsmilingly on the G.I.

"What are you drinking, fellah?"

"Do what, lieutenant?" asked the G.I.

"What are you going to have?"

"But I've got a drink, lieutenant!"

"Then have another. A short one. Do you good."

The G.I. cocked his head, elevated his brows and glanced down at the half-filled glass of beer in front of him. "Okay," he said with a succession of quick little shrugs, "make it a gin if you like."

The lieutenant slowly went out of the room, crossed the hall and descended the steps to the saloon bar. Presently he came back up and again walking with slow, almost painful precision brought a sparkling glass of gin and set it down before the G.I.

"Thanks, lieutenant!" smiled the G.I.

"Don't mention it."

Silently gazing into space the lieutenant lingered for a moment beside our table, but when he turned to rejoin his companion I saw that he'd begun to perspire.

"Strange Incident"

January 1956

The town, presumably for reasons which might have been consistent with the pattern of race relations in America, was out of bounds to "black Yanks." It also lay somewhat off the beaten track, insofar as the generality of visitors from the "dependent territories" were concerned. Even as transients non-whites of whatever variety—colonial war workers, English mulatto evacuees or West Indians in the R.A.F.—were such a novelty I had a feeling that when they did put in an occasional appearance they possessed for the local folk all the interest of an exotic, war-time phenomenon.

I passed through the empty foyer. It was deep in the dusk of a late afternoon in November, 1943. I pushed [open] the big glass door and went in.

"Did you get our postcard, Mr. X?" asked one of the clerks. No, I hadn't. The card, mailed on the previous evening, did not reach me until the morning of the third day. "One of your books has arrived."

The clerk, a blonde with golden hair and an unvaryingly polite smile, emerged from behind the counter and walked down to the front of the shop. (It was she who had taken my order about a fortnight previously.) When she got to the ladies' patterns on a stand just inside the door she proceeded along the wall behind them to the foyer. The girl out there was selling someone a newspaper. After a word with her the clerk returned and, taking no more notice of me, wandered off.

Standing there alone with the patterns, I didn't feel at all self-conscious. Not even a teeny weeny bit? I cannot be positive. The shop, in contrast with the gloom of the wintry dusk, was festooned with a beckoning array of lights. Nor was the lure of the lights abortive. There was a sprinkling of the local folk in the shop, but there was in addition a surprisingly large number of American military police conspicuous in their white helmets and white armbands. ("Snowdrops," I'd once heard a gum-chewing Negro G.I. from the camp outside the town where I was staying say, referring to the ones in his unit). There were about twelve of the M.Ps. and they were slowly moving about in groups of two or three . . . gazing up at the bookshelves . . . lingering beside a tray with Christmas and birthday greeting cards . . . gathering around the pyramids of new books on a row of tables in the centre of the room . . . coming in and going out through the big glass door behind me.

Presently the girl from the foyer appeared with a parcel for me. I handed her a ten-shilling note, pocketed the change and walked out.

Passing two M.Ps. in the foyer, I turned and strode up the street. Should I be able to accomplish all that I had planned? The doctor's surgery was open from six to seven o'clock. (A return of an old bronchial complaint.) I had a choice of two buses back: one at six o'clock and the other at six-twenty. But before I boarded the bus I wanted to stop somewhere for a cup of tea. Meanwhile I was hurrying along Church Walk to the County Reference Library! I made a rapid calculation. Even at the brisk pace at which I was going I could not get to the library under eight to ten minutes. Ahead of me and beyond the spiked railings of a high stone wall the clock on the church tower was barely visible in the dark. I peered up at it. 5:45 p.m. I decided to change my plans. Instead of going to the library (the things I wished to look up there in connexion with an historical work on which I was engaged could easily wait), I'd get a cup of tea and catch the six o'clock bus.

I started to retrace my steps. Nothing was farther from my thoughts than that I should forthwith find it necessary to step aside quickly in order to avoid a head-on collision with two ominously silent American M.Ps. I had not heard them coming up behind me. I continued on down Church Walk. When I got to the end of the passage I paused before crossing the road, took out a packet of cigarettes and lit one. The two M.Ps. emerging out of Church Walk, had stopped on the pavement of the High Street and while casting furtive glances in my direction, appeared to be trying to penetrate the blackness of a shop window.

The big store, lit up like a Christmas tree, absorbed a high proportion of the day's shoppers from the surrounding countryside. It was packed with a milling throng and trade at the buffet was brisk, incessant. The line of customers was two deep—

"Do you live around these parts?"

A large, black-gleaming shape stood beside me.

"Yes," I answered.

"Whereabouts?"

I mentioned a town on the Wiltshire Avon to which I'd moved down from London on the evening of the day Hitler's ultimatum to Poland expired.

"Let's see your identity card."

The constable looked at the card and then handed it back to me.

"What's up, officer," I said, "What's all this about?"

"We've had a complaint," he said, "that you are wearing U.S. Army shoes. Are you?"

"I don't think so."

I glanced down at my shoes. They were an old pair of brown utilities I had purchased from a well-known firm of boot and shoe dealers in a West Country town.

"Who made the complaint?" I said

"The U.S. military police."

"I see."

"They said you sounded when you walked as though you were wearing U.S. Army shoes."

For a moment I contemplated the shoes. What was it that I had done, or omitted to do to them that had made them sound on the wet, shining pavement in the darkness of an early November evening as though they did not belong to me? I looked up at the officer. It was plain from the expression on his face and in his eyes that he did not believe my story.

Half-jestingly, I said: "Shall I take them off and show you?" The officer flushed. "Yes!" he hissed, leaning over towards me. He was daring me to take off the shoes then and there. Seeing that we were not getting anywhere like that, I turned my head aside in an agony of disgust. The whole thing was so ridiculous. . . .

"I think you had better come with me," the officer then said.

I extended my foot. The M.P. bent down over it. I even pulled up the leg of my brown corduroy trousers.

"Are they U.S. Army shoes?" the constable asked.

"Yes, they are!" declared the M.P. without a moment's hesitation. He straightened up and remained standing erect and motionless with his eyes set dead ahead of him. He never once looked in my direction. He was a boy of about 19 or 20, tall and lean with light hair that stood up stiffly on the top of his head. Until I had joined him and the constable outside the store I had never seen him before.

We stood in a corridor outside the door of a small room facing a larger one with a switch board and some unoccupied desks in it. The constable was telephoning. He was trying to get someone to replace him on his beat. When he got through telephoning he disappeared up the stairs. People kept passing and re-passing before us. Girl auxiliaries in dark blue uniforms eyed us. Finally a U.S. Army Officer with a tentative air about him, slightly built and be-spectacled, appeared. The constable led us into the small room and I was motioned to a seat beside a desk.

"Let's see one of your shoes."

I took off the shoe and handed it to the lieutenant. He wasn't long examining it. He turned it over, glanced at the marks inside . . . A 199 . . . MMI . . . 62M94 . . . Size 8 . . . Shape 6-77 . . . REF 1398 . . . and then casually handed it back to me. "No," he said, "It's not a U.S. Army shoe."

When I got to the bus stop, just in time for the 6.20 p.m., an old woman crept up to me. "How did you get on?" she asked in a whisper.

"It was a case of mistaken identity," I said.

"I thought so," she said with a sigh. It was the same woman who, not for the first time, had served me the cup of tea at the buffet in the store.

"From British Guiana to Roundway"

December 1952

I was born in Georgetown, British Guiana, but at the age of eight I was taken to Barbados and thence to Colon, Panama. The interlude in Barbados lasted about two years. The island has been a British possession since 1605; many of its early settlers came from Wiltshire, and it is sometimes called, not without reason, "Little England in the Caribbean Sea."

My mother and I stayed for a time on her grandfather's place, an old sugar estate with the storm-wrecked ruins of a windmill still on it. Later, she and I moved into a cottage beside which grew a breadfruit tree overshadowing the yard.

My father, a merchant tailor, had meanwhile gone on to Colon. He'd been caught up inexorably in the stream of history, like the migrants of every race, colour and nationality then flocking to the country through which Uncle Sam was cutting a canal to link the Caribbean Sea with the Pacific Ocean.

In Colon, I early became aware of the fact that I was in a "plague-spot," one of the worst in the world. The Anglican Church on the beach, the big warehouse on its mercantile fringe, the Government Palace and the calaboose* were the only stone buildings in the town; all the others, teeming with newcomers, were tenements built of wood, while fully half of the old, coin-shaped, Indian isle of Manzanillo on which the town had sprung up consisted of a swamp.

The swamp was full of reeds, machineel, the bone white spectres of dead and leaflessly dying trees. The east wind wafted its exhalations over the town.

The cemetery at Mount Hope, beyond the causeway, contained a large proportion of the graves of some 22,000 men, mostly French, who had died on the Isthmus of malaria and yellow fever during a previous attempt in the 1880's—that of Ferdinand de Lesseps, the builder of the Suez Canal—to dig the Panama Canal.

The effect of the climate coupled with a weakened immunity to disease owing to lifelong residence in a country with only the most elementary notions of sanitation was occasionally mirrored in the faces of mestizos whom I passed in the street on the way to and from school. Faces that seemed feverish, hot to the touch, and of a pale yellow like that of the poison fruit of the machineel.

Looking back upon those early formative years on the Isthmus (after I'd left the school which I attended on the Canal Zone, and had already had one or two "office-boy" jobs) a white concrete building on a palm-fringed road in Cristobal looms up before me. Here, on the first floor, was the nerve centre of the public health service on the Caribbean side of the Isthmus.

Here, as a junior clerk, checking and filing the reports on the war to exterminate the mosquito, observing the comings and goings of the field staff, over-hearing talk about 'tenements unfit for human habitation' and about the case of the Sanitary Inspector who had involved the Department in a law suit in his "cleaning up" zeal over in Colon, I obtained a kind of "bird's-eye" view of the measures which had not only made the construction of the canal possible, but had made the Canal Zone one of the healthiest places in Latin America.

Four years after the canal was open to traffic and ten years after my arrival in Colon, I pulled up stakes and moved north. I went to New York. It was June, 1918.

My first job in New York was in the Wall Street area—correspondent in the export department of a Chicago firm of soap manufacturers. Here I first saw, and was shown how to operate an Elliot-Fisher machine.* Here, too, after the blue and gold had departed from the October sky, I saw something I had never seen before; snowflakes swiftly falling against the backdrop of the Corn Exchange Building.

The job didn't last as long as I would have liked. The war-time boom was over, the export market was "contracting," orders began falling off, and at the end of six months I was out in the street.

Getting off the 8th Avenue "El" at 42nd Street, I began the long trek eastward in deep crisp snow. My destination was the Architects' Building at No. 101 Park Avenue. Under my arm was a copy of a morning paper, "The New York Times." I was answering an advertisement which I'd seen in it.

The architect, a Southerner, wanted someone to replace a clerk he'd formerly had—a West Indian who'd enlisted in the British Forces through the British recruiting Mission in New York, and had gone overseas. The architect didn't say so in so many words but I gathered that he wanted the vacancy filled temporarily.

No one would ever be able to step into the West Indian's shoes. His job would be there waiting for him when he came back.

It was a small office—two draughtsmen and myself were the only employees, and most of the jobs on the drawing boards or recently completed were country lodges upstate; the one big, and I believe, the only job in Manhattan to the architect's credit was a hospital at the tail-end of the island.

Serving a resident population of 20,000 and a non-resident one estimated at 1,000,000 and consisting of seamen and office workers in the Wall Street district, the demands on the hospital—it was situated on the south-east corner of Broad and South Streets—had long since exceeded its limited capacity. When I appeared on the scene the architect was even engaged in drawing up plans and specifications for new additions to the hospital.

One day the young English doctor from South Africa, A.J. Barker Savage, who had founded the hospital with the backing of Herbert and James Barber, owners of the Barber Steamship Line, and who'd occupied the post of Superintendent from the beginning, came into the office. As he adjusted his pince-nez and eyed the architect I distinctly heard him say, "Neil, where did you get a man like that?"

A few weeks later I accompanied the architect on a trip to the hospital. The doctor was in the X-ray room. As we entered he turned from the plate which he had been reading and again remarked, "Neil, where did you get a man like that?"

As before, the architect ignored the question, but on the way back to the office he told me that the doctor was in need of a secretary and that, if I wished, I could have the job. He also told me that his former clerk was back in New York and had been in touch with him.

It was not long before an "accommodation," agreeable to all concerned, was reached—the West Indian returned to his old job with the architect and I went to work for Dr. Savage at the Broad Street Hospital.*

Thus began the two years which I spent in touch with 'life in a hospital.' This 'life' I touched at many points. I saw how vital to the workings of a hospital, the only one in a populous part of a big city, was a telephone switchboard for the reception and transmission of emergency calls. I saw something of the kind of patients that were admitted—seamen injured in storms at sea or in cafe brawls on the water-front, stockbrokers suffering from hardening of the arteries, an old Irish woman with cancer—fetched by the Superintendent himself in his Cadillac car from her home at Astoria, Long Island.

I even read with all the curiosity of a layman a brochure on Group Medicine which Dr. Savage had written about the experiment of the Mayo Brothers at Rochester, Minnesota; while it was my privilege, almost daily, to usher into the doctor's presence an old silver-haired English gentleman, James Barber. (A bronze plaque to the memory of his brother, Herbert, who'd passed on some two years before, stood on the wall inside the doorway.)

No hospital, dedicated to the service of humanity irrespective of financial capacity, can ever "pay its way" and the Broad Street Hospital was no exception; but thanks to the lead given by Herbert and James Barber and the widely recognised fact that the hospital was performing a great public service its existence during the early 1920's was never in danger. Its Finance Committee of which James Barber was Chairman experienced no difficulty in keeping it solvent.

It was able to enlist the support of an ever-widening circle of friends, including J. Pierrepont Morgan and Co., the National City Bank, Henry L. Doherty, a public utilities magnate, Elisha Walker of the banking firm of Blair and Co., William Hamlin Childs of the Barret Company, manufacturers of tarvia* products, and other distinguished figures in the financial and commercial life of New York.

It is a far cry from British Guiana and Barbados[,] Colon and New York to Wiltshire—a big jump in time and space from the Broad Street Hospital to Roundway.

The jump, for a "depression casualty" in the years following the Wall Street crash of 1929, is almost frightening. It is as though I'd entered a new world, a compact, almost self-contained community set in surroundings of rare beauty.

Here at Roundway I've seen a hospital functioning not on voluntary contributions but under a National Health Service—something I'd never seen before or ever dreamt of. Among my fellow patients I've seen some astonishing examples of brotherliness and self-sacrifice.

For myself, I can only say that my experience as a voluntary patient so far has been in keeping with the spirit at large in the Hospital. Kindness, sympathy and understanding are the essentials of the life I've known at Roundway.

"The Second Battle"

Excerpts, April 1956 to July 1957

VII

With the departure of the troops in the garrison there remained but a skeleton force of police to sustain the power of the Federal government in Colon. It was a contingency for which Pedro Prestan had been waiting. Organised and led by him and three of his principal lieutenants—General Portuzal, a mulatto who had taken refuge on Colombian soil from the chauvinism of an all-black regime in Hayti, "General" Souffront, a Negro from the island of St. Thomas in the Danish West Indies, and George Davis ("Cocobolo"), a Jamaican—an uprising of the Colon proletariat soon neutralized the police. Once in possession of the calaboose, a block-long, two storey structure built of wood on the edge of the lagoon in the centre of the town, Prestan turned it into his headquarters. He raided the armoury, opened the cells and led the prisoners out into the sunlight and air of the courtyard. Many of these men, fervent partisans of his, had been detained on political charges and had been lodged in cells with men with fetters on their legs. Without stopping to discriminate between one class of prisoner and another Prestan armed the lot and incorporated them into a force of his own devising for the preservation of law and order in the town[....]

A dark fusion of Spanish Creole, Indian and Negro, Prestan was not only by far the most controversial figure thrown up in the Colombian civil war of

1884–1886. He was a man who, in a violent and destructive way, exerted both directly and indirectly, a profound influence upon the fortunes of the Inter-Oceanic Canal Company. He was thirty-four years of age, a family man, short in stature and lean, almost wiry. He was first a *tinterillo* who in a short time had graduated into the ranks of the licensed advocates, then a captain in the Colombian Guards and later the founder of an incendiary weekly. On the occasion of M. de Lesseps's arrival at Colon in the steamer *Lafayette* on December 31st, 1879, Prestan was on the wharf (with Monsignor Paul, the Bishop of Panama, now the Archbishop of Bogota) to welcome the builder of the Suez Canal on behalf of the citizens of the United States of Colombia. He was there in his capacity as the representative of Colon in the Legislative Assembly at Panama [. . . .]

In 1881 Prestan was invited to join the legal staff of the Inter-Oceanic Canal Co. His duties required his occasional presence at the company's head office at Panama, he maintained a residence in a village on the line of the canal and never once relaxed his iron grip on the Liberal Party organization in Colon. When the Assembly was not in session he would return among his constituents to work for an end to the association which had begun in 1821 when the people of Panama voluntarily and of their own free will decided to join the Confederation of New Granada. Talk of a breakaway and the return of autonomy to the Isthmus did not win him converts on the other side of the political fence. Nor did the sneers of the Opposition ever fail to provide him with an opportunity to figure in gun plays and acts of violence in which the explosive spark was usually politics, no less than Latin sensibility [. . . .]

Among the men who were indifferent if not hostile to the "cause" of Pedro Prestan was one of the Cespedes brothers—Manuel, a 39-year-old merchant from Carthagena. Manuel and Jose A. Cespedes were partners in a mercantile house in Colon. Manuel was the proprietor of a business house in El Rio de Indo. In April, 1881, Manuel was charged with the management of the Colon establishment during Jose's absence in Bogota. Actuated by what was afterwards deemed the highest of motives—"the kindly act of a superior towards a subordinate" [The Panama *Star and Herald*, March 28th, 1885].* Manuel wrote a letter to one of the firm's employees, a Jamaican clerk named Briceno-Levy, "counseling him to take no notice of certain publications of Prestan." Whether Prestan could have got wind of the letter through anyone other than the employee to whom it was addressed was never established. But if the letter did not find its way into Prestan's possession, the Deputy soon learned all about its contents. He flew into a rage and resolved to demand an explanation from Manuel Cespedes.

A few days later Prestan ("accompanied by a number of individuals who were armed and ready to render assistance to him" in case of need) called at the merchant's place of business. Told that Pedro Prestan had come to pay him a call, Manuel Cespedes emerged with arm crooked above the right hip, from the interior of the establishment. The sight which met his gaze was not calculated to lessen his apprehensiveness. Briceno-Levy, who had received the visitors, stood talking to Prestan in the outer office which was filled with menacing specimens of Prestan's men. Whether he yielded to the sudden urge to do away with an employee whom he now suspected of having betrayed him, or whether he saw an opportunity to put paid to Pedro Prestan was a secret which Manuel Cespedes carried with him to the grave. At all events the crooked arm came up suddenly, and a pistol shot followed by a cry of anguish from Briceno-Levy rang out. Notoriously quick on the draw, Prestan returned the fire and Manuel's gun fell with a clatter as he slowly sank to the concrete floor, holding his stomach [. . . .]

At six o'clock on the morning of April 30th Manuel Cespedes died of his wound. ("From the first little hope of saving his life was expressed by his medical attendant. He lingered in pain and suffering for a week, although every effort was made to assuage his distress and prolong or save life.") Now charged with the murder of Manuel Cespedes, Prestan was remanded to the calaboose. A date was fixed for an early trial. On the nineteenth of May a jury of five persons was sworn in. ("It is said some of these are warm personal friends of the accused.") Four days later the case came up for trial, and the verdict of the jury was one of acquittal. Scenes of wild, unrestrained joy—shouts of "Long live Prestan!"—filled the court room. The prisoner, however, was still in active custody and when the order for his release was presented at the calaboose the officer on duty, under orders from the Prefect, Jose O. de Obaldia, refused to honour it—Don Jose alleging "informalities and irregularities in the legal proceedings." The action of the Prefect meant that the case would now be referred to the Superior Court at Panama, and that Prestan would have to stand a new trial.

A week later, however, the Legislature of the State of Panama in special session made recourse to a higher court unnecessary. It passed a resolution to the effect that the Executive should demand by telegraph the release of Pedro Prestan, "who had already been declared innocent by a jury." The Legislature went even further and demanded "that all parties who have been interested in keeping Mr. Prestan in prison shall be tried and punished according to law." With nothing to do but to comply with the Legislature's request, the Government set Prestan at liberty and the Deputy, accompanied by the jury that had acquitted him, embarked on the Colon-to-Panama one o'clock train for an unknown destination somewhere along the line [. . . .]

X

At 1.30 a.m. on Tuesday, March 31st, 1885, one hundred and sixty men of the two hundred and twenty (mostly levies of various nationalities with a "stiffening" of Colombian Army regulars) under the command of General Carlos A. Gonima in the garrison at Panama City embarked on a special train for Colon. The object of the expedition was punitive. It was to put down Pedro Prestan's rebellion and restore the authority of the National Government, and the officer chosen to lead it was Col. Ramon Ulloa, who commanded the *Boyaca,* a revenue cutter (built in the Wilmington-Delaware yards of the Pusey and Jones Company) lying off Panama and forming part of General Gonima's forces [. . . .]

About three miles from Colon the troops suddenly came under fire. Scurrying for cover, taking up positions in the ditch beside the road to repel the attack, they had been taken by surprise. The unexpected bursts of fire in the dawn had come from both sides of the road; from the woods below the cemetery on Loma de Mona (Monkey Hill) and from the guava trees, the scrap metal yard and a row of box cars lying on the other side of the spreading lines of the railway. A small party of rebels under General Portuzal had been sent to ambush and engage the troops with obviously only a limited tactical aim in view—to delay Ulloa's advance as much as possible while Don Pedro himself, knowing that he was up against an enemy superior in arms and training and therefore in discipline, feverishly got on with the night-long job of erecting barricades from behind which to contest Ulloa's entry into the town. The engagement, in which such wounds as were inflicted on either side seemed to have been insufficiently serious to affect the victim's mobility, ended after half-an-hour with the rebels retiring in two streams on Colon, hard pressed by the National troops [. . . .]

"Immediately after the American troops had taken up their positions" on the mercantile fringe at one end of the town the forces under Col. Ulloa made their appearance before the barricades at the foot of Bolivar Street and the Calle de la Laguna and in the rear of the headquarters of the revolutionary army at the other end. Joined by the survivors of the Monkey Hill rout, the main rebel force manning the barricades was under the command of Pedro Prestan, who had vowed that rather than see the town fall to the National troops he would reduce Colon to ashes [....]

Re-entering Colon, the rebels found their line of retreat virtually severed. Their barricades had been swept aside, the Commander of the *Galena* had taken the unheard of step of imposing something like martial law on the city—ordering all bars and canteens and liquor shops to be closed—and armed patrols of Yankee sailors and marines with fixed bayonets had penetrated as far south as the environs of Boca Grande. Yet no cowering air of submissiveness overhung the 'native populace.' On the contrary, the white and black and yellow-skinned mass, whether of local Spanish-speaking or foreign immigrant origin, Separatists to a man and therefore partisans of Pedro Prestan, seemed in a mood to take on both the National troops and the "Gringoes." Thus when the forces under Col. [Santiago] Brun began to move in and occupy the town the fighting was continued with pot shots being taken at them from street corner and alley, tenement door and window, balcony and rooftop.

At 4 o'clock in the afternoon when the sniping subsided and the rebels seem to have been encompassed in total defeat, a cry of horror went up:

"*Fuego!*"

Seconds later the cry, preceded by the explosion of a charge of dynamite was heard in another part of the town.

"Fire! Fire!"

The cry, followed by the futile one of "Water! Water!" was repeated again and again until it arose all over the town. In the bitter agonized moment of defeat the rebels had committed a supreme act of egoism and revenge: they had set fire to Colon.

The city, bounded on the north by the Caribbean Sea, on the west by the Bay of Limon and on the east by the Bay of Manzanillo, was three quarters of a mile long by about one third of a mile wide. It was built on a coralline foundation almost entirely of wood—Christ Church, "a Gothic edifice of classic proportions," facing the boulders piled up on the Caribbean shore, built of dark stone from the quarry at Bohio Soldado on the line of the Panama Railroad for the convenience of its employers, and the company's freight house on the Limon Bay waterfront, were the only solid stone struc-tures—and in the fine weather of the dry season it burned like kindling. (Among its public or private services there was no such thing as a fire bri-gade; a *cuerpo de bomberos* did not come into existence anywhere on the Isthmus until 1888.) The fire, fanned by a north east wind ("an awful, though grand spectacle" in the night), raged until it burned itself out on the after-noon of the following day. Ten thousand people were rendered homeless, and property estimated at twelve million dollars—not a penny of insurance on which was collected . . . was consumed in the flames. On the morrow of the conflagration the once flourishing city presented an appearance of utter desolation.

". . . . blackened and ruined walls; lands covered with ashes where once crowded tenements or prosperous stores or hotels stood; wharves in ruins with their iron piles and frames bent and broken by the intense heat; the large freight house with its valuable contents; hundreds of car tracks and frames of cars (many of which had been loaded with valuable cargoes) on the lines of rail from which the ties were burned away and the rails twisted and warped by the fury of the fire; all go to make up a picture of what hap-pened on that which was undoubtedly the darkest day in the history of Co-lombia [. . . .]

XIV

[. . .] General Reyes convened a court martial to sit in judgement on Gen-eral Antoine Portuzal of Hayti and George Davis ("Cocobolo") of Jamaica. The court returned an oral verdict of guilty and sentenced the prisoners to be hanged the same day.

The execution was set for 5.30 p.m. and from early in the afternoon a large crowd of the morbidly curious—it was to be the first public hanging in Colon since the days of Ran Runnels*—began to gather around the scaf-fold that was erected in the centre of the town. The manner in which the condemned men—diverse in character, social origin and nationality but united in their loyalty and devotion to Pedro Prestan and the cause of the Panama revolution—prepared to meet the end of their days on earth con-trasted strangely. "Cocobolo," the Jamaican immigrant, his last wish grati-fied, downed a bottle of his favourite rum and two glasses of eau de vie* and ascended the funeral car with a tipsy swagger.

"Incendiary! Assassin!"

Had he not heard the words, and sensed the undercurrent of hostility? Had he not heard the click of a photographer's camera upon his appearance in the crowd, manacled, flanked by the rifles and bayonets of Colombian soldiery? Had he not been spat at? *He would show them that he knew how to die!*

Antoine Portuzal, the mulatto political exile from Hayti, made a few dispositions concerning the future of his import and export business and then, after composing a brief note, turned to the Catholic priest in attendance upon him and asked him gently to deliver it to Pedro Prestan. A translation of the note from the French was as follows:-

"Colon, May 6, 1855.

"To Senor Pedro Prestan,

In life.

Friend Prestan:—

I die on account of acts accomplished in the burning of Colon. Although I am in the tomb do me the favour to clear me in the minds of the people of Colon that I am the author of the crime. I had already surrendered to the government troops at one o'clock when at two o'clock you placed fire in the city. The Colombians I do not blame. The Americans who captured me in the streets of Colon—they are my assassins and not the Colombians.

I die as a soldier but you know well why. It is because of you; because I had no right to political colour in Colombia.

My family remains on the earth. I have sacrificed their means and resources for you.

Farewell

Gen'l Portuzal."

Having refused to have their eyes bandaged, the men stood looking into the setting sun as the nooses were carefully adjusted under the left ear of each. There was almost no slack to the ropes and as the car was pushed from under them the bodies did not *drop* (the men made no other movement beyond an involuntary effort to clutch the ropes, but their manacled hands prevented this), but subsided slowly and turning a quarter of a circle Portuzal and "Cocobolo" died quietly by strangulation facing the ruins of the old calaboose from which for one whole fortnight in March they had collaborated with Pedro Prestan in controlling the destinies of Colon.

"What's that?"

"A portion of the wall of a gutted building over there—"

"Fallen masonry?"

"Sounds like a revolver shot to me."

"Somebody is paying off a last-minute score with the dying bravos."

Whatever it was, the crowd of nearly four thousand scattered and fled in indiscriminate haste from the lugubrious scene.

Twenty minutes after the bodies had been let down, "Cocobolo's" pulse was still beating. His companion had much less vitality and a few minutes after six o'clock both were pronounced dead, cut down and removed to Monkey Hill to be buried as they were found, uncoffined.

UNPUBLISHED WRITINGS

"Shadow in the Sun"

Short Story

[I]

The teacher put down the chalk and, turning from the black-board, dusted his hands. Adjusting his pince-nez from which a black cord dangled, the teacher—a big beefy 'old Wolmer's College boy' from Jamaica who, from the position of timekeeper with a gang of Negro ditch diggers at Tabernilla on the banks of the Chagres River early in the final successful attempt to cut the Panama Canal had progressed up the ladder of the separate school system on the Canal Zone until he was now head of the Cristobal unit—wrinkled his forehead and bent his head. His dimpled, clean-shaven chin and heavy jowls jutted over a choker of a linen collar and a thin black tie. His pongee silk suit, which he wore with a double-breasted waistcoat of white flour-bag,* hung loosely about him.

He stood gazing down at the notes on his desk. The eagerness with which the pupils had followed his little excursion into the geography of the

Isthmus was most gratifying. So far he'd had to use the cane only once—on Felix Prout, a dreamy, inattentive boy. 'MOUN-tain-ous.' Ugh! A fine example of what a rootless existence could do to a boy. All those trashy little schools which he'd attended over in Colon and half-way round the shores of the Caribbean Sea had certainly left their mark on him.

The teacher raised his head. Thirty pairs of eyes, shining in the faces of a roomful of Negro boys and girls in their early teens, stared innocently at him. "And so," he concluded softly, "orchids now bloom, flamingoes and cranes have found new centres of reproduction on the little islands that float above Tabernilla's tomb like emerald[s] on a mirror. There had been no ceremony to mark the occasion when from two sides the water rushed in. No tears had been shed. Having failed to survive the marriage of the oceans, Tabernilla now lies at the bottom of Gatun Lake."

A wave of subdued laughter rippled round the class room. Wilyan Boy jerked his head upwards. Then he leaned forward in his seat and poked Felix Prout gently in the shoulder.

"Him don't know say him* is not a timekeeper at Tabernilla now."

"Sh-h-h."

"Always gwine on about Tabernilla like him can't get the old burg out of his system, the silly old—"

"Look out. Here he comes now."

The teacher stepped down off the platform. Felix and Wilyan, without moving an eyelid, saw him stride in his white kid shoes through the door on to the balcony, heard him stalk back into the class room through the other side door and listened as the teacher, continuing the onward sweep, disappeared through yet another door on to the wide verandah running along the front of the schoolhouse and facing the Mount Hope road.

"'Old Tab' is tapping with his foot and humming 'Hearts of Oak.'"*

"A sure sign he's up to no good."

"Yes, but him don't have it, man! See it over there—"

"Where?"

"Behind the swivel chair. Leaning up against the blackboard."

Instead of the bamboo cane the teacher was clasping with one hand the tongue of a hand-bell, while in the palm of the other hand, a fat brown one, lay a gold watch. He stopped tapping and humming and looked at the watch. Then, with a clang that shattered the silence in the schoolhouse, the teacher rang the bell for the mid-morning recess.

From the low-topped (not quite ceiling high), white-walled divisions in the old Martinique workers' barracks the pupils streamed on to the wide front verandah, clattered down the steps at either end and dispersed out into the sun. All the "exotic" games which the children of West Indian parents had brought with them to Panama were soon in full swing on the two cinderdusty halves of the school's roadside playground.

Felix Prout alone remained on the verandah. The sun was moving up behind the schoolhouse, but the shadow of the projecting end of the zinc roof still reached as far out as the gutter. The footpath between the curb and the verandah was wide, wide enough to provide a mounted Canal Zone police officer with a brief respite from the sun as he slowly rode by on his beat; but unless Corporal Stroud came along the path, now coolly shaded, would become shadowless with the white dazzling fire of the sun beating down upon it.

II

"And Stroud—"

"Yes, sergeant."

"Take one of the new men with you."

"Sir?"

"One that knows a bit about the ropes. Let me see. . . ."

As he consulted the roster of "Silver" officers on duty-call the expression on the sergeant's face in the softly spreading glow of a light with a green mantle that hung low over his desk was tense.

"Yes, take Bodie Prout with you," said the sergeant. "He used to be a police constable in the West Indies. Once broke up a cane field riot almost single-handed."

Short, lean and bow-legged, a former Texas cowboy, Stroud's fingers closed in a white-knuckled grip on the railing in front of the sergeant's desk.

"A good man, Prout," continued the sergeant with a shake of the head and a frown, "Handy with a pistol too."

A pink flush crept upward from the neck of Stroud's khaki tunic.

"You two ought to get on well together," said the sergeant.

In spite of himself Stroud relaxed. He frankly did not think much of the choice. It was as if the sergeant had never seen Bodie Prout stroll into the station house in white flannel trousers, open-necked cellular shirt and green sports jacket with a cricket bat in his hand.

"Where are you off to?"

"Tabernilla Green . . . for a work-out with the boys."

Or had never heard the sounds that arose from the so called Green in the evening at dusk:

"Stroke!"

"Well played, sir!"

Or had never been tempted, just for the fun of the thing, to egg Bodie Prout into unburdening himself about his origins. No—this in explanation of his thin lips, high-bridged nose, brown skin and faintly green eyes—there was no Carib or East Indian in him. The light skinned side of him was pure Anglo-Saxon!

Or had never seen the light that would steal into Bodie Prout's eyes or heard the words that dripped like honey from Bodie Prout's lips whenever he spoke about his home in Barbados: how his father, the son of a planter in St. George's parish and a Negro slave was the only man in the island after whom a village was named; how the old mulatto once owned a couple of sugar estates and still paid taxes on odd pieces of property scattered about the island. How one hot sunny afternoon in the midst of the grinding season at Flat Rock ashes and fine grains of sand had begun floating down out of the sky. ("It happened on a Friday . . . Christ was crucified on a Friday.") Then the sky turned black. A wind rose. The lime trees wafting their perfume from the front of the estate house, the big breadfruit tree down by the lily pond, the uncut canes in the fields surrounding the house on three sides all began trembling, swaying and moaning. The sails in the windmill flew round and round with a harsh, a grating noise. The roof of the boiling house shot into a field and the rain deluged down into the vats in which the cane juice was fermenting, coming to the boil, crackling. The fires under the vats went out. The water poured as through a sieve from the loopholes in the red brick cone of the mill. The staves round the puncheons of molasses standing out in the yard fell apart and for days after the storm the water, sweet, then merely brackish, flowed over the edge of Flat Rock until it reached midway up the trunks of the golden apple trees down in the gully.

"And Stroud. . . ."

"Yes, sergeant!"

"If our 'spick-o-ty' friend should turn up tonight in the vicinity of those freight cars on Tabernilla siding for the sake of all that's dear to you don't let him see you first."

The sergeant paused. Spread out before him was a document which he appeared to be studying.

"*Soy hombre libre! No soy enganchado!*" ["I am a free man, not a contract labourer."]*

"Sir?"

"Around the Plaza Santa Anna in Panama City during the last days of our French predecessors on the Isthmus, Fonseca, the One with the Twist in his Neck, as he is known among his followers, was merely a wild-eyed demagogue. . . ."

"A what, sir?"

"Ah agitator . . . a rabble rouser . . . who never knew where his next meal was coming from, but don't let that deceive you and don't forget there's a price of $500 on his head. The moment you think you've spotted him let him have it."

"Yes, sergeant!"

". . . . 'has since blossomed out into a full-time 'Gringo'-hating *tinterillo* in a blue alpaca suit who never moves a step without a .44 Colt revolver on his hip and knows how to use it too.'"

Stroud spread his bow legs and tilted back his head. There was a twinkle in his blue eyes.

"Did you say he's got a twist in his neck?"

"Yes!"

Stroud chuckled: "We'll soon straighten that out."

"And what's more," cried the sergeant, "the crack-pot . . . by the ease with which he can walk on and off the Canal Zone cutting our telegraph wires, tearing up sections of the Panama Railroad and dynamiting our good trains . . . is holding up work on the canal. But this sabotage's got to stop or else some ignorant, big-mouthed Congressman in Washington will want to know why."

"Yes, sergeant!"

The sergeant turned to gaze through the thin wire screen in the door at the glimmer of raindrops rippling down off the roof of the station house. He had come a long way since leaving a clerical job in the police department of a small town in Illinois to join the force slowly being got together to police the ten-mile wide strip of territory, leased in perpetuity to the United States, through which the Panama Canal had been traced out and partly dug by a French company. His grasp of the essentials of what was wanted in those early days of muddle and experiment was so sure that he had been sent to an important sector of the canal to take charge of the station house at Tabernilla, a village on the Chagres River. The force which he'd gradually built up, from both the "Gold" and Silver" sides of the payroll, had started with a nucleus of white officers from the States, until it was swollen with a number of new recruits drawn from the pick and shovel gangs in the sector.

"Good night, Stroud!"

"Good night, sergeant."

"Good night, Prout."

"Good night, sir."

Buttoning on black waterproof capes over their *khaki* uniforms the two officers passed in front of the sergeant's desk, opened the wire-screened door and went out into the night.

III

"H'm! No taste for games, eh? Dreaming again, I suppose."

Startled out of his absorption in the slow ascent of the shadow-line over the curbstone, Felix caught a glimpse of the Principal hurrying with head erect into the adjoining class room. *Dreaming again?* What a strange thing for 'Old Tab' to say! It was as if, appearances to the contrary, the Principal had by some lofty means of divination penetrated the secret of the awful thing that haunted Felix every moment of each day that he spent at school. It was no dream. It was a nightmare in which a long coffin of wet between rows of box cars on a Tabernilla siding blended with the black gleams of a rain-splashed cape at the tail-end of a tense, night-long vigil and with the image of Stroud, his gun still smoking, swaggering out of the dark and kicking the warm still body of Bodie Prout over in the mud.

"Cut that out!"

Creeping up softly behind him Wilyan Boy suddenly made Felix feel as if a swarm of red ants had erupted on the verandah beneath him. Felix stamped his feet and rubbed one stockinged leg against the other.

Wilyan grinned. "Here," he said, handing Felix a tamarind switch, "I'll let you return the compliment. Fan me."

Felix grasped the switch and made as if to swish Wilyan round the legs with it. "I have a good mind to!" he cried. Then he broke the switch in half and threw the pieces over the verandah.

"Why . . . why . . . what's the matter?" quavered Wilyan. "Can't you take a little joke?"

"No!"

"Well," ventured Wilyan after a while, "Are you glad to be leaving school?"

"Oh, I don't know," said Felix.

He hadn't had too bad a time at school. He hadn't been exactly a bright pupil. Still, he had managed to collect in recognition of his all-round proficiency a few "Honour Checks" which the Supervisor of Coloured Schools had himself presented to him. 'Old Tab,' in spite of the manner in which he would sometimes pull him up—"what rubbish are you talking, boy? The word is elephantiasis . . . *Isis! Isis!*"—and before whom he'd often had to stand up, stretch out his hand and take a good stiff caning had been considerate too. In fact, the Prinicipal had been strangely partial to him from the beginning.

When, after his father's death, the problem of finding him a new school arose his mother just did not know what to do. Over in Colon where she and Felix had settled after leaving Tabernilla, since they were no longer entitled to living quarters on the Canal Zone, there was no lack of schools. Mr. Jill kept one in a lodge room on Cash Street (not the lower end), there was "Tutor" Grant's on the balcony of a tenement overlooking the "D" Street sewage canal and a cross-eyed St. Lucia spinster kept an academy with the emphasis on dramatics and folk dancing on the gallery of a house in Coolie Town. But at all these schools which Felix attended one after the other for short periods of time there was either too much frivolity and lack of discipline or the standard of instruction was only so-so. More-over, they all charged fees which she, trying to earn a living as a dressmaker, had found it increasingly difficult to pay. What was she to do? She could not afford to let him grow up without even the bare rudiments of an education.

"What about the school in the big white building at the top of Bolivar Street?" asked Miss Sobers, her next door neighbour in the Ants' Nest Building. "Plenty of West Indian boys and girls does go there. And besides, 'um is free."

"Send my boy to a Spanish school when he don't even know English good yet?" she had cried, recoiling in dismay from the thought of Felix growing up like so many real or pretended "black creoles," the Isthmus-born children of West Indian immigrants, literate only in Spanish and with nothing to distinguish them from the Negro citizens of the Republic of Panama. "Bring him up to be a 'speak-o-ty'? No, soul. His father would turn over in his grave if he thought I would do such a thing."

So, out of a feeling that she was entitled to *something* after the way she was widowed, she had taken Felix to 'Old Tab,' knowing full well that the school of which he was Principal was a Jim Crow school—set up by Uncle Sam for the free but exclusive use of West Indian employees on the Panama Canal. And "Old Tab" without asking a question had agreed to admit him just as if Bodie Prout was still alive and on the Canal Zone police force.

"Why, man alive!" cried Wilyan Boy. "Aren't you glad to be going to work? Owning a watch and a fob, a brass check. . . ."

"Oh, I'm looking forward to all that," said Felix, drumming with his fingertips on the verandah rail. His pay as a messenger boy in the Quartermaster's Department at Mount Hope would help considerably to ease the strain on his mother. The job would provide relief in another sense, too. It would place him outside of Corporal Stroud's beat. The agony of seeing the man who had killed his father riding by the schoolhouse day after day, hugging the shadow of the verandah, would be over.

"And with money to buy as much sponge cake and ice cream as you like!" cried Wilyan. "Gee, how I envy you!"

Wilyan paused, suddenly remembering that the cartons of vanilla, pineapple and chocolate ice cream and even the cake which leapt to his mind's eyes were, like iced Canadian apples* with the bloom still on them, luxuries that could only be obtained at the Canal Zone stores with scrip issued to employees as an advance on wages.

"You will get a commissary book, I suppose?"

"Book?"

"So that you won't have to wait till pay day. . . ."

"I suppose so."

As one magnetized by the shadow of an all-pervading dread Felix scanned the horizon. The traffic signals at the crossing just beyond the upper end of the schoolhouse and opposite the spot where Bolivar and 14th Streets in Colon converged upon the top of the road to Mount Hope pointed serenely to the sky. No one either on foot or horseback was crossing the tracks from the direction of the red-tiled roofs and the palm trees of Cristobal. At the lower end of the schoolhouse, beyond the broken steps and the flower boxes and the dirty sun-rags screening the porches of a curving line of Negro family quarters, the position at the crossing which, devoid of traffic signals, provided a short cut through the Cristobal machine shops to the Hindu coolie barracks and the Negro 'baby' box car hutments of Coco Tiers, all part of Corporal Stroud's beat, was the same. In front of the crossing the road—white and dusty and with no sign of a big bay horse, no sign of Corporal Stroud—began to curve out of sight; but curving in sight from a tall, round-roofed corner of the shops was the rear end of a locomotive . . . backing up the mainline of the Panama Railroad.

"What did Stroud say to the coroner's jury? Oh, yes. . . . 'You know how it blackens up just before dawn, after the gas lamps in Tabernilla go out. Well, I was standing under the lamp at the crossing when the light went out.'

"'Was it still raining?'

"'No, it had stopped raining.'

"'Go on, Stroud.'

"'The crossing was blocked with five long lines of freight cars, so when I heard a crunch, crunch, crunch on the gravel I tiptoed a few yards in the direction of the sound. Then I leaped over the couplings between two of the cars and as I turned my head I saw a shadow moving towards me. I whipped out my .45 Colt and fired a couple of shots. Then I ran up with the gun cocked and when I turned the body over with my foot I saw that it was Zone Policeman Prout. I reckon in the dark I had mistaken him for the 'spick.'

"Perhaps operating in harness, walking up and down, backwards and forwards all night long had become irksome to them, so they decided to separate. Yet someone had to say, 'I will go this way, you go that.' Whose idea was it anyhow that they should split up?"

"Whose idea is what?" cried Wilyan Boy.

Felix gulped. He moistened his lips and gazing directly across the road pointed a trembling finger at a blue-overalled Negro workman standing on the edge of the track oiling the mainline switch.

". . . . What a long spout that oil can's got on it. It's more than a foot long."

"Oh?" cried Wilyan with a swift arching of the eyebrows and a shake of the head.

"Nearer two feet."

Wilyan fell in with the mood: "It's almost time to go back in."

"Already?"

"Yeah."

"The quarter of an hour has certainly flown by."

"There's the engine for the 11 o' clock train."

"It's moving along on velvet. No smoke, no noise. . . ."

"Yeah."

"It must be 10:45."

"Yeah."

Striding on to the verandah, 'Old Tab' started to ring the bell for the end of the recess and the pupils, hot and sweaty, laughing and chatting, pushing and elbowing each other in the race back to their class rooms flooded up the verandah's broad steps out of the sun. Turning from the railing Felix and Wilyan found themselves immobilized in the crush.

"How about coming out this afternoon?"

"I'm sorry, Wilyan, but I don't think I can make it."

"Okay."

He had promised on numerous occasions to go on a Coco Tiers junket with Wilyan on some late afternoon before dusk, before it was too dark to see the snipe flying around in droves over the swamp behind the Hindu coolie barracks. It was not the distance from Colon—that was nothing—which had prevented Felix from going. It was merely that he had happened one morning to see the expression on Wilyan's face as a flock of parokeets dipping, wheeling and gaily chattering appeared in the sky above the schoolhouse.

"Oh, boy! What a party!" Wilyan had cried. And with his lips tightly compressed he had taken out his slingshot and winged one of the parokeets.

"Jesus!"

"What's up, boy?"

Across the road from the schoolhouse the horizon had suddenly darkened. The engine for the 11 o'clock passenger train from Colon to Panama was passing by, proceeding to its point of departure with a swift, easily flowing rhythm. It hardly made a sound. The driver sat awkwardly twisted round in his seat, leaning out of the window with one hand reaching up behind him on the throttle, while the arm of the other hand rested on the sill. His jaw was set as though carved out of granite. The gleam in his blue eyes under the jut of his cap was cold, remote. He was staring dead ahead of him . . . along the engine's rear and up the line to the Colon depot. As it passed the switch something in blue fluttered out from under the wheels of the locomotive, rolled over and over on the grass and then lay quite still.

Speedily and in a hush the forward movement into the class rooms was checked, then it went into reverse. One thought seemed to dominate the now backwardly flowing sweep of the pupils: how to get down off the verandah with a minimum of delay. Soon everyone was running across the road with 'Old Tab,' his elbows bent and his bald head agleam in the sun, bustling along in the front.

Teacher and pupils gathered in silence round the body of the Negro workman. Now and then the body, lying face downwards on the grass beside a dripping oil can and no longer tumbling with life and vigour, merely quivered. The big locomotive had performed a neat surgical operation upon it. One arm was cleanly severed at the shoulder and the blood was bubbling up over the meaty stump in a thick, purple dark ooze.

Hoof beats sounded on the road. The beats grew soft, then louder and urgently near on the crisp dry grass. Then a Canal Zone police officer galloped up. Instinctively the circle formed by 'Old Tab' and his charges widened out. The officer dismounted, threw the reins over the horse's head and drew his baton. He was short and bandy in the legs and he walked with a quick rolling swagger. The brim of his tasseled hat was slanted forward almost on a level with his eyes.

"Break it up!" cried the officer, as though sensing a threat to the freedom of the transit. "What do you think this is—part of your playground?"

"But officer," began 'Old Tab,' not daring to call his name, "this poor man has met with an accident—"

"Get back there, I say!" cried the officer, getting a tight grip on the baton and eyeing the mass of uncovered Negro heads with a kind of misty impartiality, "Stand back!"

The circle widened out still further.

"Come, children," said 'Old Tab' in a whisper. Then slowly and in silence teacher and pupils moved across the grass, crossed the road and mounted the schoolhouse steps. One boy failed to complete the ascent. Felix Prout who, turning with one hand on the banister, had stopped midway up the steps to gaze back across the road.

The horse, a deep chestnut, was nibbling the turf. Its mane, hanging forward, almost obscured the white spot on its forehead. Gathering up the reins the officer leapt into the saddle and turning the horse's head round in the direction whence he had come, set off at a canter, lightly using the spurs. Opposite the steps at the upper end of the schoolhouse the officer crossed the road. Then he turned and slowly rode through the cool, dark line of shadow projecting from the end of the verandah roof.

"Come on, Prout. It's time to get back into class."

"Yes, teacher."

Felix's gaze fluttered round from the figure on the horse. On the verandah, towering high above him, 'Old Tab' stood with swelling neck and jutting jaw gazing at Corporal Stroud resuming his beat along the Mount Hope Road.

"I know how you feel," said 'Old Tab' sternly, not looking at him, "but you can't stand there dreaming."

"No, teacher."

IV

The building comprised a single enormous room with a highly polished floor and bare rafters in the ceiling. (There was one small corner that was partitioned off.) It was wedged lengthwise in the flank of a hillock and supported by piles standing in tall grass beside the tracks opposite the railway station at Mount Hope. A driveway led across the tracks up to the entrance at the northern end of the building, facing a fanwise arrangement of railway lines on the eastern side of which was the road over the causeway linking *Tierra Firme* to the old island of Manzanillo on which the twin cities of Colon and Cristobal were built.

Pushing open the wire-screened door, Felix went straight to the long table jammed up against the window in the messenger boys' corner. All the other boys, with the exception of Obi Clements, the senior one, who fetched the mail twice daily from the Post Office at Cristobal were flying like bell-hops in a hotel from one white, shirt-sleeved clerk to another far back in the hazy depths of the room. To Felix, fresh from running an errand in the sun, the window was like an oven's mouth. He sat before it, mopping his face with a handkerchief.

Caught in a swirl of dust Obi was coming up the road. Much older than the other boys Obi, who was all head, shoulders and legs, was mounted on the Department's mule. The mail pouch was hitched to the saddle and Obi's long, blue-trousered legs dangled outside the stirrups. His feet almost touched the ground.

Merely to sit and watch through the window's dusty wire screen Obi and the mule struggling along in the white eddying dust and the blazing heat of the early afternoon sun was enough to make Felix's eyes smart. He closed and opened them, closed and opened them. He nodded his head drowsily. Once, twice—

What's that?

He jumped up as though he'd seen a ghost and leaning over the table, glimpsed through a corner of the screen the rump and swishing tail of a chestnut horse disappearing from view.

"It cannot be!" cried Felix, now fully awake. "It just cannot be!"

Had Corporal Stroud followed him to Mount Hope? Had he had his beat extended so that it now included the Depot? What was the officer up to? What was he trying to do? Was he looking for an opportunity to put a bullet into him too?

Running to the door Felix pulled it open and stepped down upon the landing at the top of a short flight of steps. The horse, rounding a pile of timber driven into the ground at the end of a line of track, was slowly descending the gravel path to the Printing Plant. A Canal Zone police officer was mounted on the horse but his legs were encased in puttees of a dark greenish grey, not in shining leather. His hat sat straight on his head, not tilted at the back. His neck was not thin, deeply tanned and freckled. It was thick, bull-like and jet black.

Felix crept back in out of the sun. He was feeling rather foolish but none the less relieved. It would not be at all funny if Corporal Stroud, bent on his destruction, was now lurking around the Depot.

"What's the matter? Are you deaf? Can't you hear Mr. Cornelius ringing?"

"Okay, I'll get it!"

He streaked off across the mirror of the floor, swerving to avoid a collision with what always seemed to him when he came into the room with his eyes full to blackness with the glare of the sun like an iridescent, enormously blown-up soap bubble anchored on a stand. (It was only the ice water bottle.) Around the room's dusk-filled perimeter lights shone. There was the glow of desk lamps whose green shades matched the ones which almost all the clerks wore over their eyes. The chief clerk wore an eyeshade, but not the Quartermaster or Helmut Cornelius, the requisition clerk. Old Hel' was a German from Milwaukee . . . blond, with a receding chin, a long pointed nose, an enormous waist-line and short legs.

"See that the foreman at No. 8 gets this," cried Helmut Cornelius, waddling round from behind the big roll-top desk in the corner.

Felix grasped the folded sheet of paper and kept on going. . . . pushing open the door, which continued to swing to and fro, on to a verandah and hurrying over the covered bridge—down by one side of which lay, deep in water lilies, a stagnantly oozing drain—which connected the administrative office of the Depot with the store-house.

The road curved down from Guava Ridge into the silence, the grey ghostliness, the desolation of a jungle stretching endlessly over a swamp. It was a concrete road with a rounded surface and sloping edges as if the threat of obliteration was forever lurking beside it.

Manchineel trees, laden with yellow poison fruit, lined both sides. The fallen berries, turning black in the gooey suction mud, floated like corks on a fisherman's net. Here and there through gaps in the trees appeared a wide expanse of the swamp . . . filled with the trunks of fallen trees and the leafless, bone-white specters of dead and slowly dying trees.

Ping! Ping! Ping! . . . that was the music the other boys at the Depot were now hopping and jumping to. Going from one clerk to another, from one desk to another, carrying slips of paper; or, as a kind of nerve-test, waiting upon the Quartermaster himself . . . a short, wiry little man with a gruff voice, who, in his Army captain's uniform, stumped in and out of the office speaking to no one. Tiptoe in, close the door softly and stand over him with a blotter to blot and remove the requisitions and orders piled up on the big mahogany desk before him as fast as he signed them. Knowing all the time that one false clumsy move would provoke a swift upward glance and a snarl of disgust. . . .

The ground under Felix's feet had been dredged up from Manzanillo Bay within Felix's own memory and the music of the pipelines through which the soil had flowed was still in his ears. What was it that had produced the fine churning sound, the rattle as of dry pumpkin seeds in a gourd? Oyster shells, fragments of a coral reef, the skeletons of blue-water fish?

"Oh, Felix."

"Yeah."

"Have you decided yet what you're going to put on your fob?"

"Not yet."

"How about a shark's tooth mounted in silver? It shouldn't cost so very much. Or maybe something in ivory or even gold."

"Maybe."

The lumps of reddish clay in the dirt trains hurrying down from Mindi to lay on Lesseps Beach the foundations for a row of new steel and concrete piers had often been studded with the smoke-blue gleams of sharks' teeth. Now, if the teeth could have been found on a hill so far inland—the sharks must have come to grief at some pretty remote geologic epoch, before the emergence of the Andes chain from the sea—then surely there was a good prospect of finding one or two specimens in the hard, pink and white, shell-encrusted soil pumped up only a year or two ago from the depths of a bay infested with sharks. . . .

"Hey, you!"

Felix's hopefully straying gaze rose from the ground.

"Where do you think you're going?" asked the sentry at the gate. A bayonet was fixed in the rifle over his shoulder and an automatic was strapped in a holster to his thigh. The marine's face was flushed an angry pink.

"I, sir?"

"Yes, you!"

"Back to the Quartermaster's Department at Mount Hope, sir."

Don't you know that you can't get out of here without a pass?"

"Yes, sir."

"Then where is your pass?"

"Here it is, sir."

The fruit on the thick, overhanging line of guava trees on the slope had begun to ripen. Felix reached up, picked a yellow one and bit into it.

"H'mmm!"

He went from tree to tree looking for the ripe ones within reach and devouring them. His ear tingled. He slapped his cheek. A bee buzzed. He looked up and found that he was standing beneath a hive.

"Holy smokes!"

He moved on, knee deep in the grass, pulled down a bough and proceeded to denude it of the ripe guavas. A shadow, swaying backwards and forwards, fell about him. He thought it was a kite, but who would be flying a kite in the Depot's scrap metal yard? Or from the old French Canal Company building falling into decay among the mulberry trees on the hillock? He looked up through a break in the foliage and saw a large beautiful bird fluttering overhead.

"Go away!" cried Felix, striking at the bird with his cap. But the bird pecked at the cap and kept flying up and down.

"Shoo!" cried Felix, the guava sticking in his throat; but the bird, fluttering up, plunged down again. It lunged at the hive, flew off, up and around—filling the air with bees. Still hovering, the bird suddenly fluttered down on him.

"Jesus!" cried Felix, holding his head.

He flew down the hillside through clumps of Spanish needles, crawled under the scrap cars in the yard and climbed on to the storehouse platform. When he got back to the messenger boys' corner, not at all sure that he did not have a couple of bees somewhere in his jumper, Obi was standing by the long table in front of the window surrounded by the other boys.

"I'll go," said one of the six.

"Me too," said another

"You can count me in," chipped in a third.

"Go where?" asked Felix.

Obi turned to him: "How about you, Felix? Do you want to earn five dollars extra?"

His wage, like that of the other boys except Obi, who received a little more, was seventeen dollars and fifty cents a month.

"Do I?" cried Felix." I should think so! But how . . . doing what?"

"All you got to do," said Obi, "is to go down to the Cristobal docks with us in the morning to meet the boat from New Orleans. Only you will have to strip and put on a grass skirt."

"But I haven't got a grass skirt," said Felix meekly.

"You don't have to worry about that, man, I got enough for all o' we.

"Strip? Put on a grass skirt . . ."

"You will get time off," said Obi. "The chief clerk is the one that gave us the job. They are having a convention or something."

"No, I'm sorry," said Felix, "but I don't think I can go."

The following morning before going to work Felix sneaked over from Colon to the Cristobal docks. Everything in which Obi appeared to have had a hand was in readiness by the time the boat pulled in alongside the pier. The boys, clad in grass skirts and grass anklets, formed a lane from the end of the gangway. Each one was gently waving a coconut palm. The chief clerk, a big, sandy-haired man, had on a Palm Beach suit, his usual attire; but he was now wearing a red fez with it. (There was a crescent in gilt on the fez.) As he strode about the pier, seeing to this and that, the chief clerk was closely followed by Obi carrying a spear. Obi's kinky, long-grown hair was fuzzed out over his ears and his mouth, eyes and nostrils were encircled with chalk, while a tuft of ostrich plumes adorned the bulging, uptilted seat of the little grass skirt that he wore.

When the passengers began to disembark the "Gold" employees with their wives and children on the pier, waving flags and handkerchiefs, sent up a cheer.

"Hip, hip! Hooray!"

"Hip, hip!"

When the outburst had subsided the boys, led by Obi, broke into a song and dance. "O! Bongo-lay!" they sang, stamping their feet and turning slowly round and round waving the palms. "O! bongo-lay!"

After a while Felix slipped away from the crowd of onlookers. He had to hurry if he was going to catch the 7 o' clock work train to Mount Hope.

Outside the kiosk at the entrance to the Cristobal docks a Negro police officer stopped him.

"Hey, boy, where you going?"

"To work, sir."

"Let's see your pass."

"Pass?"

"Yes, don't you know you gots to have a pass to get in and out of the Cristobal docks?"

"I didn't know, sir."

"Where do you work?"

"Mount Hope, sir."

"Let's see your brass check."

"Here it is, sir."

"What is it, Corporal?"

A white police officer with the knotted end of the tassel round his hat drooping forward over the brim, stepped out of the kiosk. His blue eyes flashed.

"A stowaway?"

"No, I am not a stowaway," cried Felix. "I live in Colon. I work in the Quartermaster's Department at Mount Hope. I just went to see the Shriners."

"How did you get through the gate?"

"When no one was looking, sir."

"Haven't I seen you somewhere before?"

"Yes, sir."

"Aren't you the son of—wasn't your father a Zone policeman?"

"Yes, sir. He got shot at Tabernilla."

Sergeant Stroud turned to the Negro officer. "I know this boy," he said. "It's all right."

"Thank you, sir!" cried Felix.

"Brine"*

Excerpts of a novel
ca. 1923

[I]

The taxi cut its way through a labyrinth of traffic. The tall, black, shadowy pillars of the elevated [train] shot past it with the velocity of a whirlwind. Her face close to the window, Nora gazed out on the creeping expanse of folk sprawling on the sidewalks of Tenth Avenue.

"Got the olive oil, Jim?" she asked, "You didn't forget it, did you?"

He shifted the baby from one leg to the other. "Here it is," he said, "yes, I got it."

He relapsed again into silence. To Nora it was unbearable. All he did was strain anxious eyes on the trundling course of the taxi.

"Hazel's getting the eczemas, too," Nora sulked, alarmed, "I don't know what I'm going to do with these children."

This created a stir within him. He spoke, without turning his head, hollowly to her. "I warned you not to let them play with those mangy children downstairs. You're too hard ears,* that's what's the matter with you. You won't listen to a thing I tell you."

Involuntarily there rose to his mind's eye the vision of Lizzie Cumberbatch's children, raggedy, scrawny, unwashed. They had been in America now about... Oh, the Lord only knows how long... but the dirt and mange and scrofula with which they [were] afflicted back in St. Eustatius* still clung desperately to them.

Jim spat disgustedly. "God, to think that I've descended to this." The thought of the Cumberbatch kids, the sores on their legs, the dirt all over them, the boils and green glazed pus spattering over them, rose to him.

Near to him, its eyes bright and gay, a cherub, for it was something of that, of gold and pearl, gorged itself with the mystery of the dusky window before it. Threading its way through the mist the taxi sped on towards the water front.

Near them, buried in the crook of Nora's arm, a girl child slept . . . was breathing softly. Looking at it, at the vision of a cow's udders on its cheeks, one thought of a bed of yellow tulips in May.

"Jim . . . you must rest . . . sleep . . . you hear what I say?"

"All right."

It didn't mean anything, his saying that to her, but Nora hadn't had time in her strenuous life in America as a married woman to know her husband that well.

"And you mustn't bother about us, you hear?"

Ready to be off, off to the West Indies, Nora was anxious to be on good terms with her husband. She wanted to go home with the burden of their life together off her shoulders. She wanted to at least make him feel that she still loved and cared for him.

Abruptly he swung round to her. "Sure the paper said two?"

"Yes," Nora replied, "I'm sure." And Nora looked worried.

Again he fastened his eyes, shifty under the strain, on the jolting trail ahead. "It'd be hell if you missed this boat," he murmured, "after all the trouble I've been through."

"That clock there says twenty to two," he remarked presently. The boat was scheduled to sail at two. And they were still fifty blocks away.

He leaned over to the driver. "See if you can't speed 'er up a bit there, old man," he yelled above the roar of the engine.

He sat back again. The baby's bonnet was awry. He adjusted it; he did it with the deftlessness of a sleep walker. A lump of coal dust, caked out of the dancing void, fell on the baby's faint vermilion cape. He flipped it off.

Nora put a hand on his arm. It crawled, trembled, felt its way up to him, that hand. "Don't forget, Jim," she begged, "to fix up the place tomorrow. You know Miss Cumberbatch, how snippy she is. Be only too glad to say, she and that old Miss Cushnie on the top floor, 'gal, she went away 'n left all she dirt for me to clean up.' So all you do don't forget to go up and tidy the place for me. Take the trash down stairs . . . after you've got a rest . . . sleep late tomorrow . . . must be so tired . . . Get some sleep, hear? And all you do don't throw away those lace curtains I sewed for Miss Green. Take 'em back to her on Bradhurst Avenue and tell her when I get to Kingston I'll drop her a line."

"Look at that child!"

The car swerved, bumped over a pyramid of stone, then kept rolling on its journey.

"Missed her by so much. These Italian kids, they set you crazy."

"Pick up the ribbon," Nora continued, unmoved by the near-tragedy, "don't let any of it go astray. I can use all those scraps at home. I can make patch work with them. Don't forget. Save all the scraps of ribbon."

He thought: patch in the crutch is nothing much but patch in the knee is poverty.

Honking tugs patroled the Hudson. From across its silvery surface came the unmistakable scent of the sea, the odor of crated cattle, of hogs and pigs buried in graves of black excretion, the grime and filth of steel mills and sugar refineries pouring forth tons of iron grey smoke; of the slow unostentatious decay of everything along the river front.

From this languishing spectacle he was forced to bring his ears to Nora talking again. "Promise me," she was saying, "please . . . tell me, Jim . . . you haven't a girl . . . tell me . . . some woman who is turning your head against us . . . tell me . . ."

In Nora's voice there was a note of pathos that always got the best of him. It reminded him of the cry of a wounded doe.

"You think money is everything," she said for want of something more to the point.

"It is," he said dryly, "in America." He bitterly went on, "After I pay the taxi man I'll have about eight cents left. Eight cents, imagine! I'll buy an apple for three and with the nickel I'll ride back to Harlem."

That seemed a trivial matter to Nora; she waved it aside. Hers was a more vital, a more fundamental approach to their problem. "Money isn't every thing," she repeated enigmatically.

He shifted uneasily. "When did you find that out?" he countered, "Just now?"

With the Caribbean dashing up on sands of gold and coral, rose and white [. . . .], to wet their unshod feet, he could have imagined Nora digging her golden toes, in it, her head drooped in modesty, as she murmured, "Last week you said you'd come to stay with us till we went home."

A wave of disgust rose within his breast. He looked at her with rancid scorn. "You seem to forget," he declared bitterly, "that I slept with you last night. Aren't you satisfied with that. . . . wasn't that enough . . . what more do you want. . . . God, what a cow you are!"

It didn't outrage Nora. Weaned to this sort of this, [sic] she gulped it down unnoticed. "But Jim . . ." she cried with that dog pity of hers, "don't you know . . . can't you realize . . . see . . . that I need to be happy . . . to be

loved ... and made much of. A woman in my condition needs the comfort-
ing arms of a man ..." She broke off, her fragile frame shook, Nora sobbed.

And Jim was moved. He felt, groped towards the girl. With a hidden passionate joy he realized that, despite their past differences, the awful tragedy
of their lives, he still had eyes to see that Nora was a woman to be desired.

It was only for a moment, however, for Jim, who had grown to steel his
heart at beauty, discovered with an uprush of disgust that what beauty there
was to be gloated over in Nora was that of a woman ... with child.

He turned and gazed out the window.

II

The taxi drew up before the entrance to the wharf. Facing the Layland pier
there stretched a queue of trucks, swollen to the ribs, waiting for the signal
from the gateman before they bolted in. The drivers, white men with faces
black and limned with the dust and dirt of rain and sun, snow and hail, toil
and murk; horses and mules with the brunt of age and suffering; the tar-
paulins shielding the rich, unwieldy cargoes; it might have been a medieval
caravan about to plunge into the teeming sands of the Sahara.

"See if you can't drive up a little closer," he said to the driver. "The
gateman says it's all right. There ... that'll do. Come Junior, we get out
here. Careful Nora, let me look after the bag. You take Hazel. Be careful
now...."

Wharf hands swarmed about the mouth of the pier. Their lips red and
greasy with victual they were clad in overalls and dungarees, and were smoking and carrying on hilariously. One of them, a prize fighter, with sunken,
scarlet eyes and large, high, swollen cheek bones, was shadow boxing. Behind a bale of cotton an old Negress, noted from the North to the East River
for her beef balls and hot biscuits—food that put hair on the strapping black
men's chests—with her mulatto girls, two fat, wide-hipped trollops, was en-
deavoring at no trivial cost to keep track of those who had paid for their
day's meal and those who had not.

The *Mozambique* was a British tramp that brought balata* and red wood
and cattle. On its return voyage it sometimes took a passenger or two.

The steward, a Nevis octoroon, in shirt and trousers, bare of arm and
browned with the sun, met Jim at the top of the gang plank [and] took Hazel
out of his arms. He was a quiet, soft voiced man, who kept his eyes on the

ground while he spoke; with large, thick shoulders, a hairy russet brown skin, and big wooden-like arms.

"I wish they'd take this medicine chest out of here," Nora murmured as the steward disappeared out of her stateroom. Jim put Hazel, who was fast asleep, on the bunk and gave Junior a tangerine.

"God, I wonder if there are other passengers on the boat," Nora kept saying as she untied the [baby's] bonnet. "I'd hate to be the only passenger on it . . . me and these two children."

Fagged out,* Jim sat on the edge of the bunk. "It's all right," he said, "there's another woman on the boat . . . an old lady going to St. Kitts. You won't be lonesome."

"Oh-o," Nora breathed, "that's more like it. For I remember when I was coming here one of those sailors started to get fresh with me. Good thing Agnes was on board with me."

"All right, Nora," he remarked, again, "you haven't anything to fear, I've arranged with the steward to see that everything'll be all right. If anything goes wrong go to him, he'll see that you're protected."

She finished untying the baby's bonnet. Having had the steward bring her trunk in the room, she opened it, took out the things, and began arranging the room which was to be her abode for the journey.

"Well," he rose at last, "I guess everything is all right, Nora. I'll run along now. Nothing more I can do. Good bye . . . Tell Agnes howdy do for me . . . don't forget. And if you're seasick, the steward will be glad to look out for you and the children. I've fixed it up with him. Good bye, Nora."

Contrary to his expectations Nora did not make an outcry. "Come kiss me, Jim," she snuffled, "kiss me good bye." She moved up to him. It was a slow, languorous movement. It possessed all the magic, all the unseen power of her being. One foot across the threshold Jim stopped. Coyless, she drew her lips to his, threw her arms around his neck, and gave him one long crushing hug.

III

He descended the gang plank besieged on all sides by motley emotions. The watchman, a gigantic Irishman, with a nose red and shiny and sprayed with warts and pus-ripe ochre, languished at the gate. A night stick swung from his arm. He strolled up and down the pier's portals like a great towering giant. A shaggy tousled head on which sat an official cap disappeared up in to the horizontal regions. From the misty roof fell the gateman's booming voice.

"Here's that rope, son."

He took it. "Oh, yes," he said, and lingered. One of Lizzie Cumberbatch's children had loaned it to him to tie the baby's carriage on to the side of the taxi. He had promised to return it to them.

The watchman swung his night stick. "Folk's goin' back t'other side?" he inquired impishly. "Yes," the black man didn't dare look up. He sensed, by that vaguely obsequious attitude people, not only menials, have of indicating their wants, that the gateman was expecting, no, actually, courting a tip. It was futile, however, for he possessed but eight cents left in his pocket. He fondled the rope. Through his erupting consciousness raced a thought; the curse of this infernal tip system. Up in the black belt where it was fierce if he went into a restaurant and spent fifteen cents he had to tip the waiter or waitress five. If he didn't she'd mark him out and should he enter there again she'd go out of her way to see to it that he obtained scant courtesy, the due of cheap skates.

The gateman interrupted his mental peregrinations. "Easier on you now, ain't it?" he observed, twirling the stick. The Negro didn't answer. He kept playing with the rope. "Folks gon' fer good?" The Irishman pursued in the manner of whites to blacks of their obvious social stratum. "No," said Jim, looking up at the other's bearded, bumpy chin, "wife's sick; sending her 'way for a change. She'll be back in a little while." "Oh, I see," the other rejoined. "Well, good luck to ye." He made to move off.

Breathing heavily the Negro bristled alertly. "So long," he said, and stumbling over a splinter of the rotting wood which, sticking up menacingly out of the pine paved pier, nearly tripped him over, disappeared into the screen of hot grainy dust which shielded the cottages and dilapidated houses along West Street.

Around the corner he stopped outside a Greek fruit store. Through the yellow window he saw a woman of the isles, old, stooping, mustard-colored, behind the counter. Close to the window he looked at bunches of luscious grapes, oranges, apples, pears. He jingled the money in his pocket.

"Give me an apple for three cents," he said, entering. Now that he was inside free of the bewitching snare of the sun he saw her as she was. She was a viper. Everything about her suggested greed . . . greed of gold . . . greed of power . . . greed of self . . . Mouse faced, she possessed lips that were a trail[,] a thread of hot glue. The eyes, sharp and piercing, were two balls of blazing fire. The nose was sharp, small, pointed, Semitic.* A wary shawl was wrapped about her gaunt chest and bony shoulders. She stood before the candy show case an animated cadaver firm as the rock of ages.

She shook her head at the Negro's request.

"A pear then," he repeated smiling. Again the eagle wagged her head. "What have you got for three cents then? Give me three cents worth of anything you've got." Without a word she bent over to the show case. She threw two rolls of sugar coated dates on the counter. He put the pennies in her outstretched palm and strolled out.

⁜

He must remember to get a blind for the window. A green one. To pull down at night, to keep the sun out of his eyes in the morning, [and] to help preserve the warmth in the room. For if he was a newcomer Nora was a newer one still with winter's baptism ahead of her.

She was shaking him.

"Jim! Get up, please. It's seven o'clock."

"H'm?"

Now that he was no longer in lodgings and there was Nora to do for him he could stay in bed a little longer, eat breakfast at home and still be in time for work.

Illusion!

He lay on his side with his face turned away from the sunbeam. 'All in'— whacked. The exertions of the last few weeks had taken so much out of him. First, he had had to take a couple of days off from work to go down to Nora's sister's and brother-in-law's place in Washington to get a line on things. (The blue and gold had gone from the October sky and light flurries of snow had already begun to powder the ground.) Then, on his return to Brooklyn, he had had to start looking around for an apartment . . . evening after evening and at week-ends until he found one: a cold-water flat, two rooms and kitchenette, on the top floor of a two storey frame house. Then he had to traipse up and down Myrtle Avenue and Smith Street to get, mostly from secondhand dealers and hire-purchase furniture stores ("Dollar down and a dollar a week"), the stuff to put into it.

"I don't know how to manage this coal stove. Come light it for me."

He threw off the covers and leapt out of bed. He had before him, energizing and enflaming him, a sudden vision of Nora's sister Agnes, her face stained with tears of foreboding, looking out the window at the leaves falling from the elm trees on "U" Street and bewailing the departure of the autumnal glories of Washington, while Nora was getting larger and larger and paler and paler.

"Here, let me show you."

He pattered out into the kitchenette, crumpled up a sheet of newspaper and stuffed it down on to the clean-swept grate.

"I only got these and the scuttle of coal yesterday afternoon," he said, untying one of the bundles of kindling. "Last thing I did before I went to the Pennsylvania Station to meet you."

He covered the paper with pieces of wood and then carefully packed small lumps of coal around the top. "No kerosene on this," he cautioned as he struck a match. "No kerosene the way you people do in the West Indies with your coalpot fires out in the yard."

"Who people?" cried Nora. Her upturned face, now flushed a golden yellow was close to his. Her black luminous eyes danced. Her lips, moulded in a disdainful curve, trembled with the imminence of a smile. She was trying to meet him halfway, to show him that she too possessed a sense of humour: a side of her which she had not much of an opportunity to reveal to him hitherto.

"You people, no?" cried Jim warily.

"As if you aren't one too!" cried Nora with a bubble of laughter.

"I am not," growled Jim with a frown, "one of you West Indian. . . ."

He wanted to use a word that was appropriate to their mood but he was not quite sure that it would not have been dangerous to do so.

"Why don't you say it?" teased Nora. "Why don't you say what you wanted to say?"

She had been in America only since the beginning of summer but she already knew that Negroes in moments of levity—even the foreign-born ones, the thing was so catching—sometimes referred to each other as "niggers."

Jim watched the flame leaping up through the smoke. "I'm a Guianese," he said. "Don't forget. A 'Mud-Head' from Demerara, if you like. I'm not sensitive about it."

"A what?"

"A Demerarian."

"Is not that the same as a Bajan?"

"No, it is not!"

186 : Unpublished Writings

He put the lid on the stove and opened the draught. Then he pattered back into the bedroom with the fire zooming and fast building up to a roar.

"I thought . . ."

"You thought!" mocked Jim, pulling his pajama jacket over his head. He tossed the garment on the bed and went round to the washstand in the corner between the head of the bed and the wall that divided the bedroom from the sitting room. He picked up the jug off the floor and started to pour water into the basin.

". . . . it was the same."

⋮

"My, this looks good, Nora!" cried Jim, eyeing the slice of melon, the plate of eggs and bacon and the steaming cup of coffee in front of him. As he ate Jim slowly came to a decision. "Tell you what I will do, Nora," he said, trying not to frown. "I will give you the money each week and let you do the shopping. I don't think I will have the time to do it and I am sure I am no good at it anyway."

Nora sprinkled a little salt on her melon. "All right, Jim," she answered gravely. "I can still move around, I guess . . . Oh, Jim!" She reached out and touched his hand. She looked into his eyes in a way that made him feel slightly uncomfortable. "Let us try and make a go of it!"

"Why, Nora!"

"Let us love and care for one another and *stick together!*"

"Why, of course, silly!"

"Let us show my folks they don't have to worry about us." She paused. Then, without lowering her gaze, she went on evenly: "Then when baby comes I am going to try and get mother to come and stay with us. Then I will go out and get a job and help you realize your ambition."

She picked up the spoon and flushed with a new-found sense of pride, resolution and faith in the future, attacked the melon.

Jim took a sip of coffee. His ambition? Nora did not know what she was talking about! He only knew that ages ago in Colon he used to attach a lot of importance to the need for a good grounding in Latin and mathematics if he was going to matriculate at an American college and then go on to Meharry* or some other Negro university to study medicine. In Colon there were no schools where a Negro immigrant boy like him could get such a grounding, but after a while he had found a way out of the difficulty: outside the door of a one-room flat in a "G" Street tenement. The balcony there, wide and gently sloping, was 'screened off.' Inside the square thus created another room of a sort had sprouted—a white glow of canvas in the night. Here on a form he used to sit, along with a handful of other boys, three evenings a week, sweltering in the heat of the oil lamp on the table as they faced a former master at Wolmer's College in Jamaica—conjugating Latin verbs, reading Caesar's Gallic Wars and wrestling with equations in algebra. If, much later on, he had not lost all his savings when the Bank of the Canal Zone failed (none of the directors was involved in any unpleasantness following the crash, in spite of rumours about the 'faulty investment of the depositors' money' in a development project that was to turn the savannahs along the road to the vine-covered ruins of Old Panama into a new Balboa), Jim also knew what would have happened. He would in all probability have been in Washington now "getting the man's stuff" in the Medical School at Howard University like Agnes' husband, Hubert Wilson.

When Nora spoke again she seemed to be impelled by a desire to let Jim into a secret which she deemed the time was now ripe to withhold from him no longer. "You know," she said, "my daddy is blind. . . ."

"Blind?"

"Yes."

"I didn't know that."

"He has been blind ever since I can remember, but instead of his affliction softening his nature it has made him cranky and disagreeable and hard to live with, the black devil!"

Jim wrinkled his forehead. Should he get up and consult the mirror on the dresser and so give himself the frivolous satisfaction of knowing there could not possibly be any confusion in Nora's mind about what he looked like and, in particular, about the colour of his skin?

"I can't help it, I suppose," she went on, but I hate very black people. I don't have any luck with them. That is why I am so sorry for my mother. She is white, all her children are away from home—either in Cuba, Central America or here—and yet she won't leave my father. And he is always making things so hard for her."

The spasm of pain and distress that was mirrored in Jim's eyes gradually transformed itself into tender, animated regard. "Look, that's not a bad idea, Nora, your mother coming here to live with us. Then we would be free to go out together often. To the movies, I mean. You and I one evening, one of us and your mother the next and so on. So that there will always be someone to stay in and look after the place."

He got up and went into the bedroom. When he came out again he had on his hat and overcoat. He took leave of her at the door.

"What time will you be back?"

"Oh, about six o'clock."

She saw him descend into the darkness of the stairs. She could not see him when he reached the bottom, but she could hear him as he turned and moved through the hall. She heard him trip down another flight of stairs, open the door and close it softly behind him. Only then did she turn and go back into the kitchenette.

"The Panama Scandal"*

Essay, ca. 1933–1934

Financial swindles of one sort or another are frequent occurrences in France. Sometimes they go by the name of Stavisky, Oustric* or Panama. But in their essential aims and objects, and in the methods employed by their principals, they all bear a singular resemblance to one another.

Forty years ago the social, economic and political life of France was stirred to its foundations by the revelation of the Panama frauds. A paltry sum of $262,600,000.00 garnered from the "small folk who lodge the results of their little economies in woolen stockings" was sunk in a canal that had to be abandoned, midway in the course of construction, through lack of funds.

The man at the bottom of the affair was Ferdinand de Lesseps, the builder of the Suez Canal.

Now Ferdinand de Lesseps was not the sort of man who would set out deliberately to swindle anybody. He was too covetous of glory, too full of patriotism and pride.

This love of glory and self-esteem, which shone through every act of M. de Lesseps, was the motive that led him, against the sober advice of friends and family, to undertake the building of the Panama Canal. It was the will-o'-the wisp that was to plunge him, at the age of 88, into irretrievable disgrace.

When asked to associate himself in the enterprise, M. de Lesseps had answered: "*Quand un général a gagné une bataille, si on lui propose d'en gagner une seconde, il ne recule jamais!*" (When a general has won a battle, if someone proposes to him to win a second one, he never retreats.)*

This second battle M. de Lesseps set out to win at any price. It was to be fought in a country of which he knew practically nothing and against the most implacable odds. A cut had to be made through the Andes range at Culebra; the Chagres River, with its numerous tributaries, had to be diverted from its course; in addition to steam shovels, dredges and excavators, even labourers had to be imported from abroad and their lives ensured against the ravages of malaria and yellow fever. And all this in a country that was savage, bankrupt, unhealthy and continually rent by civil wars.

The plan of battle was drawn up as early as 1876—by General Etienne Turr, a Hungarian army officer. [. . .] General Turr's brother-in-law was Lieut. Lucien N. B. Wyse, a French naval officer of genius. [. . .] Wyse was selected by Turr to make a survey of the Isthmus and to advise upon the efficacy of the Darien route. Wyse's labours in 1877–78 led to the scrapping of the Darien project and the substitution of a plan for a sea level canal to run across the Isthmus of Panama.

The plan was submitted to M. de Lesseps who, in the absence of a better one, accepted it. It was in reality, sound, fool-proof, air-tight.

M. de Lesseps was now ready to proceed. So ready was he that he drew up a contract with Couvreux & Hersent, a Paris firm of contractors, to dig the canal for the sum of $102,400,000.—a fact he pompously displayed in the *Bulletin* founded to sing the praises of Panama.

And to give the venture a "non-partisan" air and to disarm the Americans who were also interested in a canal to link the Atlantic and Pacific oceans, M. de Lesseps decided to call a "Congress of Savants" to deliberate upon the question.

This Congress, which met in Paris in May 1879 with M. de Lesseps in the chair, was from start to finish a miserable fiasco. Of the 135 delegates in attendance 61 were from England, the United States, Holland, Mexico, Germany, Italy and China. Of the other 74, who were all Frenchmen, 13 were employees of the Suez Canal while the balance were either "yes-men" in the pay of M. de Lesseps or parasitic nobles formerly of the court of Louis Napoleon.

As was to be expected, the Congress approved the Wyse project. Two months later M. de Lesseps secured the rights and concessions of the *Société Civile* for the sum of $2,000,000.

Everything was ready. The Americans were beaten on their own ground; the "small folk" all over France who were to bear the financial burdens of the enterprise had been properly impressed by the display of medals and titles and eminent foreigners at the Congress. After all, the show was as much for them as for anybody else.

Only one obstacle remained and that was Wyse.

M. de Lesseps was inflexible on the point. He had promised Wyse all during the work of the surveys the job of Chief of Construction Works in case the canal was ever started up. But now that M. de Lesseps felt he no longer needed Wyse, he decided to change his mind.

The truth of the matter was M. de Lesseps was apprehensive of Wyse's great ability. He was afraid if he appointed him *Chef de Chantiers* and the canal was ever built that Wyse would get the credit for it. So, as soon as the Congress broke up, he intrigued to break off relations with him.

To raise the money with which to build the canal M. de Lesseps now organized a *société anonyme*, or limited liability company, with a capital of $80,000,000. This sum was "covered" by 800,000. shares of stock which were put on the market at $100. each. Remembering the great fortunes that had been made in the Suez Canal, the public gobbled them up like hot cakes.

Early in 1881 work on the canal began.

Commander Armand Reclus, a naval officer who had served in the Wyse expeditions of 1877–78 was sent out as the Company's General Agent. His chief task was to coordinate the work of Couvreux & Hersent with that of the Company's technical and engineering staff.

A deposit of $150,000. was made with the Colombian government as a guarantee of good faith. To this sum [was] added $700,000. which the Canal Co. gave to the Colombian government partly as a loan in order that it might pay its restive, barefoot soldiery in its feeble attempts to stave off an impending civil war; and partly as a charge for augmenting the police forces at Panama.

The Grand Hotel, a modest hostel overlooking Cathedral Plaza in Panama City, was purchased for $200,000. and turned into the Company's administrative offices on the Isthmus.

A single-track railway, 47 miles long, extended from ocean to ocean along the delta of the Chagres River. It was built in 1850–1855, as a result of the discovery of gold in California, by a New York syndicate at a cost of $6,000,000. It was operating under a deficit and its stock, which had depreciated from $250. to $100. a share, was fluctuating lower and lower on the Wall Street exchanges.

To expedite the dispatch of labourers and machinery to the *chantiers*, the Canal Co. was obliged to avail itself of the services of the railway. And to combat the hostility of the owners, who pushed up their carriage rates to an exorbitant level, the French decided as an "economic measure" to buy up the railway. But the Americans, who proceeded on the hypothesis that the canal could never be built without the railway as an adjunct, were out to drive a hard bargain and extracted from the Canal Co. $25,000,000. for a controlling interest in the line.

A large army of workers, lured by the promise of high wages, was recruited in [the] open market from over as wide an area as Europe, China, Africa and the West Indies. The vast majority, however, consisted of Negroes from Jamaica.

The narrow neck of land across which the canal was to be dug was covered with a network of forests, swamps, rivers and mountains. The dark and humid forests, always lying in a state of semi-inundation, were invested with giant-sized cypresses, scrub, lianas* and parasite vines. They were perpetually alive with the chatter of monkeys and parokeets and the menace of coral snakes, wood ticks and tiger cats. The rivers, animated by the presence of electric eels, *bobo* fish and crocodiles, flowed in every direction. The swamps, full of reeds and the scarlet convolvuli,* served as a breeding place for mosquitoes and horse flies. The sunlit hills of porphyry,* at the bottom of which lay groves of wild bananas, sloped down to the edge of swamps and rivers and drank of their deadly poison.

The workers were housed in thatched cabins in clearings in the jungle; on barges, river boats, scows; in box cars shunted off on railway sidings; in shanties and mud huts and above stores and shops in the numerous villages that had sprung up like mushrooms along the railway line; in vast, hive-like tenements in the slums of Chorillo, Caledonia and Colon.

The wages of white mechanics varied from $5. to $6. per day; of black workers from $2.50 to $2.75; of common labourers from $1.00 to $1.50. [...]

At the end of two years the contract with Couvreux & Hersent was cancelled and Commander Reclus returned to Paris.

Gaston Blanchet was sent out as Director of Works and the monopoly exercised by the one-company system of contracting for the work was broken.

The excavation of the canal was now arranged for a small group of contractors—French, Dutch, British, American and Italian. The experiment was determined upon in an effort to wipe out the abuses which had existed under the old system. But in less than six months, following the death of Gaston Blanchet from yellow fever, the *chantiers* had degenerated into a rabid no-man's land of graft, thievery and corruption. In this awful state of affairs, which was of long duration, the men who profited most were the contractors.

One firm made a profit of 50% on a contract of $3,200,000.; another cleared $2,200,000. on a contract worth $9,000,000. Still another filched a net profit of $2,400,000. on a $9,200,000. contract.

But the man who outdid them all was Alexander Gustave Eiffel, the builder of the Eiffel Tower.

Eiffel had manifested an interest in the canal from the start. He was a delegate to the Congress of Savants and in 1880 accompanied M. de Lesseps on a visit to Panama. At that time he was a noted civil engineer who specialized in the construction of large metal bridges. He hadn't yet secured for himself a measure of immortality by ornamenting the Champs de Mars in Paris with a giant steel tower stretching 985 feet in the sky.

Eiffel was called in at a crucial period in the work. The big contractors had been tried and found wanting; the small ones who succeeded them had proved to be no better. Of the 120,000,000 cubic yards of earth to be excavated to give the canal the required width and depth, only 14,678,856 had been excavated up to January 1886. By this time the Company had already sunk in the canal about $230,000,000—$80,000,000 from the sale of its stock and $150,000,000 subscribed in 1883, through an emission of bond loans.

To make up for lost time,—he had promised to deliver the canal by 1888, by the latest 1889—M. de Lesseps decided on one or two drastic measures. After a long struggle with himself he was ready at last to scrap the sea level canal—it was the one that had succeeded at Suez—in favor of a lock canal. And to free himself from the tyranny and incompetence of contractors M. de Lesseps decided to call in M. Eiffel [. . . .]

Jules Dingler, the successor to Gaston Blanchet, was a jolly little rotund man with a middle class Frenchman's love of good substantial living. In France he had been a Departmental Head in the Ministry of Public Works. Later he was elevated to the post of Director-General of government railways.

Dingler was sent to Panama during a threatened cessation of work, as a result of the spread of malaria and yellow fever. The engineers and mechanics, who began early to sicken and die, were in a constant state of panic;

while the black labourers, who possessed no greater powers of immunity, died like flies. No less than 22,000 workers of all classes perished before the French abandoned the canal.

To 'give the lie' to rumours of disease and death at Panama, M. de Lesseps, in the *Bulletin* drew attention to the conditions existing at Greytown, a seaport town on the Caribbean coast of Nicaragua, where the Americans had started work on a rival canal. M. de Lesseps described Greytown as a *tombeau des européens*,* meanwhile taking great pains to give Panama a clean bill of health.

Dingler, on the eve of embarking at Marseilles, joined the efforts of M. de Lesseps to reassure the *actionnaires** on the health and well-being of the workers. "Only the dissolute take the yellow fever and die at Panama," said M. Dingler. And to show that he was determined to prove what he said, he took along his wife, their grown son and daughter and the young lady's fiancé.

On arriving at Panama M. Dingler ordered the erection of a palatial villa on the side of Ancon Hill. "Dingler's Folly," as the villa was called, cost the Company $90,000.00. A special parlour car, made in the States, was placed at M. Dingler's disposal on his infrequent visits to the *chantiers*. It cost $60,000. to assemble. M. Dingler's son, a lad of twenty, was given a sinecure as Chief of the Department of Posts. His son-in-law-to-be was assigned to one of the *chantiers* with the rank of sub-chef.* Ancon Hill, until then a refuge of wild swine and deer, was turned into a sort of Bois du Boulogne* with fountains, water falls, bridle paths and marble seats.

One M. Gapdaille, a "labour merchant" in Jamaica whom M. Dingler, by a necessary act of charity, had enabled to earn a net profit of 65 francs, or nearly $15, on every Negro sent on contract to Panama, made a gift to Madame Dingler of a fine pair of Arabian horses. After the death of Madame Dingler,—she was the first to go,—the sight of the riderless horses was too painful for M. Dingler to bear. Dingler ordered the horses put to death. For a long time nobody could be found who would do the job, until one day a native came along. The disemboweling of the horses, by the clumsy blows of a *machete*, was a savage affair, the horses expiring after hours of cruel torture. But the expenses of the killing were borne by the Canal Company, not by M. Dingler.

The deaths of the son, daughter and the young lady's fiancé followed hard by. Death, in each case, was due either to malaria or yellow fever.

When, in 1887, Jules Dingler returned to France,—a raving maniac haunted by the terrifying nightmare of Panama,—it was only to be clapped in the mad house.

Late in 1885 M. de Lesseps, again hard pressed for cash, appealed to the French government to come to his aid. He wanted authority to issue *valeurs à lots*, or lottery bonds, to the extent of $120,000,000.00 in an endeavor to raise the money necessary to complete the canal. This was during the second ministry of Jules Ferry. The Minister of Finance, Waldeck-Rousseau, to whom M. de Lesseps was referred, suggested that the request be incorporated in a Bill and presented to the Chamber. As a hereditary noble and a second cousin of the Empress Eugenie, M. de Lesseps, though "the Grand Old Man of France" to the masses of French people, was not in great favour with the Deputies in the Chamber. The Chamber, as then constituted, was dominated by the Radicals and Socialists, who, in addition to their objections to M. de Lesseps on personal grounds, were inclined to look upon the Panama Canal as an imperialistic undertaking.

At its first reading the Bill was hotly opposed from the Left, and in the vote of confidence which followed the government lost its majority and resigned.

On the formation of a new ministry the Bill was again introduced, but before putting it to the vote, the Government proposed to send a naval engineer, M. Armand Rousseau, to report on the condition of the canal works.

M. de Lesseps, who decided to accompany M. Rousseau, represented the trip in the *Bulletin* as a sort of triumphal march. M. Rousseau, he said, was going to Panama "to inaugurate the period of final execution of the maritime canal."

M. Rousseau spent a total of 3 weeks on the *chantiers*. In the report that he submitted to the government in April 1886 he differed with M. de Lesseps on the length of time and amount of money necessary to finish the canal, but expressed no opinion which was calculated to prejudice the Chamber against the Lottery Bond Bill. But the Chamber did not get a chance to vote on the Bill then; it adjourned for the summer recess and M. de Lesseps withdrew the measure.

M. de Lesseps then turned to the "small folk," who seemed to have an inexhaustible store of ready funds, and extracted from them, through the emission of a new series of company bonds, an additional sum of $70,000,000.00. He was "going into society more than ever (since the downfall of the Empire) and was at a dance or dinner almost every evening." His mission to

Berlin to decorate the French Ambassador with the Grand Cordon of the Legion of Honour was timed to coincide with the opening of Bismarck's African Conference.* His decision to dine with the Iron Chancellor was not calculated to stir up friendly feelings in the French Chamber of Deputies, but possibly that was of minor consequence to M. de Lesseps.

The adoption of the lock canal in 1887,—a concession to the views of M. Rousseau and the engineers at Panama,—produced a "favorable reaction" in government circles and M. de Lesseps was advised to resurrect the Lottery Bond Bill and submit it to the Chamber.

In June, 1888, the revised measure, asking for permission to float *valeurs à lots*, or lottery bonds, to the amount of $155,000,000.00, was presented to the Senate, which approved it. The Bill did not just naturally pass the Senate, it was *bribed through it*. But the existence of corruption in the highest legislative body in France and the methods used by M. de Lesseps and his financial agents in lubricating the Senatorial palm were not exposed until long afterwards.

When the Bill came up for discussion in the Chamber it met with a gathering storm of opposition. This opposition, which was manifested in violent anti-imperialistic tirades from the Left, was confused and strengthened from outside the Chamber by manoeuvres on the Bourse,* attacks from the press and the hostility of certain financial combines. But the opposition, which was to end by sealing the doom of Panama, was most serious on the Bourse.

It was a tradition on the Exchange that the 1st and 5th days of each month were "settlement days." On one of these days, during the exciting debates in the Chamber, a rumour was circulated to the effect that M. de Lesseps had fractured a leg while riding in the Bois du Boulogne. Immediately the market price of Suez and Panama Canal shares fell. A few days later a stock brokerage firm sent something like 500 cables to various parts of the world announcing the death of M. de Lesseps. The stock quotations on Suez and Panama declined still further. The agitation and excitement rose to Vesuvian violence. The tactics employed outside Paris by the opposition forced M. de Lesseps to mount the rostrum in a wild endeavor to calm the shareholders. And in October, 1887, M. de Lesseps filed a $1,000,000.00 damage suit against a Paris news agency for issuing a bulletin to the effect that the interest payments on Panama Canal shares had been suspended.

Two months later M. de Lesseps, too old and discouraged to carry on the hopeless battle, threw in the sponge. He resigned from the presidency of the Panama Canal Co. and asked the courts to appoint a receiver to go on with the Canal.

On the following day the Chamber, by an overwhelming vote, rejected the Lottery Bond Bill.

A petition in bankruptcy was filed by the Directors of the Company and a Liquidator appointed by the Courts. Work on the Canal was suspended early in January 1889 and the high-powered plant in operation at Panama abandoned to the tender mercies of the tropic jungle.*

No sooner had the suspension of work been decided upon than a frenzied cry went up from the stock and bond holders. Could this be the end of Panama, the fate of their hard-earned savings? Profiting by the growing feeling of insecurity and unrest, the *Libre Parole*, an anti-Semitic paper, circulated among the investors a petition to which 20,000 signatures were soon secured, accusing the promoters of Panama of "abuse of confidence" and "swindling." The petition was sent to the Procurer-General who, after months of delay, forwarded it to the Minister of Justice. Meanwhile, the campaign started by the *Libre Parole* was taken up with vigor by a widening circle of Paris journals. Public opinion was fanned to fever pitch. Rioting broke out in the provinces and an abortive attempt was made on M. de Lesseps' life. The excited state of the people forced the Minister of Justice to recognize the petition and the necessity of taking action. On the basis of the charges made a bill of particulars was drawn up against M. de Lesseps and his associates and submitted to the Chamber. The passage of the Bill, which was defended by the Right to the utter dismay of the Left majority, set the machinery in motion for the prosecution.

That afternoon Jules DeLahaye, a Deputy enrolled in the ranks of General Boulanger's supporters, gave notice of an interpellation* on Panama which was to be made on the following day. In the corridors of the Palais Bourbon there was unconcealed apprehension as to the nature of the revelations promised by the young deputy.

Between twelve o'clock that evening and one o'clock the next morning Baron Jacques de Reinach, in his lavish flat near the Parc Monceau, took a fatal dose of cyanide of potassium. The Baron, a Frankfort Jew, was the senior partner in the stock brokerage firm of Levy-Cremieux, the fiscal agents of the Panama Co. Reinach was no ordinary banker, or stock broker; he was an *entrepreneur* on a Homeric scale. He was keen, scholarly and energetic with a fluent command of five languages—French, English, German, Italian and Spanish. He owned and developed large tracts of land in the south of France; he was the promoter of the South Algerian Railway; he was interested in coal mines, subways and railway projects in England, Portugal and Venezuela. The opening of the Suez Canal in 1869 had brought him into contact with M. de Lesseps. To him the Orient loomed like another El Dorado. He was soon drawn into a whirlpool of plans and schemes for promoting trade with that corner of the globe. He financed the canal at Corinthia and drew up plans for another to run across the Malacca Peninsula, with the object of drawing trade from Singapore and of shortening the ocean route to China. Indeed, Reinach's sinister activities in the Orient brought him into conflict with the British government and hastened, in 1886, the annexation of Burma.

Reinach had asked the Panama Co. to place at his disposal the sum of $1,000,000.00 to be used in buying off opposition to the Lottery Bond Bill. This money was distributed in bribes to 150 senators and deputies and 10 of the leading newspapers of Paris. Reinach, whose nephew Joseph was a Deputy in the Chamber, was afraid of DeLahaye's revelations. He was afraid, too, of Cornelius Herz who, by intimidations, threats and blackmail, had extricated from him millions of dollars belonging to the Panama Co. Reinach's Italian barony, according to Maurice Barres in *Leurs Figures*, had been purchased by acts of treason to France. Herz was the only person who knew the Baron's secret and to keep it inviolate he made the Baron pay and pay until he was nearly penniless. Then, to save himself from the ignominy of exposure, the Baron committed suicide.

The news of the Baron's death, which stirred all France, resulted in speeding up plans for the prosecution. The government's case was set forth in a ponderous dossier of "500 pages of folio written on both sides with an appendix of 300 more." Warrants to appear before the Court of Appeals were promptly issued to Messrs. Ferdinand and Charles de Lesseps, Marius Fontane, Baron Cottu and Alexander Gustave Eiffel.

Notified of the Court's order, M. de Lesseps *père* "rose and dressed and asked that the cross of the Legion of Honour be pinned on his breast." The examination at the Palais de Justice was only a perfunctory affair, but "on his return home he was seized with a fever and became delirious. In his delirium he fancied that he was being dragged before magistrates to be harassed with questions. 'I shall go to England!' he cried in his despair, 'where the Queen at least would recognize my work.' When the fever fell his wife persuaded him that the examination was but a bad dream. He believed her for some time after. He would beg her when he felt himself going off into a doze to awaken him should he rave about a scene at the Palais de Justice. Then he suddenly fell into a state of dotage from which no one has had the courage to rouse him."

This state of senility and raving lasted all during the trial.

Alexander Gustave Eiffel, who received altogether $14, 600,000.00 from the Panama Company, was fined $4,000.00 and sentenced to one year in prison. Baron Cottu, one of the directors, and Marius Fontane, the Secretary, received terms of two years and fines of $1,200.00 each. Fontane was the officer who was directly in charge of the distribution of $4,000,000.00 in subsidies to the press, on the occasion of the emission of the Company's various bond loans.

Ferdinand de Lesseps and his eldest son Charles, who was the Vice-President of the Panama Co., received the maximum penalty prescribed by French law in cases of "abuse of confidence" and "swindling"—i.e., five years in jail and a fine of $1,200.00 each. The court's verdict was withheld from M. de Lesseps *père*, who lay seriously ill at La Chesnaye, the family chateau near Indre. Charles de Lesseps, after serving six months in Mazas prison, was transferred to St. Louis Hospital with an acute attack of dyspepsia. His sentence was later revoked by the courts. The elder de Lesseps died Dec. 7, 1894, at the age of 89, totally unaware of the sensational details of the trial or the verdict of the court.

NOTES TO THE TEXT

A variety of sources were consulted in compiling these notes. The following were particularly helpful: Aberjhani and Sandra L. West, *Encyclopedia of the Harlem Renaissance* (New York: Clearmark Books, 2003); Richard Allsopp, *Dictionary of Caribbean English Usage* (Oxford: Oxford University Press, 1996); F. G. Cassidy and R. B. Le Page, *Dictionary of Jamaican English*, 2nd ed. (Kingston: University of the West Indies Press, 2002); Frank Collymore, *Barbadian Dialect*, 6th ed. (n.p.: Barbados National Trust, 1992); Cary D. Wintz and Paul Finkelman, eds., *Encyclopedia of the Harlem Renaissance*, 2 vols. (New York: Routledge, 2004).

Harlem on My Mind

Harlem Shadows and Spring in New Hampshire: are not identical texts. *Harlem Shadows* includes additional poems such as "If We Must Die" that McKay had omitted from *Spring*.

Housmanic order: in the style of Alfred Edward Housman (1859–1936), an English poet known for his lyricism.

T. S. Stribling: Thomas Sigismund Stribling (1881–1965), a white Southern author who won a Pulitzer Prize in 1932 for the novel *The Store*. His novel *Birthright* (1922), presenting a portrayal of the Negro from a black perspective, influenced many Harlem Renaissance authors. Walrond wrote a favorable review of it in *Negro World* (Apr. 22, 1922): 4.

Cohen: Octavus Roy Cohen (1891–1959), a Jewish writer of comic fiction featuring caricatures of African American speech.

Shake That Thing: popular blues song written by Papa Charlie Jackson (ca. 1885–1938).

Odum's *Rainbow Round My Shoulder*: (1928), the work of American folklorist and sociologist Howard W. Odum (1884–1954). Walrond wrote a favorable review of it entitled "Black Rambler," *New York Herald Tribune* (Mar. 11, 1928): sec. 12, p. 3.

Boody Lane: name for the Rue de la Bouterie, a crime-ridden section of Marseilles.

Morand: Paul Morand (1888–1976), French diplomat, fiction and travel writer. His works include the novel *Ouvert la Nuit* (1922), translated as *Open All Night* (1927) by Vyvyan Holland, and *Magie Noire* (1928), translated as *Black Magic* in 1929 by Hamish Miles. Walrond dismisses Morand as uninteresting and lacking understanding of blacks in his interview with Jacques Lebar.

Juan-les-Pins: a town in southeastern France known for its casino, nightclub, and beaches.

Camorra: a mafia-like criminal organization that originated in Naples.

Lincoln Theater: located in Harlem on West 135th Street between Fifth Avenue and Lenox Avenue. It was an important entertainment venue for blacks in the 1910s and 1920s.

café au lait: light-skinned.

Strivers' Row: a Harlem neighborhood located on 138th and 139th Streets between Seventh and Eighth Avenues that was home to some of Harlem's most notable residents.

Harry Wills: (1889–1958), "the Black Panther," largely thought to have been denied an opportunity to challenge for the heavy-weight title—even though he was the number one contender—because of his race.

Rawlins' Paradise: Walrond is possibly referring to the famous Small's Paradise which opened in 1925 and was one of the most popular night clubs in Harlem. It catered to a largely white audience.

Cotton Club and **Connie's Inn**: the Cotton Club, on Lenox Avenue and 142nd Street was the most famous of the Harlem night spots; Connie's Inn, on 7th Avenue and 131st Street, was another popular Harlem club. Both the Cotton Club and Connie's Inn generally excluded black patrons even though most of the performers were black.

ofay: generally derogatory term for whites.

bump the bump: a sensual dance popular in Harlem marked by swaying the hips to the front and back. See Rudolph Fisher, *The Walls of Jericho* (New York: Alfred A. Knopf, 1928), 110.

Tammany Hall: the often corrupt Democratic Party political machine that helped shape New York City politics in the nineteenth and first half of the twentieth century. Its most famous figure was William "Boss" Tweed (1823–78).

Jazzbo Brown: a semilegendary character, referred to in DuBose Heyward's *Jasbo Brown and Selected Poems* (1924).

Manhattan Casino: (later the Rockland Palace), a large hall used for dances, sports, and other events. It was located at 280 West 155th Street and Eighth Avenue.

Rhone: Arthur "Happy" Rhone established an elegant nightclub located at Lenox Avenue and 143rd Street.

Sugar Hill: an exclusive area in Harlem extending from 145th Street to 155th Street, and from Amsterdam Avenue in the west to Edgecombe Avenue in the east.

canaille: the masses or proletariat.

"pearl divers": dish washers.

lamp: to look at, often in a sexual manner.

black and tan: dark and light complexioned African Americans.

high yellow . . . fast black: light and dark complexioned blacks respectively.

Fugitive Stories/Sketches

pollera: a shirt; also a large colorful skirt once popular with Spanish women.

John: generic name for a Chinese man.

Déboisement: (French), deforesting.

black vomit: dark vomit of digested blood, often a sign of yellow fever.

camino real: (Spanish), the main street, literally the royal road.

jalousies: windows with adjustable shutters.

Zamba: (also Sambo), offspring of a black person and a Native American; generally used pejoratively.

Chantier: (French), building site.

Decauville car: manufactured by a French company founded by Paul Decauville.

Cuartel: (Spanish), literally a barracks. Walrond probably intends *cárcel*, a jail.

Alcalde: (Spanish), mayor.

assafoetida: (asafetida), a yellowish plant. The resin, with an unpleasant odor, is often used in folk medicine and sometimes employed to ward off evil spirits.

Tinterillos: (Spanish), clerks, pen-pushers or shyster lawyers.

quinine: used to treat malaria.

Cabildo: a Spanish colonial administrative council.

fo': can mean either "for" or, as in this case, "to."

tereckly: directly, right after.

comado: an unmarried person who lives with his/her partner.

out o' he hand: out of his hand. In Creole English, subject, object, and possessive pronouns are used in various sentence positions. In the clause "me is next," for example, "me" takes the place of the subject pronoun.

forced-ripe brat: precocious youngster.

chopine: a type of shoe. Walrond probably intends chopin, a liquid measure ranging from half a pint to a quart.

black puddin' an' souse: black pudding is a popular delicacy, made of pig's intestines often stuffed with rice or sweet potatoes, pepper, pig's blood, and seasoning. Souse is made with the pig's head and feet, which are pickled and well seasoned.

sow gran'murrer: the sow's grandmother. In Creole English, the possessive is not marked by an apostrophe.

aggle: upset.

krolick: colic.

coppers: money, copper coins.

gill: a quarter of a pint.

trampo: *tramposa* (Spanish), a crook; a cheat.

teef it: [steal it], a person can't even pick up a pepper to look at it without all of you thinking I am going to steal it.

eddoes and cassavas: root vegetables. Cassava is also known as yucca.

sapodillas: small apple-shaped fruit, brown-skinned with a sweet yellow pulp.

pap: soft food given to infants or invalids.

Allez . . . allez . . . zut!: (French), Get out . . . get out . . . damn it!

contre-maître: foreman.

fellahs: laborers or peasants in some Arabic-speaking countries.

"Is fight yo' want, fight?": a grammatical feature called front focusing, when the speaker wants to emphasize a point. The main verb or clause of a sentence is introduced, then repeated in the sentence in normal position.

Panama: as opposed to the U.S. controlled Canal Zone.

Ants' Nest: a six-story tenement in Colón.

napa: (Spanish), an imitation leather.

singlet: a man's sleeveless undershirt.

adz-faced woman: an adz is an ax-like tool.

Cholo: a Spanish American Indian, often derogatory.

yadda: other.

fowl cock: rooster.

ackee bush: an ackee is a pear-shaped fruit with black seeds and creamy, edible flesh. It is often served with salt fish.

fomembah: remember.

gunga peas: dark green peas often cooked in stews. Also known as pigeon peas.

farrim: for it.

kiss-me-ears: (also kiss-me-neck), a strong curse or oath.

Babu: an old Indian man, often derogatory.

tayche: (sometimes tache), a copper pan used in converting sugar cane juice into sugar.

Negro admiral with a land ship: The Barbados Landship is "[a] sort of friendly society which frequently holds organized parades of its members all dressed in naval uniforms" (Collymore 59–60).

conoce: (Spanish), literally, "to know."

chigger: (also chigoe), a flea whose bite causes severe itching.

goblet: in this context, a clay vessel used to keep liquids cool.

quattie: a small silver coin.

form fool: to act like a fool.

fifty pound: there is often no plural inflection in Creole when the noun is modified by a number greater than one.

don't do: Walrond probably means "don't go." The repeated lines may be a printing error or they may be given for emphasis.

bobo fish: a flat, freshwater fish.

pappy show: someone or something foolish.

fi' nyam: to eat.

a next: another.

Fugitive Journalism

costumbres del pais: (Spanish), customs of the country.

vieux anglais: (French), a pseudo-Englishman.

Froude, Spenser St. John: J. A. Froude was the author of *The English in the West Indies* (1888), a controversial travel book denigrating black culture and maintaining that white West Indians, because of their isolation from England, were unfit to rule. Sir Spenser Buckingham Saint John, the author of *Hayti; Or, the Black Republic* (1884).

Gallegos: people from Galicia, in Northwest Spain.

Cocolo: A term used by some Spanish-speaking communities in the Caribbean to refer to non-Hispanic persons of African ancestry, as well as those from the Anglophone and Francophone territories.

Jutland: the British suffered heavy casualties in this naval battle with Germany off the coast of Denmark on May 31 to June 1, 1916.

Pukka Sahib: a true gentleman. Sometimes seen as a pose, as in George Orwell's *Burmese Days* (1934).

Eton: the most famous and the largest of England's public independent schools.

Charles I: King of England from 1625 to 1649.

Cibao: the region in the northern part of the Dominican Republic. The people there are known for their patriotism and spirit of independence.

Monroe Doctrine: a policy established in 1823 by President James Madison that the Americas were no longer open to colonization by outsiders. The United States would consider any attempt to colonize these territories as an aggressive act.

Mona Passage: a strait that separates Hispaniola from Puerto Rico.

Faustin Soulouque: 1782–1867. Elected President of Haiti in 1847, he pronounced himself Emperor Faustin I in 1849. He made several unsuccessful attempts to capture the Spanish part of Hispaniola. After a revolution in 1858, he abdicated the following year.

Captain Rafael Trujillo y Molina: Trujillo (1891–1961) was President of the Dominican Republic from 1930 to 1938 and from 1942 to 1952. He also ruled as an unelected military dictator until his assassination in 1961.

take an awful lot of beating: be difficult to defeat.

rapine: despoiling a country in warfare.

General Arias: Desiderio Arias, a guerilla leader widely admired in the northwest Dominican Republic. He was assassinated by Trujillo in 1931.

the "Big Stick" Latin-American Policy: "Speak softly and carry a big stick." A policy established by President Theodore Roosevelt as a corollary to the Monroe Doctrine.

Roundway Review (Fiction, Caribbean)

turpentine mango: one with the smell of turpentine.

water-course: body of flowing water.

wall pockets: decorative receptacles fastened to walls for storing objects.

midnight cry: Evangelical groups such as the Plymouth Brethren saw this as a sign of the apocalypse. See Matthew 25: 6 ("And at midnight there was a cry made, behold, the bridegroom cometh; go ye out to meet him").

Sea Wall: a dyke built by the Dutch when they settled Guyana to keep the sea out.

Bush Negro: escaped slaves (maroons) who fled to the interior of Suriname (Dutch Guiana).

Baba: baby.

stand-pipe: "A source of piped water-supply mounted on a concrete stand and placed at the side of the road for the convenience of the public" (Allsopp 527).

poor great: "[p]oor but haughty in appearance or conduct" (Allsopp 448).

Plymouth Brethren: see note 29 of our notes to the introduction.

Chichi: chicken.

pepper-pot: In many places in the region, a soup, but in Guyana, it is more of a stew consisting of casareep (a thick, black cooking sauce made from cassava extract), spices, and meat, usually beef.

foo-foo: (fufu), a thick paste or porridge usually made by boiling cassava or yams and then pounding them with a mortar and pestle until they reach the desired consistency.

hefted: to judge the weight of something by lifting it.

Do: please, as in "Do Mistah Bee don't chase me 'way/Fo' de gals nex' do' will laugh at me" ("Panama Gold," *Tropic Death*). See Cassidy and Le Page 152.

went to: intended or meant to.

knock down: in Creole English, the Standard English regular past tense inflection "ed" is usually deleted.

Lamaha . . . Canal: a central manmade waterway located in Georgetown.

Houses . . . on stilts: Because Guyana is below sea level, many houses are built above ground to prevent flooding.

fustic: a tropical hardwood tree that yields a yellow dye.

star apple: a purplish fruit with seeds arranged in a star pattern. It is not a variety of apple.

cus-cus grass: usually khus-khus, a hardy grass once used for a variety of purposes by Caribbean householders.

the Hindu had given the planters the slip: Indians had been brought over to British Guiana as indentured labor after the emancipation of slaves in the British colonies in 1834.

palings: "property fence[s] made of wooden staves or of galvanized sheeting" (Allsopp 424).

Nelson's statue: the statue of Lord Horatio Nelson was unveiled in Bridgetown, the capital of Barbados, in 1813.

Careenage: an arm of the sea that stretches inward. It was formerly used in Barbados for docking ships and unloading merchandise.

soul: a friendly form of address used mainly by elderly women.

Gap: a narrow roadway leading off a main road.

Demerara: a county in Guyana in which the capital, Georgetown, is located.

Jenkin's Insane Asylum: Barbados' lone psychiatric hospital, opened in 1893.

shack-shack tree: also shak shak or woman tongue. It is named for the noise its thick seed pods make.

ratoons: new shoots from the base of the sugar cane.

Old Jojo: Joseph Benjamin Prout; see note 30 of our notes to the introduction.

Flat Rock: see note 30 as cited above.

Mess House: see note 30 as cited above.

pimpler: (plimpler), a thorn.

jook: poke.

kiskadee: a small bird "known for its clear, insistent call from which its name is derived" (Allsopp 331).

silkerchief: silk handkerchief.

cane peeling: the thick skin of the sugar cane plant.

bat and ball: an improvised version of cricket.

Sargasso Sea: a part of the Atlantic Ocean between the West Indies and the Azores. Its calm waters and gulfweed have made it become a graveyard for numerous ships.

There's a young girl in the ring: Well known Caribbean children's game. The line is often give as "there's a brown girl in the ring."

soldier crabholes: homes of the hermit crab.

manchineel trees: tall, poisonous evergreen trees that tend to grow in coastal areas.

poky: cramped.

Cho': an expression denoting anger, impatience, disappointment.

kiddy goat: young goat.

"tra-la-la" buggy: "[o]ld-fashioned two wheel gig" (Collymore 110).

"Arise": see note 30 of our notes to the introduction.

alligator pear: a species of avocado with rough skin.

two and six: two shillings and sixpence, about thirty U.S. cents at today's rate of exchange.

tea: any hot beverage. It can also mean breakfast.

Wolmer's College: in reality, a high school. Some West Indian high schools that offer tuition to Advanced Level (first year university) are known as colleges.

speak-o-ty: speak to.

bills of lading: documents used to acknowledge receipt of a shipment of goods.

Porfirio Diaz: also Porfino Diaz (1830–1915), controversial president of Mexico from 1876 to 1880, and from 1884 to 1911 who encouraged foreign investment in the country.

rass: strong curse word.

Jamaica turkey: the carrion crow, or john-crow. Popular etymology has it that a Barbadian "when he came to Jamaica and saw a john-crow for the first time, remarked 'Jamaica turkey does fly high.'" (Cassidy and Le Page 242).

Bajan: Barbadian.

Bottle Alley: (officially Avenida Balboa), a thriving, but often dangerous commercial strip in Colon. Walrond mentions this street in many of the narratives set in Panama.

cow-catcher: a device attached to the front of a train to clear obstacles off the track.

lora: a flower.

cayukas: small boats, kayaks.

"Ah treat him friends them": "Them" is a plural Creole marker. The sentence means "He is treating his friends."

tell him say: "tell say" is a Creole phrasal verb. In this case the phrase means "tell him that."

hafta: after.

rope-soled "pusses": canvas shoes that would normally have rubber soles. That these are made with rope instead indicates a relative poverty although having shoes at all implied a certain degree of wealth.

hard tack: an inexpensive, long-lasting biscuit or cracker.

duppies: ghosts, called jumbies on some islands.

shaddock: a large variety of citrus fruit.

golden apple: despite its name not a variety of apple, but a roundish fruit with a spiny seed, often eaten with salt. It is known in Jamaica as Jew Plum, and in some other islands as *pomme cythere* (French Creole), literally apple of the earth.

Great-Aunt Muriah: Most probably a reference to Anna Maria Cheeseman, one of J. B. Prout's many paramours who resided at the "Mess House." She was not related to Walrond or his mother, Ruth.

drag it along: shuffle, might indicate elephantiasis, a condition in which limbs become grossly enlarged owing to obstruction of the lymphatic vessels, especially by nematode parasites.

Plaisaunce: a village in Demerara, a few miles outside Georgetown.

bucks: name for aboriginal Amerindian natives of Guyana, often derogatory.

matti: a close friend.

obeah: "A set of systems or secret beliefs in the use of supernatural forces to attain or defend against evil ends" (Allsopp 412).

brown man: In Jamaica especially, a light-skinned, middle class person; the term is associated with privilege, color and class prejudice.

sprawl: spread, that is wide and flat.

picknee: children. Unlike in the United States, in the Caribbean, the term is often used with affection.

doctor's surgery: office

W.C.: literally, water closet, hence modern plumbing facilities.

Jamaican mento: rural folk music probably derived from Africa.

... you been bleachin' again: lightening his skin.

sucking his teeth: to make a sound of annoyance, displeasure or disrespect (Cassidy and Le Page 428).

blood-hole: Jamaican curse word.

Roundway Review (Fiction, United States)

peckish: hungry.

sea eggs: the flesh of the sea urchin, a Barbadian delicacy.

unna: all-you; plural form of second person pronoun "you."

wunna: plural form of the second person pronoun "you." Also possesive "your."

Love was once a little boy: song by Irish composer Joseph Augustine Wade.

begrudgeful: more familiarly grudgeful, "maliciously envious" (Allsopp 271–72).

vamping: blatantly using one's body to attract a man.

Off-Side Brethren: a sect of the Plymouth Brethren.

Saba: an island in the Netherlands Antilles.

toime: Barbadian Creole English, where the vowel sound in "time" is pronounced as the diphthong /oi/. Walrond's Barbadian characters also use the "oi" sound for the personal pronoun "I" throughout *Tropic Death*.

Wo-lay! Wo-law!: "expression[s] denoting despondency, grief" (Collymore 118).

patois man: one who speaks Caribbean Creole.

wire screen: to keep out disease-bearing mosquitoes; wire screens are ubiquitous in Walrond's writings set in Panama. They are especially present in the homes and offices of the Europeans and Americans.

spick-o-ty: sometimes spick; derogatory term for persons of Latin American descent.

. . . a contract labourer: Walrond's translation.

puttees: (also puttie), a strip of cloth covering wound spirally around the leg from ankle to knee.

foine: find

ownwayish: stubborn, obstinate, head-strong.

cou-cou: (coo-coo), a Barbadian delicacy made with okra, cornmeal, and butter (and occasionally peas).

Bohack's: a supermarket chain no longer in business.

cyclamen-hued powder: most commonly, a pale pink.

dolphin: dolphin-fish, commonly known as mahi-mahi or dorado.

buckra: (often backra), a poor white person.

congeners: toxic chemicals formed by the fermentation of alcohol.

celluloid collar: made of cellular, a type of cotton.

harmonium: a small keyboard instrument.

pram: perambulator, an infant's carriage.

lisle: smooth, fine cotton.

Gold Dust Twins: The popular marketing logo of Gold Dust Washing Powder (Walrond had worked for the Gold Dust Soap Company) featured two stereotypical black boys, Goldie and Dustie, on the box.

starter: a starter in manual elevators regulated the speed and started and stopped elevators.

pongee: a thin, soft woven cloth.

paysanos: peasants, citizens, countrymen.

Max's Busy Bee: an inexpensive eatery chain in New York City mentioned in several Walrond pieces, including "Vignettes of the Dusk."

When the moon shines over the cow shed: from "K-K-K Katy," a popular song composed by Geoffrey O'Hara and recorded in 1918 by Billy Murray.

Roundway Review (Nonfiction)

calaboose: a prison.

Elliot-Fisher machine: a typewriter manufactured by the Elliot Fisher Company. It was designed to type on flat surfaces. The typebasket sat below the keyboard, which moved to the right when typing.

Broad Street Hospital: this hospital merged with St. Gregory's Free Emergency Hospital in 1945 to form the Beekman Downtown Hospital. After other mergers, it is now known as the New York Downtown Hospital.

tarvia: road surfacing material made with asphalt.

Panama *Star and Herald*: quotations from various issues of the newspaper are footnoted in Walrond's text.

Ran Runnels: Randolph Runnels, born in Texas ca. 1830, was hired to quell labor unrest in the Panama Isthmus in the 1850s, often using brutal tactics. See Michael L. Coniff, *Panama and the United States: The Forced Alliance*, 2nd ed. (University of Georgia Press, 2001).

eau de vie: brandy.

Unpublished Writings

white flour-bag: a crocus bag made of jute in which flour was packed. The sack was often used to make clothing.

him don't know say him: In Creole English "say" can be used to mean "that" when combining two main clauses. The phrase here means "he doesn't know that he."

"Hearts of Oak": the official march of the Royal Navy of the United Kingdom.

. . . a contract labourer: Walrond's translation. Part of this section is virtually identical to "Success Story." It allows us an opportunity to examine how Walrond reworks his material.

iced Canadian apples: apples packed in ice and transported to the Caribbean, where they were considered a treat since they did not grow in the region.

"Brine": Although it is impossible to know Walrond's design for the organization of "Brine," internal evidence seems to suggest that he was experimenting with the idea of presenting the story in flashbacks. Thus, we have arranged the excerpts we use with the "ending" of the story (the breakup of the couple) first.

hard ears: stubborn or disobedient.

St. Eustatius: part of the Netherlands Antilles, east of Puerto Rico.

balata: a durable timber from an evergreen found in some of the Caribbean territories.

fagged out: tired out.

Semitic: Walrond had an anti-Semitic streak running through much of his work. See for example "On Being Black" and "City Love."

Meharry: founded in Nashville, Tennessee, in 1876. It was the first medical college in the South for African Americans.

Panama Scandal: the scandal involving the sale of stock in the Panama Canal Company rocked France in 1892–93. Many important figures were convicted of taking bribes and hundreds of thousands of stockholders were defrauded. Ferdinand de Lesseps was fined and sentenced to jail. Although the jail term was overturned, his reputation was sullied forever.

Stavisky, Oustric: Alexandre Stavisky, who had connections with high-ranking government officials and members of society, sold worthless bonds. After a series of trials, he died under mysterious conditions in 1934. Albert Oustric was a wealthy French banker who bought out companies, merged them, and then sold them at a high price. He, and many who invested in his companies, lost their fortunes in the Great Depression.

. . . he never retreats: Walrond's translation.

lianas: long stemmed vines.

convolvuli: herbs and shrubs of the morning-glory family.

porphyry: a purplish variety of igneous rock.

tombeau des européens: (French), the tombs or graves of the Europeans.

actionnaires: (French), investors, shareholders.

sub-chef: a sous chef, a person directly under the executive chef. He is second in command of the entire kitchen production.

Bois du Boulogne: a large park in Paris.

Bismarck's African Conference: The Berlin Conference (1884–85) called by German Chancellor Otto von Bismarck to divide Africa among the European powers.

Bourse: the Paris Stock Exchange.

tropic jungle: An example of this decay is seen in Walrond's story "The Palm Porch" in *Tropic Death*.

interpellation: a procedure in some legislative bodies for asking a government official to explain an act or policy.

Louis J. Parascandola, professor of English at Long Island University, Brooklyn, is author or editor of seven previous books, including *"Winds Can Wake Up the Dead": An Eric Walrond Reader; "Look For Me All Around You": Anglophone Caribbean Immigrants in the Harlem Renaissance; Amy Jacques Garvey: Selected Writings from the Negro World, 1923–1928;* and, with Carl A. Wade, *Eric Walrond: The Critical Heritage.*

Carl A. Wade, former senior lecturer in English at the University of the West Indies Cave Hill Campus, is coeditor with Louis J. Parascandola, of *Eric Walrond: The Critical Heritage* and has also published extensively on other Caribbean American authors and American fiction.

www.ingramcontent.com/pod-product-compliance
Lightning Source LLC
Chambersburg PA
CBHW031053020726
47495CB00007B/1864